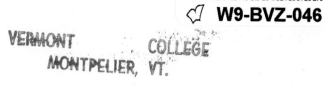

NATIONS OF THE MODERN WORLD

CEYLON

S. A. Pakeman
Formerly Professor of Modern History, Ceylon University College, Appointed Member, House of Representatives, Ceylon, 1947–1952

ENGLAND

John Bowle
Professor of Political Theory, Collège d'Europe, Bruges

MODERN INDIA

Sir Percival Griffiths
President, India, Pakistan and Burma Association

MODERN IRAN

Peter Avery
Lecturer in Persian and Fellow of King's College, Cambridge

IRAQ

Brig. S. Y. Longrigg
Formerly of the Goverment of Iraq and the Iraq Petroleum Company and one time Political Officer, Iraq
and
Frank Stoakes
Formerly of the Iraq Petroleum Company, Lecturer in Government, Manchester University

JAPAN

Sir Esler Dening
H.M. Ambassador to Japan, 1952–1957

MALAYA

J. M. Gullick
Formerly of the Malayan Civil Service

PAKISTAN

Ian Stephens
Formerly Editor of The Statesman *Calcutta and Delhi, 1942–1951 Fellow King's College, Cambridge, 1952—1958*

SOUTH AFRICA John Cope
Formerly editor-in-chief of The Forum *and*
South African Correspondent of The Guardian

SUDAN   K. D. D. Henderson
REPUBLIC   *Formerly of the Sudan Political Service*
            and Governor of Darfur Province 1949—1953

TURKEY   Geoffrey Lewis
            Senior Lecturer in Islamic Studies, Oxford

THE UNITED H. C. Allen
STATES OF   *Commonwealth Fund Professor of American*
AMERICA   *History, University College, London*

YUGOSLAVIA Muriel Heppell
              and
            F. B. Singleton

NATIONS OF THE MODERN WORLD

YUGOSLAVIA

YUGOSLAVIA

By
MURIEL HEPPELL
and F. B. SINGLETON

FREDERICK A. PRAEGER, *Publishers*
NEW YORK · WASHINGTON

BOOKS THAT MATTER

Published in the United States of America in 1961
by Frederick A. Praeger, Inc., Publishers
111 Fourth Avenue, New York N.Y. 10003

Second Impression 1966

© Muriel Heppell *and* F. B. Singleton 1961

Library of Congress Catalog Card Number: 61-6385

Printed in Great Britain

Preface

YUGOSLAVIA is a country of great interest to the peoples of the non-Communist world and it is fortunately the most easily accessible of the East European countries to travellers from the West. Since the 'great schism' of 1948, when the Yugoslav Communist Party was expelled from the Cominform, Yugoslavia has become the centre of the Revisionist heresy which proclaims that Communism can develop in complete independence of the Soviet Union, politically, economically and militarily. The recent struggles of this small Balkan country to assert its right to decide its own way in the world have aroused wide interest, and evoked many conflicting emotions. Some see the issues in terms of a Yugoslav David defying a Russian Goliath; others study with interest the methods by which a rigid, centralised state machine has attempetd to liberalise itself, and there are yet others who affirm that the leopard cannot change its spots, and that Communism, whether national or international, whether Titoist or Soviet, is always the implacable foe of democracy.

Our aim in this book is not to pass final judgements on these matters. We feel that there is a great need for a book which will attempt to explain how the Yugoslav people reached their present position, and to offer to the intelligent reader a picture which is not too heavily coloured by national or ideological bias. We realise that strict objectivity is an unattainable ideal, and that no one has a completely open mind on the writing of the history, whether ancient or modern. We have striven hard to be fair minded, but we cannot claim that in a matter as complicated and controversial as the history of Yugoslavia we have always succeeded in eliminating our own prejudices. One bias to which we must both plead guilty is that we have both fallen under the spell of the country about which we have written, but we hope that our love for the Yugoslav people is not an uncritical passion.

In a book which appears under the names of two authors,

the reader is entitled to know how the work has been divided betwcen them. Dr. Heppell, who has taught English in the University of Novi Sad since 1956, was formerly a post-graduate student of London University, where she made a special study of the influence of the Byzantine Empire in the development of medieval Slavonic culture. She has written the chapters dealing with the history of the Yugoslavs up to the early part of the nineteenth century. Mr. Singleton – who has spent some part of every year since 1948 in Yugoslavia, first as a volunteer worker on a construction project, and later as a student of geography and as an adult educationalist – is responsible for the second part of the book, which deals with modern Yugoslavia. The introductory chapter and that on the nineteenth century have been written by both authors. We have been helped greatly in our task – or perhaps that is too formidable a word for so pleasant an occupation – by a number of Yugoslav friends. In particular we should like to express our thanks to Dr. Slavko Gavrilović of the University of Novi Sad, for advice and help with Chapters III and IV. For some of the material in the second section of the book we are indebted to a number of friends in the University of Ljubljana and in the Workers' and Peoples' University of Slovenia and Croatia. Discussions with them and with other friends in Bohinj, Piran and Ljubljana have been of great value to the author of this part of the book. They are too numerous to mention here, but our thanks to them are not less sincere because they are given anonymously.

A number of English people with an interest in Yugoslavia have been good enough to read the proofs and to make helpful suggestions. Amongst them are Mr. G. F. Sedgwick, Mr. A. J. Topham, M.A., and Mr. E. E. Dodd, M.A. of the Yorkshire (North) District of the W.E.A. Mr. A. J. P. Taylor, M.A., F.B.A. of Magdalen College, Oxford, looked through the later chapters, and made a number of valuable comments. To Mr. and Mrs. E. E. Dodd a special word of thanks is appropriate, for they introduced the two authors to each other during a W.E.A. Summer School in Ljubljana in 1958. Without this introduction the book would never have been written.

We should like also to thank our cartographer, Mr. G. Bryant, of Leeds University, for his excellent maps, Messrs Hughes and

Denton of Ernest Benn Ltd. for their unfailing courtesy, Miss E. Tweedie, Mrs. M. Tomlinson and Miss E. Barron for their efficient typing of the manuscript, Mr. Nichols, Miss Sykes and members of the Leeds City Reference Library staff for their help with the bibliography, and finally Mrs. Singleton and the children for putting up so cheerfully with the domestic upheaval occasioned by having an author at work in the house.

Without the help and encouragement of all the above, and many others, this book could not have appeared. For all expressions of opinion and for any shortcomings or errors, however, the authors alone are responsible.

M. H.
F. B. S.

Contents

Maps

Drawn by G. BRYANT
(*Department of Geography, University of Leeds*)

Guide To Pronunciation

SERBO-CROAT spelling is phonetic, that is each letter of the alphabet always represents the same sound. The following guide to pronunciation is based on the Croatian alphabet, which uses the Latin script. Diacritic marks are used with certain consonants to indicate sounds which have a separate sign in the Cyrillic alphabet, used in Serbia, Macedonia and Montenegro.

A	as in English	*a* in *father*
B		*b* in *bed*
C		*ts* in *cats*
Č		*ch* in *reach*
Ć	– a sound between *ch* in *reach* and *t* in *tune*	
D	as in English	*d* in *dog*
Dz		*J* in *John*
Đ	(Dj) – a sound between *d* in *duke* and *dg* in *bridge*	
E	as in English	*e* in *let*
F		*f* in *full*
G		*g* in *good*
H	as in Scottish	*ch* in *loch*
I	as in English	*i* in *machine*
J		*y* in *yet*
K		*k* in *kite*
L		*l* in *look*
Lj		*ll* in *million*
M		*m* in *man*
N		*n* in *net*
Nj		*n* in *new*
O		*o* in *not*
P		*p* in *pet*
R		*r* in *run* (slightly rolled)
S		*ss* in *glass*
Š		*sh* in *she*
T		*t* in *tap*
U		*u* in *rule*
V		*v* in *veil*
Z		*z* in *zebra*
Ž		*s* in *pleasure*

14

Introduction

As a modern state, Yugoslavia is a young country, with the vitality, and sometimes the crudity, of youth. Yet in parts of it, notably on the Dalmatian coast, one feels much closer to ancient Rome than in our own islands, while the mountainous country of south Serbia and Macedonia is full of reminders of medieval Byzantine civilisation; and though the present state is of recent origin, its people have their roots deep in the past. This juxtaposition of old and new is pleasantly stimulating to the discerning visitor and contributes in no small measure to the fascination of the country.

The state of Yugoslavia came into existence in 1918, as the result of the amalgamation of the small Balkan states of Serbia and Montenegro with certain provinces from the dismembered Austro-Hungarian and Turkish empires. Slovenia, Croatia, Bosnia and Hercegovina and Vojvodina came from the Austro-Hungarian Empire: Macedonia was detached from the Turkish Empire just before the First World War. After the Second World War the frontiers were further extended to include Zara, on the Dalmatian coast and the peninsula of Istria at the head of the Adriatic. In the Trieste area the final boundary with Italy was not settled until 1955. The area of the present state thus occupies 98,767 square miles, and has land frontiers with Austria (200 miles), Hungary (390 miles) to the north; Rumania (346 miles), and Bulgaria (333 miles), on the east; Greece (163 miles) and Albania (288 miles) to the south; and Italy (125 miles) to the north-west. In addition to these land frontiers the country has some 500 miles[1] of coastline on the Adriatic Sea.

Present-day Yugoslavia is a federal republic, the official title of which is *Federativna Narodna Republika Jugoslavije* (usually abbreviated to FNRJ), that is the Federal People's Republic of Yugoslavia.[2] It consists of six separate republics: *Serbia* (capital,

[1] Excluding coastline of the islands.

[2] For convenience the initials of the English translation will be used when required in future references.

Belgrade); *Croatia* (capital, Zagreb); *Slovenia* (capital, Ljubljana); *Bosnia and Hercegovina* (capital, Sarajevo); *Macedonia* (capital, Skopje); and *Montenegro* (capital, Titograd). The People's Republic of Serbia includes two autonomous provinces: Vojvodina in the north-east and Kosovo-Metohia in the south; the ethnical composition and past history of both these provinces is somewhat different from those of the rest of Serbia. The decision to establish a federal republic in Yugoslavia was taken during the war, at the second meeting of the Anti-Fascist Council for the National Liberation of Yugoslavia held in the small Bosnian town of Jajce (once the capital of the medieval Bosnian kingdom, then the headquarters of the Partisans) in November 1943. The official 'birthday' of the new state was November 29th, which is now celebrated as a national holiday. The six separate republics are not arbitrary territorial divisions, but distinctive national entities with very varied political and cultural traditions; and as such they afford the best framework in which to study the very complex history of the whole state.

In its original Turkish form the word 'Balkan' signifies a range of mountains, and Yugoslavia, the largest of the Balkan states, is predominantly a land of mountains; yet most of its eighteen and a half million inhabitants[1] live as peasants, farming the plains of the Danube and its tributaries. Yugoslavia has a magnificent coastline on the Adriatic, with a number of fine natural harbours, but the sea plays little part in the life of its people. High mountains and barren plateaus shut off the plains of the interior from the coast, so that the peasants and city-dwellers of Croatia and Serbia have tended to look to East and Central Europe rather than to the sea for their contacts with the outside world. The few available routes through the mountains have an added importance because of their rarity, an importance which has been recognised by soldiers and merchants throughout history. The Postojna Gap between Ljubljana and Trieste, and the Neretva route by way of the Ivan Pass to Sarajevo were both used in Roman times, and are still used today for roads and railways. The way south from Belgrade, along the Morava and Vardar valleys to the

---

[1] The estimated population for 1960, according to the Yugoslav Federal Statistical Office.

Aegean port of Salonika, was used in the amber trade between
the Baltic and the Aegean before the Hellenes came to Greece;
today it is followed by the Simplon-Orient Express on its
journey from Belgrade to Athens. In all these routes the steepest
gradients are on the seaward slopes. Towards the Danube basin
the valleys descend gradually to the plains round Belgrade. The
headwaters of the Sava, the Bosna and the Drina are all less
than a hundred miles from the Adriatic, and the Sava is navigable for over two hundred miles. Only two important rivers
flow away from the Danube – the Neretva, and the Vardar –
and neither is navigable for more than a few miles. With these
two important exceptions, all the rivers of Yugoslavia flow
towards the vast, marshy plains in the north-east corner of the
country, where the areas inhabited by Slavs, Magyars and
Rumanians meet. In this area is Belgrade, the capital of the
federal republic.

THE MOUNTAINS OF YUGOSLAVIA

Most of the mountain ranges of Yugoslavia are of the same
age as the Alps of Switzerland and Austria. The main trend line
of the Alps is west-east through Switzerland and Austria, then
curving in a great 'S'-shaped loop through the Carpathians and
the Transylvanian Alps, and continuing across the Danube in
the Balkan mountains of Bulgaria. Another series of ranges
associated with the same mountain-building episode runs from
north-west to south-east behind the Dalmatian coast of Yugoslavia and on into the Oros Pindos of Greece. The west-east
trend of the main Alpine system is represented in Yugoslavia by
the mountains of the north-west corner, near the meeting-place
of the Austrian and Italian frontiers. Part of this system, the
Karawanken range, is followed by the Austro-Yugoslav
boundary, between Ratece and Jesenice. South of the Karawanken Alps, across the broad, glaciated valley of the Sava
Dolinka, lie the majestic peaks of the Julian Alps. Here the
limestone has been fretted into sharp ridges and gaunt, lonely
peaks. From the deep valleys of Planica, Vrata and Vršič
massive grey walls rise to heights of over 8,000 feet, the grey
turning to dazzling white as the dawn light strikes the bare
rock, and to glowing pink in the rays of the setting sun.

Towering above the Julian Alps, and commanding views of the Adriatic to the south and to the snows of Grossglockner in the north-west, stands the three-headed giant Triglav, whose summit reaches 9,400 feet. From the snowfield below the summit of Triglav the melting water percolates underground to emerge in the tarns of the Valley of the Seven Lakes which feed the waterfall Slap Savica. Slap Savica gushes forth from a cave in the sheer wall of Komarča, at the western end of the deep basin of Lake Bohinj. The Sava Bohinjka which flows out of the lake joins its sister stream, the Sava Dolinka, a few miles south-west of the holiday resort of Bled, and together they form the main stream of the Sava. Most of the magnificent ranges of the Julian Alps are held between the arms of these two tributaries of the River Sava.

Beyond the mountain rim which encloses the southern edge of the Bohinj basin lies a plateau bounded on the west by the valley of the river Soča and in the east by the flat-floored Ljubljana basin. Here the west-east trend lines of the main Alpine system meet the northern edge of the Dinaric system, and the grain of the land changes, and runs NW-SE from Slovenia through Dalmatia to the Albanian and Greek frontiers. For hundreds of miles the Dinaric chains rise above the clear waters of the Adriatic, shutting off the mild influences of the Mediterranean from the valleys and plains of the interior, and restricting the dominion of the olive, orange and lemon to a narrow ribbon along the shore, and to the sun-bathed islands of the littoral. The islands themselves are but the surviving fragments of foundered mountain chains. Beyond the mile-high ramparts of the coastal ranges is a belt of mountainous and high plateau land which is in places over a hundred miles wide. Between the mountain chains, the soluble limestone has been attacked by the forces of erosion, and enormous depressions have been formed. These depressions, known as '*polja*'[1] are often as much as fifty miles in length, but only four or five miles across. When the snows melt on the neighbouring peaks the underground watercourses in the limestone overflow and the floors of the *polja* are flooded. During the summer heat the water dries out, and the *polja* floors become arid, dusty plains, their cracked, parched surfaces thirsting for the water which a

[1] The plural of the Serbo-Croat word for *polje* = field.

few weeks earlier had been present in such embarrassing abundance. Because of the capricious nature of the water supply, the peasants who farm the *polja* are forced to live in villages scattered round the foothills of the steep mountain rims, often miles away from the cultivated patches.

The soil which has collected on the floor of the *polja* has been washed down from the slopes of the surrounding mountains and plateaus, now denuded to provide these rich accumulations. In places there are hundreds of square miles where the only visible vegetation is the few tufts of coarse grass and isolated shrubs which cling to the tiny pockets of soil scattered about the arid wastes of limestone. Here is the scenery known to geographers as '*karst*'. This word is a Germanic corruption of the Slav word *kras*, and it means a region of bare limestone pavements, of underground caverns and of intermittent streams plunging below the surface by way of deep sink holes. In such a region permanent lakes and streams are rare, but occasionally local irregularities permit their formation. Thus the deposition of lime from the headwaters of the river Korana has formed barriers of insoluble material behind which the beautiful lakes of Plitvice have arisen. At Skadar, on the Albanian border, the water supply is sufficient to maintain a permanent lake in the floors of a *polje*. Only one important river, the Neretva, maintains a course which cuts across the *karst*.

In contrast to the limestone scenery of the Dinaric ranges, the mountains of southern Serbia and Macedonia form part of a great *massif* of hard, crystalline rocks of a similar age to the granites and schists of the Scottish highlands. The general height of these ancient block mountains is below that of the younger Alpine chains, but there are many peaks which rise to a height of over 5,000 feet. Some of the highest points are along the Greek, Bulgarian and Albanian frontiers. Yugoslav Macedonia is a region of wild mountains, the lower slopes of which are thickly forested. Above the deep valleys of the Vardar and its tributaries the wooded slopes rise to heights of over 3,000 feet. Higher still tower the rugged masses of crystalline rocks, with hardly a trace of vegetation to soften the grandeur of their desolate summits. Along the Albanian frontier, where the limestones of the Dinaric system meet the ancient *massif* of Macedonia, geological disturbances have resulted in the formation of two lakes, Ochrid and Prespa, each with an area of over 100 square miles.

Just as the Dinaric mountains have been folded against the western edge of the resistant block of Macedonia, so the southern extension of the Carpathians has been thrust against its eastern edge. From the Iron Gates on the Danube, an arc of mountains extends into north-eastern Serbia, to continue over the Bulgarian frontier as the Stara Planina. Complex folding and faulting, the extrusion of masses of lava and the metamorphosis of rocks under the intense heat and pressure of some remote geological upheaval have all worked to produce a varied and complicated structure. In some areas *karstic* scenery like that of the Dinaric system is to be found; in others the landscape resembles that of the wild valleys of southern Macedonia. Although the general level is not much more than 3,000 feet, these brown and crumpled mountain chains present a formidable obstacle to human movement.

The Rivers of Yugoslavia

Out of the mountains which cover the greater part of Yugoslavia flow the rivers along whose banks live most of the people. From the snows of Triglav, the lakes of Plitvice, the springs of Ilidže and the alpine torrents of the Stara Planina the waters descend to the mile-wide flood of the Danube. Apart from the Vardar, the Neretva and the Soča, all the waterways of Yugoslavia are tributary to this mighty river which crosses the north-eastern corner of the country. The Danube enters Yugoslavia from the plains of Hungary and winds across the marshy lowlands of Bačka and Banat for less than 100 miles before it reaches the Carpathians. In this short distance it receives the waters of the Tisa, the Sava, the Drava and the Morava. Each of the streams enters from a different direction, and their valleys give access from Belgrade to all parts of Yugoslavia. The Sava is the most important of the Yugoslav tributaries. In its 600-mile journey from Mount Triglav to Belgrade it passes the cities of Ljubljana and Zagreb, and its valley thus provides the main routes by road and rail between the federal capital and the two largest provincial capitals. Belgrade, as has been mentioned, is situated at the confluence of the Sava and the Danube. Immediately above the confluence is a large park named the *Kalemeg-dan* which has been constructed round a former Turkish fortress; and at one end of this park is a wide terrace which commands an excellent view of the confluence. From this point the milky waters of the Sava can be seen mingling with the darker stream of the Danube. Four important tributaries join the Sava between Zagreb and Belgrade, each providing a route deep into the mountains: the Una, the Vrbas and the Bosna, which rise in the remote fastnesses of central Bosnia, and the Drina, which has its source in the lonely peaks of Montenegro. The Morava, flowing northward from the Macedonian border, joins the Danube east of Belgrade. Its headwaters are only a few miles from those of the Vardar, which flows south to enter the Aegean near Salonika. The Vardar-Morava route through Serbia and Macedonia is one of the great highways of European history, as it provides one of the few lines of communication between the fertile Pannonian plains of the central Danube and the mountain-encircled basin of the Mediterranean.

The rich alluvial deposits brought down by the great rivers which converge on the plains near Belgrade, combine with the fertile loess drifted by the winds from across the vast Hungarian plain to make the rich soils of Bačka and Banat. These plains, which cover less than one-eighth of the area of Yugoslavia, contain nearly half the population of the country and provide the means of sustenance for many more. From the vantage point of a tall building in one of the villages of the plain there is in summer a view of a vast expanse covered with plots of maize, wheat and sunflower, stretching for mile after mile towards the far horizon. Near the banks of the rivers the dazzling gold and yellow of the ripening crops is broken by the green of trees and grasses growing in the swampy ground of the flood plain, and again, near the villages, the green of plum trees breaks the monotony of the otherwise unbroken carpet of yellow. Certainly this area has not the dramatic beauty of the mountainous parts of the country which are most visited by tourists; but to those who know it well it has a subtle, characteristic charm of its own. This has been sensitively interpreted by a contemporary painter, Milan Konjević, who lives in the small town of Sombor in Vojvodina, near the Hungarian frontier.

The Climate of Yugoslavia

'Climate' is an abstraction thought up by geographers. 'Weather' is what we experience day by day, and what we in Britain talk about day and night. Climatic generalisations based on average figures of rainfall, temperatures, winds and pressures, often 'corrected' to smooth out local variations, have their uses, but they can be misleading. They are especially so in a country like Yugoslavia, where the variety in the relief of the land and in the configuration of the coast introduces into the 'normal' pattern a thousand local complications. Thus the Mediterranean type of climate, experienced on the Adriatic coast, is often summed up in the words 'warm, wet winters and hot, dry summers'. But this description must be considerably modified before anything like a true picture of the conditions prevailing in this area emerges. Although the average winter temperatures in places like Split and Šibenik may be in the mid-forties (Fahrenheit) – well above freezing-point – sometimes the temperature falls dramatically to the mid-twenties and remains below freezing-point for several days. These are the times when the *bora* blows – the cold wind from the Balkans which sweeps down from the mountains, freezing out the milder influences from the sea. The *bora* blows with great force, sometimes reaching over 100 miles an hour; and in places its baleful influence inhibits the growth of trees and brings human activity to a standstill. A few miles from the coast its fury is spent, and many of the outer Dalmatian islands hardly notice its icy breath. In contrast to the *bora* the warm, moist *sirocco*, brings damp fogs to the islands and often makes navigation along the coast impossible. In summer the heat of the day is sometimes tempered by violent thunderstorms in the afternoon or evening, especially in the coastal areas of the bay of Kvarner at the northern end of the Adriatic.

The plains of the interior experience a 'continental' type of climate, similar to that of Hungary and the Ukraine. For two or three months in the winter the temperature is seldom above freezing-point. In the spring there is a rapid thaw, and by May the monthly average temperature is as high as 65° F. The average remains between 65° and 75° for the rest of the summer; sometimes it rises as high as 100° F. Then in autumn there is a rapid cooling off, and frost is common by the middle of October. Because of their remoteness from the sea the plains do not have a heavy total rainfall and, despite the low temperatures in winter, snow falls on only about twenty-five days in the year. Most of the rain comes in summer in the form of sudden thunderstorms. In June and July Belgrade experiences thunderstorms at the rate of about two a week. These storms usually occur late in the afternoon and they often last for less than an hour. They bring a sharp drop in temperature for a while, but the sun often breaks through again for an hour or two before sunset, bringing back some of the afternoon's warmth.

The average figures do not show, however, that as well as the extremes of summer heat and winter cold, there are local variations from day to day, especially during the winter months, which can be very trying to the human body. In October and November cold, biting winds from the Hungarian plains to the north east or from the Serbian mountains to the south east can cause sudden drops of temperature of over 25° F. Occasionally a belt of warm air covers the Danube basin for a few days and causes equally dramatic increases in temperature.

Between the extremes of the 'continental' type of climate and the milder climate of the coast there are many local variations, the peculiar features of which can be attributed mainly to the relief of the land. In general the mountains and plateaus of the Alpine and Dinaric ranges have a climate which is transitional between the Mediterranean and continental types. The areas with a winter maximum of rainfall lie to the west of the Adriatic-Black Sea watershed, and those with a spring or summer maximum to the east; but the total amount of rain or snow in the mountain areas is higher than it is either on the coast or in the plains of the interior. Often there is a sudden increase in rainfall in passing from a station at sea-level on the Dalmatian coast to one a few miles inland in the mountains. Thus Crkvice, ten miles from the coast near the Bay of Kotor has an annual rainfall of over 180 inches – the wettest place in Europe – but at sea-level in the same district only 30 inches is recorded. On the higher parts of the mountains snowfalls are frequent and some of the higher peaks have permanent snowfields. Bjelašnica (6,000 feet) near Sarajevo, in the same latitude as Nice and Monte Carlo has snow for over a hundred days of the year and frost every day until late May. The Moslem shepherds of this region make use of the snow by storing it in deep holes in the *karst* to provide water for their flocks as they move from pasture to pasture during the heat of summer.

NATURAL RESOURCES

The natural resources of Yugoslavia are abundant and varied. Most striking is the variety of mineral deposits, which include gold, silver, platinum, iron, copper, nickel, bauxite, chromium, tungsten and manganese. Copper, chromium and bauxite are particularly important for the country's economy; Yugoslavia already holds the second place in Europe in copper production, and has the highest reserve of chromium so far known (estimated at 1.5 million tons), while her bauxite deposits, which have a high aluminium content, are among the richest in the world. Yugoslavia possesses both coal and oil. Most of the coal is lignite, or 'brown coal', bituminous coal being found only in a few places in Istria and Slovenia. The working of oil is largely a post-war development; almost 300,000 tons were produced in 1956, as compared with 28,835 tons in 1946 and 1,122 tons in 1939. The mineral wealth of the country was well known and partially worked even under the Romans and in the Middle Ages, and contributed considerably to the wealth of the most powerful Serbian kings (see Chapter 2). Many of these mineral resources are only now beginning to be exploited, and they are likely to play an increasingly important part in the country's economic life.

Another natural product with which Yugoslavia is well supplied is timber; as has been already mentioned, many of her mountains are richly wooded, and in fact about a third of the whole country is covered with forest. The annual yield of timber is estimated at 15,000,000 cubic metres and wood and wood products occupy an important place in the country's export trade. The swift-flowing rivers provide a source of hydro-electricity which is being rapidly developed.

Although the greater part of Yugoslavia is mountainous, the country possesses some very good agricultural land, and agricultural products still hold the highest place among its exports. Agriculture is practised mainly in the plains, that is in central Croatia, central Serbia. and Vojvodina, where the soil is particularly fertile. The chief crops are wheat, maize, barley, oats and rice. Industrial plants are also extensively cultivated, including hemp, flax, sunflowers, sugar beet, castor-oil plants, cotton, tobacco and a large variety of medicinal herbs. Temperate fruits are also produced in considerable quantities, notably plums, which are used to make the *rakija*[1] familiar to all visitors to Yugoslavia; many plums are also exported in the form of prunes. This brief sketch gives only a bird's-eye view of the richness and variety of the country's resources, many of which are only beginning to be systematically developed.

POPULATION

According to the census of March 1953 the population of Yugoslavia was 16,927,275 – 8,211,284 males and 8,715,991 females. Comparison with earlier statistics shows that in spite of the very heavy loss of life during the Second World War (estimated at 1,706,000, that is 10.8 per cent of the total population), the population has increased steadily since 1921. The majority of the inhabitants of Yugoslavia belong to groups of the South Slavs from which the country derives its name (*jug* = south); Serbs, Croats, Slovenians, Macedonians. However, owing the the geographical position of the country and its complex history there are a number of national minorities, the most important being the Shqiptars[2], Hungarians, Bulgarians, Rumanians and Italians. The largest of these groups is the Shqiptars, most of whom live in Kosovo-Methohia in south Serbia. They are of Albanian origin and most of them are Moslems; the men can easily be recognised by their round caps of white felt, which look like old-fashioned English pudding basins. The Hungarians, as might be expected, are most numerous in the Autonomous Province of Vojvodina which adjoins Hungary, and most of the Italians are found in the coastal towns of Istria. The national minorities, in addition to

---

[1] *Rakija* is a word used for various kinds of spirits made from fruit; the commonest kind is *šlivovica*, or 'plum brandy' (from *šliva* = a plum).

[2] This is the correct official spelling, used in the handbooks published by the Yugoslav Federal Statistical Office; it is derived from the name *Shqipĕrija*, as Albania is called in the Albanian language. For general purposes a simplified spelling, 'Shiptar' is frequently used.

enjoying full equality with all other Yugoslav citizens, all have schools, including secondary schools, newspapers and radio programmes in their own languages. In 1953 there were altogether 1,112 schools giving instruction in various minority languages, all staffed, controlled and inspected by members of their respective national groups; and seventeen newspapers and periodicals in minority languages. There are also theatres which present plays in Hungarian, Rumanian, Slovak-Italian and Shqiptar.

The majority of the population of Yugoslavia live in small towns and villages. There are only thirteen towns, mostly administrative centres, with a population over 50,000 : Belgrade (542,000), Zagreb (470,000), Sarajevo (176,000), Skopje (167,000), Ljubljana (155,000), Novi Sad, the administrative centre for Vojvodina (97,000), Rijeka (87,000), Split, the largest port in Yugoslavia (84,000), Maribor (84,000), Subotica, (80,000), Osijek (75,000) and Niš (74,000).[1] Consequently the country has so far avoided the more negative features of a highly urbanised society; even in the larger towns something of the intimacy which is more characteristic of smaller units still prevails in social life.

The story of how the people now living in Yugoslav territory came to develop a separate national consciousness, and finally to be welded into a single state, is a very complex one with some sad chapters. Yet even during periods of most acute national calamity, the spirit of the people has never been broken; and the creation of the modern state represents a triumph of courage, endurance and vitality of which all Yugoslavs are justly proud, and which members of other nations cannot fail to admire. The details of this story will be unfolded in the following chapters.

[1] The figures are for 1959. See *Statistical Pocket-Book of Yugoslavia*, Federal Statistical Institute, Belgrade, March 1960.

PART ONE

The History of the Yugoslav Lands up to the Outbreak of the First World War

by MURIEL HEPPELL, M.A., PH.D.

Chapter 1

The South Slav Kingdoms in the Early Middle Ages

BY THE beginning of the first century A.D. the territory of present-day Yugoslavia was part of the Roman Empire, where it comprised the provinces of Noricum, Pannonia, Dacia, Dalmatia, Moesia and Macedonia. The life of these provinces under Roman rule was very similar to that in Roman Britain at the same period; there were the same abortive risings on the part of the native inhabitants – the Illyrians and the Celts – and, as in Britain, they themselves became 'Romanised' in time, at any rate those who came into direct contact with Roman civilisation. The Romans built roads and fortresses, and founded several towns, including Singidunum (on the site of present-day Belgrade), Sirmium (present-day Sremska Mitrovica, now being systematically excavated), Naissus (Niš), Pola (Pula, in Istria) and Salona (near present-day Split). Towards the end of the fourth century, the emperor Theodosius (378–95) divided the Empire into two parts, thus bringing into existence an East Roman Empire and a West Roman Empire. The division was approximately according to the prevailing languages, i.e. the Western Empire was the area in which the Latin language prevailed, while the Eastern Empire was predominantly Greek speaking. Actually the dividing line – which ran from Budva (on the southern Dalmatian coast) to the upper reaches of the river Drina, and thence followed the Drina to its confluence with the Sava, and after that the course of the Sava and the Danube – ran through present-day Yugoslavia, so that part of this area was included in the East Roman Empire (more commonly known as the Byzantine Empire) at the time of the barbarian invasions. This was in fact the beginning of the 'east-west' orientation of this part of Europe, a fact which was to have considerable influence on its future history.

However the period of Roman rule, though it has left impressive material traces – such as Diocletian's palace at Split, which still forms the nucleus of the modern town, and the fine amphitheatre at Pula – should be regarded as a prelude to the history of Yugoslavia rather than as an integral part of the main story. The most convenient starting-point for this is the migration of the Slavonic tribes, whose descendants form the majority of the inhabitants of the modern state.

The Slavs are a branch of the Aryan-speaking peoples; their homeland appears to have been in the region between the Carpathians, the lower reaches of the river Vistula and the upper part of the river Bug, that is the south and centre of present-day Poland and Ukraine. The first references to them in historical sources are found in Greek and Latin writers of the first and second centuries A.D.: Pliny the Elder, Ptolomy and Tacitus. Their remarks are brief and relate mainly to the geographical distribution of the Slavs; Tacitus, however, says a little (not very complimentary) about their way of life:

> 'As for the tribes of the Peucini, Venedi[1] and Fenni, I am uncertain whether to count them as Germans or as Sarmatians – though the Peucini, who are also known as the Bastarnae, behave as Germans in their language, culture, and in their settled way of life and in their methods of house-building. All are dirty and lethargic. Owing to intermarriage the chiefs bear to some extent the degraded aspect of Sarmatians. The Venedi also have contracted many Sarmatian habits. They live by plunder, infesting all the hills and woods lying between the Peucini and the Fenni. And yet these people are better regarded as Germans, for they have a settled way of life and carry shields and delight to use their feet for running at speed – all traits completely different from those displayed by the Sarmatians, who live on horseback or travel in wagons.'[2]

The Slavs probably began to move out of their homeland sometime in the fifth century A.D. This movement eventually developed into a huge fanwise migration towards the west, south and east, which resulted in the ultimate settlement of the

---

[1] Both Pliny and Tacitus refer to the Slavs as *Venedi*, a name which they presumably heard from the Germans as it was never used by the Slavs themselves.

[2] Tacitus, *Germania*, Chapter 46.

Slavs in the lands corresponding to modern Czechoslovakia, Poland, the greater part of the Balkan peninsula and present-day Ukraine, which formed the nucleus of the earliest Russian state. It is not known when or why this migration started; but as there appear to have been some Slavs in Attila's army it would seem that the movement had already begun before the middle of the fifth century, though it had not then acquired its subsequent force and momentum. Possibly pressure from population movements farther east helped to set the Slavonic tribes moving; more probably their numbers were increasing, and as their methods of agriculture were primitive they had to find more land.

By the latter part of the fifth century, large numbers of Slavs had already settled on the left bank of the lower Danube; thus they were on the border of the East Roman, or Byzantine Empire, and it is in the works of Byzantine historians that we find most information about their subsequent movements in the Balkan peninsula. To the Byzantine rulers, already hard-pressed by a series of long-drawn-out wars with Persia, the approach of the Slavs presented a further threat to the security and territorial integrity of the Empire. The first reference to them in Byzantine sources relates to the reign of Justin I (518-27). In the reign of his more famous successor Justinian I (527-65) a small group of Slavs made many raids into imperial territory, and in 540 even penetrated as far as the walls of Constantinople. During these early raids the Slavs acted in conjunction with an Asiatic people known as the Bulgars. At first, like the Angles, Saxons and Jutes in their early visits to the Roman province of Britain, the Slavs and Bulgars were content to raid Byzantine territory in search of plunder and then retire beyond the Danube with their spoils; but it was not long before groups of them began to settle. Both the raids and the settlement were made easier for them by the inadequate defences of the Empire. Justinian did indeed order the construction of a strong chain of fortifications behind the Danube frontier, but owing to his ambitious programme of reconquest in North Africa and Italy there were not enough troops to man them. Consequently throughout the sixth century the Slavs continued to ravage the whole of the Balkan peninsula as far south as the Gulf of Corinth. The activities of the Slavs were re-enforced by those of

c

the Avars, who, like the Bulgars were an Asiatic people, vigorous and energetic in destruction but without the capacity to adapt themselves to civilised life. They fairly soon disappeared from the historical scene without leaving any permanent traces of their existence; but during the sixth and seventh centuries they were a serious menace to the Byzantine Empire. In 579 they captured the important fortress of Sirmium on the river Sava; and seven years later, in conjunction with the Slavs, they besieged Salonika, the second city of the Empire, but without success. It was not until c. 591-2 that the Empire, after making peace with Persia, was able to begin a serious counter-offensive. The Byzantine armies, with their superior equipment and discipline, won some victories over the Slavs in pitched battles, but they were unable to contain them beyond the Danube. After 602 war broke out once more between the Byzantine Empire and Persia, and the campaign against the Slavs virtually ceased. After this they began to pour into imperial territory in increasing numbers; and by the early decades of the seventh century they had settled in the greater part of the Balkan peninsula, including the north-west, which lay outside imperial territory. They pushed as far as central Greece and the Peloponnese, and some of them even penetrated as far as the Greek islands and Crete. But the Slavonic settlements in the Peloponnese were not so intensive as those in the Balkan peninsula, and after the beginning of the ninth century the Empire regained control of this area, most of whose inhabitants gradually became 'hellenised'; but throughout the Middle Ages there are references to 'pockets' of Slavs in southern Greece.

Byzantine historians naturally saw the Slavs primarily as a threat to the Empire, and most of their remarks about them are concerned with their penetration into imperial territory and attempts made to check them. However at the same time their historians provide some information about their material culture and social organisation at the time of their settlement in the Balkan peninsula. It appears that the Slavs supported themselves by agriculture, including stock-breeding; land was owned collectively by a tribe and not by individuals. They knew how to weave cloth and work metals, which they used for weapons, domestic utensils and ornaments. There are many references to their skill in making *monoxila*, or boats fashioned from a single tree-trunk; it was boats of this type that constituted the 'merchant marine' of Kievan Russia; the annual journey of these boats down the Dnieper is vividly described by the tenth-century emperor and historian Constantine Porphyrogenitus (913-59).[1] Their houses were small huts made of earth, those of a large family being connected by covered corridors. As regards their social relations and political organisation, the historian Procopius of Caesarea remarked that they did not acknowledge one man as ruler, but decided all important matters by communal discussion. Another Byzantine writer observed that they had many chiefs who frequently disagreed among themselves; that the decisions of tribal meetings were frequently disregarded and that blood-vengeance was a common feature of their social life. Even these fragmentary observations show a freedom-loving but undisciplined people; these same characteristics can be seen in their later historical development, and eventually contributed to their subjugation by the authoritarian Ottoman Turks. Five hundred years were to elapse before they were able to assert once more the ancient traditions of their race.

Their weapons were simple: lances, bows and arrows and shields. They frequently resorted to the tactics of guerrilla warfare against the better-armed Byzantine armies; and women and even children took part in their campaigns. They fought mainly on foot, but there are references to individual Slavs who served in the Byzantine cavalry.

Very little is known about the religion of the primitive Slavs. Procopius of Caesarea mentions that they regarded the god of lightning, whom they called Perun, as the creator of the universe; however, modern research suggests that they had many gods, connected with different aspects of their life or of the external world, such as the sun, spring and cattle; but there is no evidence that they ever developed any coherent body of religious views or elaborate ritual.

At first sight, the settlement of the Slavs in the Balkan peninsula appears to be a very similar historical process to the settlement of the Angles, Saxons and Jutes in the island of Britain.

[1] See Constantine Porphyrogenitus, *De Administrando Imperio*, ed. .Gy. Moravcsik, Eng. trans. R. J. H. Jenkins, Budapest, 1949, Chapter 9, pp. 56-63.

But the future development of the two regions was very different, and provides an interesting example of the significance of geographical factors on historical evolution. The Angles, Saxons and Jutes settled in an island on the periphery of the former Roman Empire; and although the territory they occupied was overrun by the Danes in the ninth century and brought under the political control of the Normans in the eleventh, they had excellent conditions in which to develop their own political institutions in comparative freedom from external pressure. On the other hand, the Slavs who settled in the Balkan peninsula, right from the time of their settlement formed a huge wedge between the Byzantine Empire (whose subjects most of them nominally were) and the rapidly expanding Frankish kingdom. Moreover they were continually subject to pressure from invaders from farther east: first the Avars, then the Magyars (who ultimately settled in the north-east of the Balkan peninsula and formed the state of Hungary), the Tartars and finally the Turks. Another important external factor was the growing power of the city-state of Venice in the early Middle Ages, and her ambition to control as much as possible of the Adriatic coastline in order to expand her commerce. Thus the Slavs in the Balkan peninsula did not enjoy favourable conditions for the development of independent political institutions.

When the Slavs first settled in the Balkan peninsula they had no political organisation; in fact most of them paid tribute – a primitive sign of political subservience – to the more ruthless and powerful Avars. It was the need to protect themselves from more onerous subjugation to the Avars that gave rise to the first rudimentary Slav 'state': a union of a large number of tribes in the middle of the seventh century under a leader called Samo. The nucleus of Samo's 'kingdom' was the middle Danube region inhabited by the West Slavs, who were the immediate neighbours of the Avars; these tribes formed an alliance under Samo's leadership in 623. Soon after this – actually following the defeat of the Avar attack on Constantinople in 626, if not before – the Slavs who had settled in the eastern Alps and the upper reaches of the river Sava also recognised his leadership. Thus the area under Samo's control came to correspond roughly to modern Austria, the Czech lands, Saxony and Slovenia. But as often happens with primitive political structures, Samo's kingdom disintegrated soon after his death in 658; and the only part which retained any political cohesion was the region known as 'Carantania' (cf. the district of Carinthia in present-day Austria). At its largest, Carantania occupied an area approximately co-extensive with modern Slovenia and the south of Austria and Hungary. This territory was then inhabited entirely by Slavs; indeed because of its central position in the whole Slav-inhabited area, the name Carantania was often used by early medieval chroniclers to designate the whole body of Slavs. Although the details of the history of Carantania are complex and obscure, its general trend can be briefly summarised: a gradual absorption, first into the Carolingian Frankish kingdom, and later into the Germanic Holy Roman Empire.

For nearly a hundred years after Samo's death, Carantania managed to retain its position as an independent Slav principality ruled by hereditary princes. Then in the middle of the eighth century a revival of Avar power forced Carantania to make an alliance with its western neighbour Bavaria. In 743 the Bavarians recognised the Frankish king Carloman as their overlord, and two years later Carantania had to do the same, as the price of Bavarian help against the Avars. However, it did not become a Frankish province, but retained, until the ninth century, the right to choose and invest its own princes, subject to the approval of the Frankish king. The ceremony of investiture was an interesting one. The ruler, who is described as a *vojvoda* (= duke), was chosen by an assembly elected by the *kosezi*, or free peasants. After his election the *vojvoda* was solemnly dressed in peasant clothes, lifted on to a horse – which was thereafter never used again for agricultural work – and led three times round a special stone known as the 'prince's stone" while his subjects sang songs of praise and acclamation. At first Carantania preserved its own system of land tenure, which was less highly feudalised than that obtaining in lands under the direct control of the Frankish monarchy. Nevertheless some infiltration of Frankish influence was inevitable, especially after the introduction of Christianity. The conversion of Carantania was the work of Bavarian clergy; thus Carantania came under the cultural influence of Western, or Latin Christianity while the Slavs in the southern part of the Balkan peninsula became members of the Eastern, or as it is more generally called, the Orthodox branch of the Christian Church.[1] Christianity, with its Latin liturgy and international organisation, introduced an alien element into the primitive culture of the Slavs of Carantania; and as usually happens in such circumstances, the new cultural influence was more strongly felt and quickly assimilated by the higher classes of society, that is the *vojvoda* and his retainers, and the more powerful landowners. Indeed the acceptance of Christianity contributed towards the process of social and economic differentiation which eventually crystallised into the feudal system. Sometimes the Church of a newly converted state may help towards the development of political maturity, if the region concerned is made into a single ecclesiastical unit with its own archbishop; but this did not happen in Carantania, which for the purposes of ecclesiastical administration was divided between the Patriarchate of Aquileia and the archbishopric of Salzburg.

The final stage in the political history of Carantania was its transformation into a *grofovija* (= earldom) of the Frankish monarchy. This happened after the Carantanians took part in a rebellion against the Frankish king Louis the Pious in 819. The rebellion was crushed, and as the price of their participation the Carantanians lost their privilege of internal self-government, symbolised by the right to choose their own princes, and Carantania became a fief of the Frankish monarchy and finally part of the Holy Roman Empire. Its administration, and even its inhabitants, became increasingly Germanised; the part of its territory corresponding to modern Austria was almost entirely German by the end of the thirteenth century. The south-west of Carantania – roughly speaking the area corresponding to modern Slovenia – remained ethnically Slav and its inhabitants retained their Slavonic language; but they were politically and culturally separated from the Slavs farther south until the creation of the Yugoslav state in 1918. Naturally their development was rather different from that of the other South Slavs; even their language, Slovenian, is different from, though closely

[1] Although there were at this time differences in ritual, custom and outlook between the Christians of the eastern patriarchates (Constantinople, Antioch, Jerusalem and Alexandria), and those under the jurisdiction of Rome, the Christian Church was undivided, and remained so until the middle of the eleventh century.

related to, the Serbo-Croat spoken by the majority of the inhabitants of Yugoslavia.

A similar, though not identical pattern of historical development can be seen in the history of the Slavs who settled in the area immediately south of Carantania; this was known in the Middle Ages as Croatia, now the name of one of the constituent republics of the FPRY. The name Croatia is derived from that of the Croats, a group of Slav tribes who settled in this region sometime during the first half of the seventh century.[1] Here, as with the Slavs farther north, the first stage of political development was the formation, probably in the seventh century, of some kind of tribal union. Very little is known about its origin, but in the first instance it seems to have been limited to the tribes living in the north-western part of modern Croatia, that is between the Velebit mountains and the river Cetina; but its scope soon extended. At this time the Croats appear to have acknowledged the nominal overlordship of the Byzantine Empire, though there was no Byzantine administrative authority outside the 'Roman' towns of Split, Trogir and Zadar. In 803 inland Croatia acknowledged the suzerainty of Charlemagne; the coastal towns did the same in 806 but were restored to the Byzantine Empire by the Peace of Aachen in 812. However, the Croats, like the Carantanians, were allowed to elect their own princes, subject to the approval of the Holy Roman Emperor. As a sign of submission the Croatian princes had to provide the emperor with military help when required and send him gifts. The acknowledgment of the political overlordship of the Frankish emperor was followed by the acceptance of Christianity. Very little is known about this aspect of Croatian history, but it is thought that the first Croatian bishopric was established at Nin, now a small town to the north of Zadar; the see of Nin was under the ecclesiastical jurisdiction of the Patriarch of Aquileia. Thus the Croats, like the Carantanians, received their Christianity from the West.

Charlemagne's authority also extended over the area between

[1] A considerable controversial literature exists relating to the origin of the Croats (and also the Serbs) and their settlement in the Balkan peninsula. There is a full summary of this, with critical comments, in G. Ostrogorsky, *History of the Byzantine Empire*, trans. J. M. Hussey, Oxford (Basil Blackwell), 1956, p. 94, n. 3.

the Sava and Drava rivers, which was known as Pannonian Croatia. Actually the power of the Frankish king was more strongly felt here than in the more isolated region of Dalmatian Croatia; and in 818 Ludevit, Prince of Pannonian Croatia, rebelled against the emperor Louis the Pious. The rebellion was crushed, but only after four years' of fighting, and eventually, as a result of the disintegration of the Carolingian Empire, the Croatian princes became virtually though not legally independent. Meanwhile the power of the Byzantine Empire in the Balkan peninsula was growing stronger, and about the middle of the ninth century the towns of Zadar, Trogir, Split, Dubrovnik and Kotor, together with the islands of Krkô, Lošinj and Rab, were incorporated into the Dalmatian 'theme' of the Byzantine Empire.[1] The themes were districts under the direct administrative control of the Emperor, whose authority was represented by an official called a *strategos*;[2] the *strategos* of the Dalmatian theme had his headquarters at Zadar. The Emperor Basil I (867–886) also tried to bring Croatia under his direct rule, but without success.

From 910–930 Croatia was ruled by a prince named Tomislav, who *c.* 925 proclaimed himself king, with the approval of the Pope, though the Byzantine emperor refused to recognise his title. Under Tomislav Croatia successfully withstood the attacks of the Magyars, who had settled in the middle Danubian basin, and the powerful Bulgarian king Symeon (893–927).[3] In 926 Tomislav decisively defeated Symeon in battle; thus indi-

---

[1] The date of the establishment of the Byzantine theme is uncertain; Ostrogorsky (*op. cit.*, p. 209) attributes it to the later part of the decade 860–70, after the Byzantine fleet had helped Dubrovnik to repel an Arab attack from the sea.

[2] The theme as an administrative unit, primarily military in character, was established in the seventh century by the Emperor Heraclius (610–41); see Ostrogorsky, *op. cit.*, p. 87.

[3] The Bulgarian state grew up in the eastern part of the former Roman province of Moesia (between the mouth of the Danube and Thrace) as the result of the migration there of an Asiatic people known as the Bulgars, who succeeded in imposing their hegemony on the Slavs who had already settled in the region. Gradually the two races fused and the Bulgarian state emerged. As early as the late seventh century the Byzantine Empire was forced to recognise the independence of the new kingdom; later, especially under the vigorous and aggressive rulers Krum (803–14) and Symeon (893–927) Bulgaria became a powerful state and a serious menace to the Empire.

cating that Croatia's military strength was considerable at that time.

Meanwhile an interesting development was taking place in the Croatian Church. In the latter part of the ninth century and the early tenth century the Liturgy and parts of the Gospels were translated into Slavonic by the 'Apostles of the Slavs' Constantine-Cyril and Methodius and this disciples.[1] The Slavonic Liturgy was first used in the principality of Moravia, but before the end of the ninth century Methodius and his fellow workers (Constantine died in Rome in 869) were expelled from the country owing to the jealousy of the German bishops. They then came to the Balkan peninsula, and some of them found a refuge (which proved to be temporary) in Croatia and introduced the Slavonic Liturgy there. But their work had the same fate in Croatia as in Moravia, and in 925 its use was virtually forbidden by an ecclesiastical council held at Split, which forbade the ordination of priests who used the Slavonic Liturgy; this represented a triumph of international 'Latin' cultural influence over the growing Slav culture.

An important reason for this decision was that Tomislav was anxious for political reasons not to lose the goodwill of the Pope, as he wished to incorporate the Dalmatian coastal towns into his dominions. By this time an increasing number of Slavs had begun to settle in these towns. During the eleventh century this infiltration increased in intensity, and in 1075 Zvonimir, who was then ruler of Croatia, was proclaimed 'Prince of Croatia and Dalmatia' with the approval of the Pope. Zvonimir chose his time well, for the Byzantine Empire was powerless to oppose him, being at that time hard pressed by the Seljuk Turks who in 1071 had inflicted a severe military defeat on the Byzantine army at Manzikert in Asia Minor.

Unfortunately for the future development of the Croatian state, by 1102 there was no direct heir to the throne, and the Croatian crown passed to a certain Prince Koloman (the nephew of Zvonimir's wife Helen), who was heir to the throne of Hungary. From that time Croatia ceased to exist as an independent political unit, and its history was thenceforward bound up with that of the Hungarian kingdom.

A few words must be said about the peninsula of Istria, to

[1] See below, Chapter II, p. 68-70.

the north-west of the Balkan peninsula. Istria, together with the towns on the Adriatic coast, was nominally Byzantine territory when the Slavs first began to settle there at the end of the sixth century. Like Carantania and Croatia, Istria came under the control of the Frankish monarchy, actually in 788. An important result of this was that the coastal towns of Istria – Pula, Poreč, Kopar and Novigrad – which were still inhabited by Romans or Romanised Illyrians, lost their rights of municipal self-government and became subject to Frankish feudal overlords, lay or ecclesiastical. The Slavs, meanwhile, were regarded merely as cultivators of the soil, and had no opportunity for cultural or political development. In 952 Istria was incorporated into the kingdom of Otto I and Frankish feudal overlords were replaced by German. However these were usually absentees, so their effective influence was not very great. More important to Istria was the growing power of Venice, which was already pursuing a policy of vigorous expansion along the Adriatic coast. Being without adequate naval defence forces the Istrian towns were forced, in the course of the tenth and eleventh centuries, to make treaties with Venice which made them virtually Venetian dependencies. Thus Istria developed within the Venetian orbit, just as Carantania developed within that of the Holy Roman Empire and Croatia within that of medieval Hungary.

The Serbs, like the Croats, appear to have settled in the Balkan peninsula during the seventh century.[1] Before the end of the seventh century it seems that a group of them had already been transported to the province of Bithynia in Asia Minor, in accordance with the imperial policy of transferring troublesome (to them) elements in the population of the Empire; their name is preserved in that of the town 'Gordoservona'[2] mentioned in a Byzantine source under the year 680. This is the first reference to the Serbs as a separate people.

Very little is known about their early history. The Byzantine emperor Constantine Porphyrogenitus, in his 'guide' to the outlying provinces of the Empire (*De Administrando Imperio*) says that the Serbs inhabited the mountains region of the Drina,

---

[1] See Ostrogorsky, *op. cit.*, p. 94, n. 3.

[2] i.e. 'the town of the Serbs' (from the Slav word *gorod* = town).

Ibar and Western Morava valleys (described in later sources under the name of Raška); also Bosnia, that is the upper reaches of the river Bosna; the area between Dubrovnik and the mouth of the river Neretva, and its hinterland, known as Zahumlje and the region between Boka Kotorska and its hinterland, known as Travunija.[1] Of course it must be remembered that Constantine Porphyrogenitus was writing some three hundred years after the original settlement of the Serbs. Politically they appear to have been nominally subjects of the Empire, although the territory in which they settled was not part of the imperial theme system; hence they were not subject to direct imperial control.

Nevertheless the Serbs must have been subject to Byzantine influences of various kinds, as can be seen from the fact that soon after their settlement individual Serbs were converted to Christianity. The process of conversion seems to have continued gradually during the eighth and ninth centuries, although nothing is known about the earliest ecclesiastical organisation among the Serbs. The important thing is that the Serbs received the Christian faith from Byzantium, not from Rome; consequently they never came directly under the cultural influence of Western Christendom, as did the Slavs of Carantania and Croatia. This was to have far-reaching effects on their future history, and its consequences can still be felt in present-day Yugoslavia.

The first signs of political organisation among the Serbs can be seen about the middle of the ninth century, under a ruler named Vlastimir. It seems that he was able to establish his personal authority over the Serbs owing to the need for a strong defensive polict, to prevent them from being absorbed into the rapidly expanding Bulgarian kingdom; by the middle of the ninth century Bulgaria had already absorbed Macedonia, and extended its control as far north as Belgrade. Vlastimir was able to prevent Bulgaria from subjugating the Serbs; and during his 'reign' the region of Travunija became part of his dominion as a result of his marriage with the daughter of the *župan* of Travunija. Unfortunately the further political development of Serbia was hindered by quarrels among the members of the princely family after Vlastimir's death; and both the Byzantine

---

[1] See *De Administrando Imperio, op. cit.*, pp. 152–4.

Empire and Bulgaria took advantage of these dissensions to try and increase their political influence over the Serbs. Finally Byzantine influence proved stronger, and this caused Symeon of Bulgaria to launch a direct attack against Serbia. But his army was defeated; then, about the year 924, in order to secure his own country against the threat of an attack from the rear, he undertook another campaign with a much larger force. This time the Bulgarian army so devastated Serb territory that the Serbs were forced to submit to Symeon. However their submission was of short duration; under Symeon's weak successor Peter (927-69) the Serbs regained their independence, though they remained nominally subject to the Byzantine Empire.

Nothing further is definitely known about the history of the Serbs until the rise of the kingdom of Duklija (Dioclea), which derived its name from that of the Roman town of Doclea, the remains of which are near present-day Titograd, the capital of Montenegro; in fact the medieval kingdom of Duklija was approximately co-extensive with the later kingdom of Montenegro. During the eleventh century Duklija was usually called Zeta, from the river Zeta which runs through its territory.

Until about the middle of the eleventh century the princes of Zeta had to acknowledge the overlordship of the Byzantine Emperor, but Prince Stephen Vojislav (*c.* 1040 – *c.* 1052) was able to assert his independence. He was succeeded by his son Mihailo (*c.* 1052 – *c.* 1081), who was obviously on good terms with the Empire: at the beginning of his reign he was given the title of *protospatarios*, and inscribed among the 'friends and allies of the Roman Empire'; this was typical of Byzantine methods of securing the goodwill of 'barbarous' but impressionable subjects, or dubious allies. In 1077 Mihailo was sent royal insignia by Pope Gregory VII, a sign that his political position was established and recognised. But the kingdom of Zeta did not retain its power very long; after the death of Mihailo's successor Bodin in 1101 it rapidly disintegrated, partly as a result of quarrels among members of the princely family – a recurrent feature in the history of the earliest Balkan kingdoms. In the twelfth century political ascendancy in the Serb lands passed to Raška (Rascia), north-east of Zeta (see above). Raška, like Zeta, derived its name from a river; in addition it is preserved today in the name of a small town on the branch railway line between Belgrade and Skopje, which is the nearest railway station – though not actually very near – to the famous Sopo-čani frescoes. Throughout the twelfth century, the princes of Raška, like their predecessors in Zeta in the previous century, struggled to assert their independence of the Byzantine Empire; without success, however, until the reign of the Grand Župan Stephen Nemanja (*c.* 1167 – 1196), the founder of the greatest dynasty of Serbian rulers. His reign marks the beginning of the most important and glorious phase in the history of medieval Serbia.

To the south of the region occupied by the Serbs lay the territory known as Macedonia. In early medieval times this name applied to a much wider area than present-day Yugoslav Macedonia, and included a considerable part of what is now western Bulgaria and northern Greece.[1] This area was settled by the Slavs early in the seventh century; and they must have settled in considerable numbers, and early formed some kind of rudimentary political organisation, as can be seen from their repeated attacks on the important Byzantine city of Salonika, next to Constantinople the most important commercial centre in the Empire. However they never succeeded in capturing it, although in the course of time many individual Slavs penetrated into the town and settled there. The Macedonian Slavs, by reason of their geographical position, and their energy in warfare, represented the most acute danger to the Byzantine Empire of all the Slavs, and therefore bore the fiercest brunt of the Byzantine counter-attacks; this inevitably hampered and indeed frustrated their independent political development. The history of the Macedonian Slavs is, for practical purposes, part of the history of the Empire.

During the seventh century, this history is a story of attack and counter-attack: repeated attempts by the Slavs to capture Salonika, and at least two large-scale Byzantine offensives against the Slavs (in 658 and 688) as a result of which the inhabitants of Macedonia were compelled to acknowledge the authority of the Emperor, although they appear to have retained

---

[1] i.e. the area between the Šar and Albanian mountains to the Rhodope range on the east; and from the Rila Mountains in the north to the river Bistrica. (*Istorija Naroda Yugoslavije*, Zagreb, 1953, p. 279, n. 1.)

the right to choose their own princes. Then in the eighth century Macedonia became a battle-ground in the long-drawn-out struggle between the Byzantine Empire and Bulgaria. Some time before 802 the Byzantine government established a theme in Macedonia,[1] and in order to strengthen Byzantine influence a number of military colonists, or *stratiotes* were settled there. But later in the ninth century, in 864, a considerable part of northern Macedonia (as far north as Lakes Prespa and Ochrid) was ceded to Boris of Bulgaria in order to secure the religious allegiance of his country to the Patriarch of Constantinople instead of to the Pope. Thus the greater part of Macedonia was incorporated into the 'First Bulgarian Empire'. Actually this Empire did not last very long; from the first it was the object of the determined hostility of Byzantium, and was in fact conquered and annexed by the Emperor John Tzimiskes in 971. But this subjection proved only temporary for in 976 a rebellion broke out against Byzantium; and at this point the centre of unrest was the recently acquired Macedonia, not the 'Old Bulgaria' to the north-east. The rebellion was led by four brothers known as the Cometopuli, so called because they were the sons of the 'comes', or provincial governor, Nicholas of Macedonia. Soon the leadership of the rebellion devolved on the youngest brother Samuel. The Byzantine emperor at that time was Basil II (976–1025), an able, strong-willed and ruthless ruler whose whole life was dominated by the desire to crush the internal and external enemies of the Empire and to increase the power of the central authority. The struggle between Basil II and Samuel has a grim, epic quality. At the beginning of his reign Basil was unable to concentrate his full military strength against Samuel, first owing to a serious revolt against his own authority in Asia Minor, and then because of a war in Syria against the Fatimid Caliphate of Egypt. Thus for some time Samuel was not only able to maintain his independence but also to extend the territory under his nominal control as far north as Zadar; but even he failed to capture Salonika. It was only at the beginning of the eleventh century that Basil was able to begin systematic action against Samuel. For thirteen years, from 1001 to 1014 he waged incessant war on Samuel's territory, as a result of which Samuel's position gradually weakened. The

[1] See Ostrogorsky, *op. cit.*, p. 172, n. 1.

climax of the struggle came in 1014, when Samuel's army was surrounded in the mountain passes of the district of Kleidon near the river Struma. Samuel himself managed to escape, but many of his troops were killed and more taken prisoner. Basil inflicted a savage punishment on the defeated army; the prisoners (said to number 14,000 though this figure is probably exaggerated) were all blinded, except for one man in every hundred who was left with one eye to guide the rest of the soldiers to the town of Prilep, where Samuel had fled. This cruel act caused Basil II to be known as 'Bulgaroktonos', the Bulgar-slayer.

The shock of seeing his former army in such a plight killed Samuel, and his Empire did not survive him for long. The inevitable dissensions broke out among the members of his family, and in 1018, after the death of Samuel's nephew John Vladislav, Basil II made a ceremonial entry into Ochrid, Samuel's capital, and received homage from his widow and the surviving members of his family. The Macedonian 'empire' had been destroyed; and for the first time since the infiltration of the Slavs into the Balkan peninsula the whole area acknowledged the authority of the Byzantine Empire.

There is some controversy among historians as to whether Samuel's Empire should be considered as a continuation, or brief revival, of the First Bulgarian Empire crushed by John Tzimiskes in 971, or as a new political unit, not Bulgarian but Macedonian. Samuel himself was a Macedonian, and under him Macedonia was the centre of the Empire; his capital, Ochrid, was a Macedonian town. But the change was one of orientation rather than of character or policy; moreover it was at least partly accidental that the Macedonian Samuel retained the leadership of the revolt against Byzantium.[1] Thus Samuel's Empire should be regarded not so much as a specifically Macedonian state, but rather as part of a larger Slav 'nationalist' movement usually associated, in the early Middle Ages, with

---

[1] After the conquest of Bulgaria by John Tzimiskes the Bulgarian tsar Boris II and his brother Romanus were taken to Constantinople as captives; at the time of the rising in Macedonia they escaped, but Boris was killed (by Bulgarian sentries who did not recognise him), and Romanus could not be recognised as ruler of Bulgaria as he had been castrated by the Byzantines. (Ostrogorsky, *History of the Byzantine Empire*, p. 267.)

the name of Bulgaria. This is the view of the eminent Byzantine historian Professor Ostrogorsky.[3]

'If Basil II showed his ruthlessness on the battle-field,' writes Professor Ostrogorsky, 'in his subsequent treatment of Samuel's Empire he showed himself a good statesman.'[4]

Two new themes were established on the conquered territory: *Paristrion*, including the lands between the Balkan Mountains and the Danube, with its capital at Silistria; and *Bulgaria*, with its capital at Skopje (now the capital of Yugoslav Macedonia). The patriarchate of Ochrid, established by Samuel, was reduced to the rank of an archbishopric, but an archbishopric of the type known in Byzantium as 'autocephalous', that is, subject only to the Emperor, and not to the Patriarch of Constantinople. The old Dalmatian theme, including Zadar and Dubrovnik, was revived; but the Serbs living in Dioclea (Zeta), Zahumlje, Raška and Bosnia were allowed to retain their native princes; thus their status was that of vassal principalities of the Empire rather than provinces. The inhabitants of the new themes were allowed to continue paying taxes in kind, although payments in gold were being increasingly demanded in the more economically developed parts of the Empire.

Yet, in spite of these moderate measures discontent continued to smoulder in Macedonia, and in 1040 it flared up into open rebellion. The causes were mainly economic: after the death of Basil II tax-farming was introduced, which bore hardly on the peasantry, and payment of taxes in gold was demanded; in addition an increasing amount of land passed into the hands of large landowners, ecclesiastical as well as secular. The rebellion was crushed, and a period of more repressive government followed. Another rising broke out in 1072; this time conditions were more favourable to the rebels, as the imperial forces had just recently been defeated by the Turks at the battle of Manzikert, and the Empire was also weakened by internal quarrels. In addition the rebels were supported by the prince of Zeta, Constantine Bodin. This rebellion was also crushed, but not without difficulty. After this the Macedonians made no further attempts to free themselves from Byzantine rule.

The religious history of Macedonia, like its political history, was bound up with that of Bulgaria. The official conversion of

[1] *Ibid.*, pp. 267–8. [2] *Ibid.*, pp. 275.

Bulgaria took place in the reign of Boris I (852–889). He, like Prince Vladimir I of Kiev over a hundred years later, felt that the time had come to abandon paganism and adopt Christianity, in order to enhance his position as a civilised ruler; but if possible he wanted an independent ecclesiastical organisation for his country. He first approached the Frankish king Louis II; this action provoked an immediate reaction in the Byzantine Empire, which did not want to see either Frankish political influence or Roman ecclesiastical jurisdiction established so near imperial territory. By means of a prompt display of naval and military force, accompanied by the promise of valuable territorial concessions in Macedonia (see above, p. 44), Boris was induced to accept Christianity from Constantinople instead of Rome, and was baptised in 864, taking the name of Michael, after the Byzantine emperor who acted as his sponsor. But differences of opinion soon developed on the subject of church organisation; Boris wanted an independent Bulgarian church, under its own Patriarch, whereas the Emperor wished it to be under the control of a Greek bishop. Boris then made overtures to the Pope, but without success; Papal legates were sent to his court, but no practical steps were taken towards the creation of an independent Bulgarian church. Boris once more approached Constantinople; and this time the Emperor proved more compliant, and allowed the Bulgarian church a status which, though not completely autocephalous, was more privileged than that of an ordinary archbishopric.

It was only after the conversion of Bulgaria that Christianity began to spread rapidly in Macedonia, largely thanks to the energetic missionary and educational work of the disciples of Methodius, especially Clement, Bishop of Ochrid, and Naum (a monastery dedicated to St. Naum still exists at Ochrid). Yet, in spite of their work, by the middle of the tenth century, Macedonia was seriously affected by heresy. This heresy, known as Bogomilism (from the name of a Slav priest called 'Bogomil', the Slavonic form of the Greek name Theophilos) was a form of dualism, similar to, and no doubt influenced by, the Massalian and Paulician heresies which already flourished in Asia Minor.[1]

[1] Colonies of Paulician heretics had been settled in Thrace as far back as the eighth century; and according to the Byzantine historian Theophanes they were responsible for the spread of heretical ideas there. (See D. Obolensky, *The Bogomils*, 1948, p. 60.)

The Bogomils considered that the whole created, visible world was under the dominion of Satanael, or the Devil, whom they regarded as a fallen angel. They therefore rejected all outward forms of ecclesiastical organisation and religious ritual as being expressions of the powers of evil; they were, on the same grounds, opposed to all representatives of secular power, such as princes, officials and landowners; thus, though primarily a religious movement, Bogomilism was undoubtedly fed by social unrest. Altogether it was a very disruptive force, and the more difficult to detect and eliminate since the Bogomils preached and practised an ascetic, 'spiritual' way of life which made them appear to be good Orthodox Christians. In spite of the vigilance of both ecclesiastical and secular authorities, Bogomilism continued to spread throughout the Middle Ages, and affected, in various forms, Bulgaria, Serbia, Bosnia (where it gained a very strong hold) and the Empire itself. Although the circumstances of its origin are obscure, there is reason to think that it began in Macedonia.[1]

In spite of wars, revolts and heresy, the cultural life of Macedonia flourished. Ochrid in the late ninth and early tenth century was an important centre of literary activity, mainly the translation of Greek ecclesiastical texts into Slavonic, to which the future development of Slavonic literature was much indebted. Monumental wall-painting (entirely ecclesiastical as to subject matter) also developed vigorously. Early examples of this art, as may be expected, show strong Byzantine influence, but the eleventh century saw the development of a more specifically 'Macedonian school'; one of the finest examples of this is the decoration in the church at Nerezi, a small village not far from Skopje. It is also probable that wood-carving, which later developed as a typically Macedonian art, was also practised in the early medieval period, though no examples have survived.

It remains to say something about one part of Yugoslavia not mentioned so far – Bosnia and Hercegovina. Bosnia is mentioned as a separate entity in the work of Constantine Porphyrogenitos, who says that it was inhabited by the Serbs (see above); he refers to it as 'the small land of Bosnia', and in all probability

[1] See Obolensky, *op. cit.*

the area concerned was limited to the upper reaches of the Bosna and Vrbas rivers – much less than the present Bosnia and Hercegovina. Possibly it was at one time part of the Croatian kingdom, and then of Samuel's Macedonian-Bulgarian Empire; later, like Serbia and Zeta (whose prince was ruler of Bosnia for a time) it was under the nominal rule of the Byzantine Empire; but by the twelfth century it appears to have been an independent principality. However, its independence was always precarious, since it was continually threatened by the kings of Hungary, who, since the beginning of the twelfth century had controlled Croatia (see above, p. 39), and was finally destroyed by the Turks. In addition the internal political development of Bosnia was frustrated by the weakness of the central rulers and the power of the feudal barons. This circumstance was largely due to the peculiar religious history of Bosnia.

Nothing is known of the circumstances in which Christianity was introduced there; but it appears that it never took a very strong hold, perhaps because Bosnia was the meeting-place, on Yugoslav territory, of Roman and Byzantine ecclesiastical influence. By the late twelfth century a heresy, akin to but not the same as Bogomilism, had begun to gain adherents in Bosnia. Unlike Bogomilism in Macedonia, the Bosnian heresy, usually known as the 'Bosnian Church', had considerable support from the nobles and landowners, though it was also popular with the common people because it did not collect tithes. It soon acquired its own hierarchical organisation: at the head was the 'bishop of the Bosnian Church'; then a group known as 'gosti' (guests), and lower still the 'starci' or elders. All these were chosen from people who followed a quasi-monastic way of life, who were known as 'krystjani' (Christians); these included women. The krstjani were the true driving force of the Bosnian Church; according to fifteenth-century sources they were frequent visitors at the houses of noble families, and were sometimes employed on state business and sent as envoys to other parts of Yugoslav territory.

Naturally it was not long before the Papacy began an energetic campaign against the Bosnian Church. In 1221 a Papal Legate was sent to Bosnia, and the native bishop, who was suspected of sympathising with the heretics, was replaced by a foreigner; at the same time the Dominicans, who had proved

themselves strenuous opponents of the heretical Cathars in
France, were sent to the country. These ecclesiastical measures
were supported by the military power of Hungary, whose
rulers were only too glad of an excuse to extend their political
power over Bosnia. The Hungarian campaigns had some success until Hungary itself was attacked by the Tartars in 1241;
this gave Bosnia a short respite. Then in 1244 the Hungarian
king Bela IV invaded Bosnia with a large army and forced the
'ban' (or ruler) of Bosnia and his nobles to submit. However,
although Bosnia remained under Hungarian political influence
until the end of the thirteenth century, the ecclesiastical authority of the Catholic Church was not effectively strengthened
there, as can be seen from the fact that the bishop of Bosnia was
always obliged to reside outside Bosnian territory, at Djakov in
Slavonia, which was under direct Hungarian rule.

Towards the end of the fifteenth century, the Hungarian
monarchy was weakened by succession quarrels, and Bosnia
came under the control of a princely family named Bribirski,
who also controlled Croatia and Dalmatia at that time. But
their power did not last long, and early in the fourteenth century Bosnia was once more ruled by a native ban, Stephen II
Kotromanić. His son, Tvrtko was destined to be the most
powerful ruler of Bosnia, and in 1377 was crowned King of
'Serbia, Bosnia and the Primorje (i.e. the coastal territory)
and the western lands'. The growth of Tvrtko's power was due
to a combination of various circumstances: the King of Hungary was too much occupied elsewhere to challenge him; the
rapid disintegration of Tsar Dušan's Greco-Serbian Empire
after his death in 1355[1] enabled Tvrtko to extend his control
over a considerable part of Serbia; in addition he claimed,
through female descent, to be the true heir to the Nemanjić
dynasty; finally he was able to persuade the Bosnian nobles to
give him effective support in his policy of territorial expansion.
Nevertheless the Bosnian army remained virtually a collection
of feudal levies whose loyalty to the central ruler was inevitably
precarious. However, towards the end of the thirteenth century,
Tvrtko was able to extend his territory still farther; after the
death of Louis of Hungary in 1282 he acquired parts of Croatia
and Dalmatia, including the coastal towns of Kotor and Split,

[1] See below, Chapter 2, p. 61.

but not Dubrovnik; his title was appropriately widened to 'King of Serbia, Bosnia, Dalmatia, Croatia and the Primorje'. Thus Tvrtko united under his rule the majority of the Croats and Serbs. But his kingdom, like those of earlier Slav rulers in the Balkan peninsula, did not last long; even while he was at the height of his power the forces of disintegration were at work, notably the relentless advance of the Turks in the Balkans.

Immediately after Tvrtko's death in 1391 the Bosnian nobles reasserted themselves by choosing as king not Tvrtko's son, but a relative, Stephen Dabiša (1391–3) who was already an old man, and moreover without the capacity to govern such a difficult country. He soon agreed to rule as the vassal of the Hungarian king Sigismund. The authority of the central government was further weakened in the brief reign of his wife, who succeeded him. Thereafter the Bosnian rulers, though always chosen from the Kotromanić family, were in fact puppets of the powerful nobles.

Clearly such a state was in no condition to withstand the double pressure of Hungary and the Turks. Sigismund of Hungary made repeated attacks on Bosnia in the early fourteenth century and compelled most of the leading nobles to accept him as their overlord. His success was partly due to the fact that some at least of the Bosnian nobles, despite their inability to see beyond their own individual interests, realised that the Turks represented an even greater threat to Bosnian independence than did the Hungarian king. On the other hand, some of the adherents of the 'Bosnian Church' preferred subjection to the Moslem Turks rather than to Catholic Hungary, since it was at the hands of the Catholics that they had experienced the fiercest persecution.

Hungarian power in Bosnia was successfully challenged by the Turks in 1415, and the unhappy country became a prey to anarchy and bloodshed. Now many of the nobles agreed to become Turkish vassals, and the king, Tvrtko II, owed his position to Turkish support. During this troubled time one of the most powerful Bosnian nobles, Stephen Vukšić, managed to establish a semi-independent state in the southern part of Bosnia, in the region of the Neretva valley. He took the title of Herceg (= duke) of St. Sava, in honour of St. Sava, a son of Stephen Nemanja and the founder of the independent Serbian

Church, who was buried in his territory; his title has survived in the present-day name of this region, Hercegovina.

Turkish pressure on Bosnia increased steadily in the early decades of the fifteenth century, mainly in the form of plundering expeditions and interference in the frequent quarrels among the nobles and members of the royal family. After the conquest of Constantinople in 1453, and the final subjugation of the Serbian kingdom in 1459, it was clear that what remained of Bosnia's independence could not last long. Nevertheless Stephen Tomašević, the last King of Bosnia (1461–3) put up a brave resistance. But when the armies of Mehemet the Conqueror made a determined attack on Bosnia in 1462 they subdued the country in less than a month. However the Turkish victory did not remain unchallenged; the next year both the Herceg of St. Sava and King Matthias Corvinus of Hungary counter-attacked, and succeeded in liberating some parts of Bosnia, including Jajce, the old capital, from Turkish control. But in time the Turks recaptured these areas, though the *banovina* of Jajce held out until 1521. After that the whole of Bosnia and Hercegovina became part of the Turkish Empire, and remained under Turkish rule until 1878.

Perhaps because of its stormy religious and political history, Bosnia made little contribution to the development of art and literature among the Balkan Slavs during the Middle Ages. But one curious form of artistic expression was highly developed, and is now regarded as typically Bosnian, namely the carving of tombstones, known as *stecchi*. It has been wrongly assumed that these were exclusively or mainly connected with the 'Bosnian Church', but this view is now no longer accepted. A large number of them have survived in Bosnia, many in remote places; but they can also be studied in the *Zemaljski Muzej* (Regional Museum) of Bosnia and Hercegovina in Sarajevo, which has an interesting collection.

Chapter 2

The Rise and Fall of Medieval Serbia

WITH proclamation of Stephen Nemanja as 'Grand Župan' of Raška *c.* 1169 an important new chapter in Serbian, indeed in medieval Balkan history begins. We have seen that the kingdoms of Carantania, Croatia and Bosnia collapsed or disintegrated (or, in the case of Croatia were amalgamated with other states) before they attained political maturity and power. With Serbia it was otherwise. Serbia, like Bulgaria in the ninth and tenth centuries (the period of the so-called 'First Bulgarian Empire'), and again in the thirteenth century (the period of the 'Second Bulgarian Empire') became a powerful state not only territorially but also economically and culturally. For a short time it even seemed possible that Serbia would replace the rapidly declining Byzantine Empire as the leading power in Eastern Europe and the main bulwark against Turkish aggression.

Just how and when Stephen Nemanja established his authority in Raška is not known. As Grand Župan he made several determined attempts to free himself from Byzantine suzerainty; first he was supported in these efforts by the King of Hungary, but later the Emperor Manuel Comnenus (1143–80) made an alliance with Hungary, so that Nemanja could no longer count on Hungarian help. Nor did an alliance with Venice prove any more effective; for in 1172 Manuel invaded Raška with a large army and compelled Nemanja to recognise his authority. But Nemanja did not give up, and during the Third Crusade, when the Emperor's attention was diverted elsewhere he again asserted his independence. Once more, however, the Serbs were defeated in battle by the imperial forces (in 1190); but the Emperor was not strong enough to follow up his victory, and from that time Serbia was virtually independent. Nemanja also added the region of Zeta to his dominions, including the coastal towns of Bar, Skadar, Ulcinj and Kotor, placing it, together with Trebinja, under the rule of his eldest son Vukan; thereafter it became the custom for Zeta to be ruled by the heir to the Serbian throne, or at least a member of the royal family. However, his attempt to incorporate Dubrovnik as well was not successful. Thus the principality he established was roughly square in shape, stretching from the Southern Morava to the Adriatic, from east to west, and along the Adriatic from south of Ulcinj almost to the river Cetina, but excluding Dubrovnik. (See map opposite.)

Like many early medieval rulers, Nemanja was not only an able military leader and administrator, but also a man of deep piety. He founded many monasteries, the most famous being Studenica (where he was buried) and Hilendar, the Serbian monastery on Mount Athos. In 1196 he abdicated and himself became a monk, taking the name of Symeon; his monastic life was spent first at Studenica and later at Mount Athos. It might even be claimed that his piety was his greatest political asset, for he quickly became the object of a 'cult', zealously fostered by his sons Sava (later destined to be the first archbishop of an independent Serbian church), and Stephen, his successor and the first Serbian ruler to have the title of king. Both Sava and Stephen wrote biographies of their father, in which they not only stressed his personal sanctity but also his ability as a ruler.[1] Shortly after his death he was canonised; thus his successors enjoyed the advantage – a considerable one in medieval Christendom – of being *svetorodni*, 'born of holy stock'.

When Nemanja abdicated in 1196 he was succeeded as Grand Župan by his younger son Stephen, although Vukan, the eldest son, retained control of Zeta. The main achievements of Stephen's reign were the acquisition of the royal title, for which reason he is known as *Stephen Prvovenčani*, 'Stephen the first-crowned', and the establishment of an independent arch-bishopric in Serbia; both these changes considerably enhanced the political prestige of the young state. It was actually the Pope, Innocent III, who sent Stephen the royal insignia, at his request in 1202. His new title was immediately challenged by his northern neighbour, King Emeric of Hungary, who, naturally enough, did not look very favourably on the growth of the Serbian state; and for a short time Stephen's brother Vukan was king, supported by Hungary. But Stephen soon recovered

[1] For further details of these works, see below, p. 72.

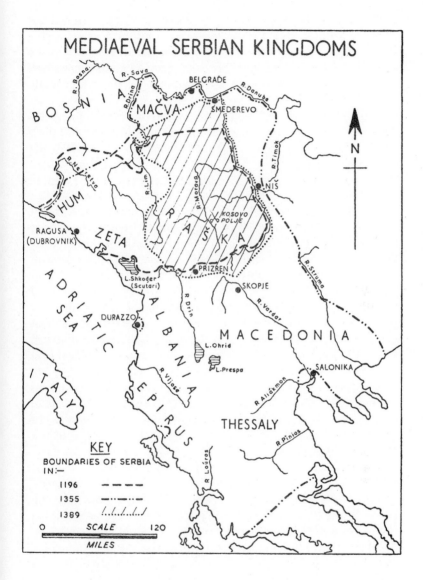

MEDIAEVAL SERBIAN KINGDOMS

KEY

BOUNDARIES OF SERBIA
IN:—

1196 — — —
1355 —·—·—
1389 /·/·/·/·/

0 SCALE 120

MILES

his position with the help of Bulgaria, now entering on its second period as a powerful state.

The independent, or autocephalous (to use Byzantine ecclesiastical terminology) archbishopric was established in 1219. Its first headquarters was at a place called Žiča, where Stephen had founded a monastery. This monastery, situated about two miles from the small town of Rankovičevo (on the branch railway line from Belgrade to Skopje) is still a striking landmark by reason of the rich red colour of its brick, visible for some distance away against a background of rolling hills. The first archbishop was Stephen's younger brother Sava, who was consecrated to his new office by the Patriarch of Nicea, since Constantinople was at that time the capital of the 'Latin Empire' established after the Fourth Crusade. Hitherto the Serbian church had been under the jurisdiction of the bishop of Ochrid, in Byzantine territory. Not unnaturally, the change was distasteful to the bishop of Ochrid, whose authority and prestige was thereby lessened; so he wrote a letter to Sava in which he protested against his new title and reproached him for leaving the life of a monk on Mount Athos (as a young man Sava had been tonsured in the Serbian monastery of Hilendar established by his father) in order to concern himself with worldly affairs. However Sava ignored this protest and addressed himself to the task of reorganising the Serbian church, in which he showed considerable administrative skill. He established several new bishoprics, all of them connected with monasteries. The creation of a virtually independent, well-organised church in Serbia both stimulated the growth of national self-consciousness and enhanced the prestige of the Nemanja dynasty.

For half a century or so after Stephen's death in 1227 the Serbian state made no notable political progress; this was partly due to the rapid change of rulers, and also to the growing power of the Second Bulgarian Empire, which forced Serbia on the defensive. Meanwhile the country's economic strength was developing rapidly, mainly as a result of the exploitation of her rich and varied mineral resources. The wealth which later Serbian rulers acquired from the mines on their territory was an important factor both in the military power of the state and in its cultural progress.

The next important Serbian ruler was Milutin (1281–1321). In his reign Serbian territory was extended southward, at the expense of Byzantine Macedonia; the Byzantine Emperor, Andronicus II, was too weak to offer any effective resistance. Once the Emperor showed himself willing to accept this territorial expansion of Serbia, Milutin was ready on his side to maintain friendly relations with the Empire; the result was a marriage alliance between Milutin and the Emperor's daughter Simonis. This was one of the strange marriage alliances of history; for Simonis was a child of six, reared in a totally different atmosphere from that to which she was sent as a bride. Portraits of Milutin and Simonis are preserved on two pillars in the church of the monastery of Gračanica which Milutin founded.[1]

Partly because of this marriage, but also as a result of the incorporation into Serbia of territory formerly under Byzantine administration, there was a marked increase of Byzantine cultural influence in Serbia in Milutin's reign. The military and political power of the Empire was declining rapidly at this time; indeed, despite the recovery of Constantinople in 1261 by Michael VIII Paleologus, Emperor of Nicea, the Empire remained permanently weakened after the blow inflicted on it by the armies of the Fourth Crusade in 1204. Bulgaria and Serbia, the two young and vigorous Slav states on its borders profited from this weakness; but even while they seized imperial territory, they remained culturally very strongly under the influence of the Empire. At the beginning of Milutin's reign, life in Serbia was, by Byzantine standards, primitive, even at court. But a Byzantine official who visited Milutin just before the end of the thirteenth century reported a quite different situation: Milutin himself was sumptuously dressed; his court glittered with silk and gold; and the visitor was served with choice food on gold and silver dishes; in fact everything, he said, was in accordance with 'Roman' (i.e. Byzantine) taste and the ceremonial of the imperial court. Another way in which Milutin copied Byzantine customs was by the introduction of Greek

---

[1] Like many similar portraits, these are now unfortunately defaced. The damage has been traditionally (though not necessarily accurately) attributed to the deliberate destructive activity of the Turks; this tradition forms the subject of a moving poem 'Simonida' by the Serbian poet Milan Rakić.

terminology into official documents, and the use of the numerous and complicated Byzantine honorific titles in the Serbian court.

Milutin also founded many monasteries. His building activity extended even outside Serbia; he not only rebuilt Hilendar on Mount Athos, but also built a Serbian monastery in Jerusalem and churches in both Constantinople and Salonika, the 'second city' of the Byzantine Empire. It was the wealth derived from the mines in his territory that made it possible for him to carry out this lavish building programme.

Milutin also extended Serbian territory northwards, at the expense of Hungary. The northern part of his kingdom was ruled by his brother Dragutin, who had his headquarters at Belgrade, destined to be the capital of the revived nineteenth-century Serbia and of the present-day federal republic. Relations between the brothers were frequently strained, for Dragutin behaved towards foreign rulers as though he were an independent sovereign. By the beginning of the fourteenth century they were in open conflict and Milutin was forced to promise that Dragutin's descendants would inherit the throne of Serbia. But in 1316 Dragutin died, whereupon Milutin imprisoned his son Vladislav and himself took possession of the territory formerly ruled by his brother. This caused the King of Hungary to intervene; he occupied Belgrade and forced Milutin to surrender much of the territory that he himself had wrested from Hungary earlier.

Milutin's death in 1321 was followed by quarrels over the succession between his sons Stephen and Constantine and Dragutin's son Vladislav. The victor was Stephen, known as *Stephen Dečanski* after a monastery he founded at Dečani.[1] During his father's lifetime Stephen had been blinded for attempted rebellion – blinding for political offences was yet another sign of Byzantine influence, destined to disqualify its victim from imperial, or in the case of Serbia, royal office. But the operation had been imperfectly performed on Stephen (perhaps deliberately so) and he was therefore able to establish his claim to his father's throne. During his reign Serbian territory

[1] The monastery of Dečani, situated in beautiful mountain scenery in the south-west of present-day Serbia, not far from the Albanian frontier, is well known to art historians on account of its very rich collections of frescoes, which include nineteen cycles of illustrations, one containing 365 separate scenes.

was further extended in Macedonia, where Serbia and Bulgaria were rivals, but a Bulgarian army was decisively defeated by the Serbs in 1330. The next year Stephen was dethroned and imprisoned by his son Dušan, and shortly afterwards strangled, whether with Dušan's knowledge or not is not known. Under Dušan (1331–55) medieval Serbia reached the zenith of its power. Dušan continued the expansionist policy of his predecessors in Macedonia, and in the course of his reign practically the whole of Byzantine Macedonia was absorbed into Serbia. Internal disorders in the Empire contributed to some extent to Dušan's success; for a time, after 1341 there was even civil war in the Empire. But Dušan aimed at more than territorial expansion. The area ruled by the Byzantine Emperors after the recovery of Constantinople in 1261 was pitifully small, and they had neither the military nor the economic resources to extend it; moreover, even the continued existence of the Empire was precarious, threatened as it was by the vigorous military power of the Turks who were advancing steadily from Asia Minor, and the growing strength of Bulgaria and Serbia in the Balkans. It was Dušan's aim not only to acquire imperial territory, but to accede to the imperial throne; and to rule from Constantinople a Greco-Serbian Empire in which the ancient culture of Byzantium should be revitalised by the wealth and vigorous military power of his own young state. It was, perhaps, unfortunate for the future history of the Balkan peninsula, indeed for the whole of Europe, that he did not succeed.

Dušan made careful diplomatic preparations, making alliances with both Bulgaria and Dubrovnik. Then he began his advance into Macedonia, actually at the suggestion of an eminent Byzantine general opposed to his government at that time. By 1334 Dušan had occupied the whole of western Macedonia, approximately as far south as the present-day boundary between Greece and Yugoslavia. The Emperor Andronicus III was too weak to resist and allowed Dušan to keep his conquests. The region thus acquired included the ancient ecclesiastical centre of Ochrid, which Dušan subsequently made his capital. After this there were a few years of peace between Serbia and the Empire, though Dušan was at war with Hungary for a short time. In 1341 Andronicus III died and civil war broke out in the Empire between the regents for his young grandson, John V and John Cantacuzenus, a powerful and ambitious Byzantine noble. Cantacuzenus appealed to Dušan for help, and made an agreement with him that they should jointly attack the Imperial Government, each keeping the towns occupied by his armies; this gave Dušan an excellent opportunity to extend his territory still further at the expense of the Empire. By 1343 his agreement with Cantacuzenus had broken down, but his conquests of imperial territory continued. By 1348 he was master of the whole of Albania, Epirus and Thessaly, and most of eastern Macedonia; only Salonika and its immediate hinterland eluded his grasp.

The year 1345 was the climax of Dušan's career, when he was solemnly crowned 'tsar (emperor) of the Serbs and Greeks'; shortly afterwards the archbishop of Serbia was raised to the rank of a Patriarch. Dušan's son Uroš was proclaimed 'King of Serbia' and put in charge of the northern part of his father's Empire. At the same time, the court ceremonial became more rigidly Byzantine: Dušan's half-brother was styled 'Despot of Epirus' and other relatives responsible for other parts of his dominions were given appropriate Byzantine titles. On the other hand, some Greek landowners in Macedonia were replaced by Serbs, so that the Slav ethnic element was strengthened at the same time as Byzantine cultural influence increased; this was quite in accord with Dušan's aim to establish a Greco-Serbian Empire. His assumption of the imperial title was just the first step in this project. But before he could accomplish the whole of his 'grand design', he died suddenly, in 1355, still in the prime of life, with the final object of his ambition unattained.

Dušan's energy was not confined to territorial expansion. In 1349 he promulgated at Skopje the first part of a *Zakonik*, or Legal Code, which was completed five years later – the first work of its kind to be produced by any Slav ruler. Its provisions were comprehensive, and were clearly designed to protect and strengthen the existing social institutions: the monarchy, the Orthodox Church, the feudal nobility and the courts. Punishments were mainly fines, in money or in kind, and, following Byzantine custom, physical mutilation of various kinds – the cutting off of hands, tongue, nose or ears, blinding and branding. There is no evidence that the death penalty was used at the time of the promulgation of the code, and punishment by exile and deprivation of property appears to have been rare. This Code, as well as being the most enduring memorial of Dušan's energy and versatility as a ruler, is also of great interest for the picture it gives of the social and economic life of Serbia at that time.

Dušan's Empire quickly disintegrated after his death, and none of his successors aspired to imperial power. Even during Dušan's lifetime it would seem that at least some of the great feudal barons were becoming more powerful and independent, and the process of disintegration was hastened by the inevitable succession quarrels. Eventually Dušan's son Uroš (1355–71) succeeded in establishing his claim to his father's throne; but he lacked Dušan's strength and energy and was unable to hold his own against ambitious feudal nobles such as 'King' Vukašin, who controlled most of western Macedonia and in practice behaved like an independent ruler.

Meanwhile the Turkish menace was gathering strength; the Turks had already gained a footing in Europe and now threatened Macedonia. 'King' Vukašin and his brother John Uglješ, the 'Despot' of eastern Macedonia, both realised the danger, and John Uglješ tried, without success, to form a coalition to resist the Turks. In the end the two brothers faced the Turks alone with only their own resources, and were decisively defeated at the battle of Marica in 1371, in which both Vukašin and Uglješ were killed. As a result of this battle, Turkish power was effectively established in Macedonia, first by the recognition of Turkish overlordship on the part of the Macedonian feudal landowners and later by their replacement by Turks. A famous, half-legendary personality belonging to this unhappy period of Balkan history was Vukašin's son 'Kraljević' ('Little King') Marko, a kind of Balkan Robin Hood, whose adventures form the theme of a cycle of songs in Serbian National Poetry.

Uroš was succeeded by Prince Lazar, the last direct descendant of the Nemjanjići, whose modest title aptly signified the reduced territory under his control; this was in fact limited to the north-western part of Dušan's Empire, since Macedonia had fallen to the Turks, and Zeta was once more independent (see below). The most powerful Balkan ruler at that time was

Tvrtko of Bosnia (see above, p. 50), whose prestige was enhanced by his claim to be descended from Nemjanja through a collateral branch.

Looking back, it is almost impossible not to see the whole of Prince Lazar's reign as overshadowed by the catastrophe that ended it, the battle of Kosovo in 1389. Like Vukašin and Ugleš before him, Lazar realised that his territory would soon be directly threatened by the Turks, who were steadily advancing through the Balkan peninsula in a north-westerly direction: Serres was captured in 1383, Sofia in 1385, Niš in 1386, and in 1387 even the hitherto impregnable Salonika fell to the Turks after a long siege.

Lazar made careful diplomatic preparations for the defence of his realm, as Dušan had made for its expansion not so many years before. He made an alliance with the King of Hungary, and with Tvrtko of Bosnia; indeed in 1386 a Turkish army was defeated by a joint Serbian-Bosnian force. But this proved to be only a temporary set-back for the Turks, and in fact provoked the large-scale campaign which culminated in the battle of Kosovo.

The Turkish Sultan Murad planned this campaign with a thoroughness which shows that he regarded the subjugation of the South Slavs as a vitally important political objective. Finally the forces of the two protagonists, Murad II and Prince Lazar, met on St. Vitus Day (Vidovdan) 1389 at Kosovo Polje (the 'Field of the Black-birds'), a small plateau in the hilly country of south Serbia.[1] The size and composition of the opposing armies has been variously estimated, and even now it is impossible to speak with certainty on this subject; but it is clear that Prince Lazar's army included contingents from other nations and was not just a national Serbian force.[2]

The battle of Kosovo proved to be a victory for the Turks from which the Serbs never really recovered. Because of its fateful significance in the history of Serbia, and the obscurity

---

[1] Kosovo Polje is now the name of a small and desolate railway junction in south Serbia on the branch line from Belgrade to Skopje.

[2] A monograph on the preliminaries leading up to the battle of Kosovo and the battle itself has been recently published with an English summary: Gavro A. Škrivanić, *Kosovska Bitka* (The Battle of Kosovo), Historical Institute of Montenegro, Cetinje, 1956.

which still surrounds certain dramatic events in the battle itself, the battle of Kosovo is still to some extent shrouded in a legend of sombre mystery. There is for example the suspicion of treason connected with the name of Miloš Obilić, which historical investigation has not yet fully clarified; and the assassination of Murad by Obilić just before the battle, perhaps inspired by a desperate determination to convince his accusers of his patriotism. Then there is the fact that, although the Turks were victorious, and Prince Lazar himself and many of the leading Serbian nobles were killed, the extent and significance of the Turkish victory were not at first fully grasped, in fact the first contemporary reports of the battle suggested that the result was indecisive.

Perhaps the reason for this was that the new sultan, Murad's son Bayazit, did not immediately follow up his victory in the field. But it was not long before the results of this became evident: Prince Lazar's successor Stephen Lazarević was forced to surrender a considerable area of territory to the Turks, including Skopje and its neighbourhood, and, what was more serious, to accept the status of a tributary prince; that is to pay the sultan an annual tribute, to receive Turkish garrisons in the chief towns of Serbia, and to supply Serbian contingents to fight in the Turkish armies.

However it was not long before Stephen Lazarević was able to free himself from this humiliating situation and once more declare the independence of his state. The reason for this was that at the beginning of the fifteenth century the Turks themselves suffered a crushing military defeat in the battle of Angora (1402) at the hands of Tamurlane and his immense Tartar army. It is significant that these barbarian hordes from Central Asia accomplished what a succession of European armies had failed to do; for only six years before an international army composed of Hungarian, French, German and some English troops had been decisively defeated by the Turks in the battle of Nicopolis.

Stephen Lazarević, together with a contingent of Serbian troops, had taken part in the battle of Angora as Bayazit's vassal. After the battle he visited Constantinople, where the Emperor, Manuel II Paleologus, conferred on him the title of 'Despot', the next in importance to that of emperor in the

E

Byzantine hierarchy of titles; and this title was the one used by Serbian rulers until the last remnant of the Serbian state was conquered by the Turks in 1459. Stephen established his capital in Belgrade, which was an important strategical centre because of its situation at the confluence of the Sava and the Danube. For this reason it had been recently claimed by King Sigismund of Hungary, but he was at this time harassed by internal troubles and therefore prepared to surrender the town to Stephen in return for his alliance. Stephen strengthened the defences of the city and made it into a powerful fortress, manned by mercenary troops and artillery. He also built a church and a hospital, and encouraged Serbs from other parts of his dominions to come and settle there.

The period of the Serbian despotate (1402–59) has its own characteristic atmosphere, a kind of sunset splendour increasingly overshadowed by the doom of extinction. The political and economic situation was gloomy; but art and literature flourished, and the spirit of both rulers and people remained unbroken to the last. During the latter part of his reign (after 1413) Stephen Lazarević was again compelled to accept the status of a vassal prince, but this at least gave Serbia a period of rest from Turkish attacks, from which economic and cultural life benefited.

In 1427 Stephen Lazarević was succeeded by his nephew George Branković. Right from the beginning he was faced with troubles from which he was to have little respite throughout his long reign (1427–56). Indeed for a great deal of this he was a Despot without a Despotate, compelled to wander through neighbouring states – Hungary, Dubrovnik and Venice – seeking for help to restore his shattered kingdom. Yet he never gave in. Even before his accession he was forced to surrender Belgrade to Sigismund of Hungary and Niš and Kruševac to the Turks; at the same time the Bosnians attacked Srebrenica, an important mining centre in the eastern part of Serbia. Deprived of Belgrade, the Despot built a new fortified capital at Smederovo, farther down the Danube, the ramparts of which can still be seen overlooking the river. For some years a precarious peace was maintained with the Turks; but after 1438 the sultan began a serious campaign against Hungary, in the course of which Smederovo was captured and Serbia cruelly plundered. Meanwhile George Branković had lost his estates in Hungary owing to his interference in succession quarrels in that country. In 1444 the tide turned a little in his favour; by an agreement with Sultan Murad II he secured the return of Kruševac and the other districts which he had been obliged to surrender to the Turks. But he was unable to stem the increasingly strong tide of Turkish aggression under Murad's vigorous and ambitious successor Mehemet the Conqueror. Ten years after George Branković's agreement with Murad II Serbia was once more overrun by Turkish troops. Unable to get any help from Hungary or Austria, the Despot was forced, not long before his death, to conclude a treaty with the sultan which left him only a pitifully shrunken territory north of the Western Morava. In 1456 he died, and his tiny state was rent by bitter succession quarrels. The sultan naturally took advantage of this situation. In 1459 Smederovo was captured, and Serbia as a political unit ceased to exist.

The economic situation was also bad, although in 1433 the French traveller Bertrandon de la Broquière described Serbia as a rich and progressive country. Probably the reason for this was that both mining and commerce flourished, providing the Despots with considerable wealth.[1] But agriculture was badly disorganised, as a result of constant war and plundering. The condition of the peasants became wretched, and many of them preferred to find work in the towns or in the mines, where they were in fact cruelly exploited. At one time conditions were so bad that the wretched peasants revolted. Moreover, although commerce, and consequently town life, flourished, the development of municipal self-government independent of feudal land-owners was hindered by the presence of foreign 'colonies', especially of 'Dubrovćani', who jealously guarded their own sectional privileges. The prosperity observed by de la Broquière was more apparent than real.

Even before the end of the fourteenth century, individual Serbs had begun to emigrate from their homeland, and after the fall of the despotate, this migration increased considerably. Most of the emigrants went either to the towns of the Dalmatian coast, especially Dubrovnik, or to the districts of Srem, Bačka

[1] The most important mining centres were Novo Brdo, famous for its silver mines, Srbrenica and Rudnik, which had silver, copper and lead mines.

and Banat in southern Hungary; the Hungarian king Matthias Corvinus estimated that about 200,000 Serbs settled in southern Hungary between 1479 and 1483. Even if this figure is exaggerated, the influx was in any case considerable. Thus this part of Hungary, roughly corresponding to the present-day Autonomous Province of Vojvodina in the federal republic of Yugoslavia, became ethnically mixed, and remains so to this day, though the population has long been predominantly Serb. The emigrants were welcomed by the Hungarian rulers, since after the fall of Serbia, Hungary itself lay open to Turkish attacks which increased in intensity after the beginning of the sixteenth century, and the Serbian immigrants provided the backbone of the Hungarian frontier forces. Most of the immigrants were peasants, but there were also members of the few Serbian noble families who had survived the long struggle against the Turks; and many of these were given estates in Hungary. After the final subjugation of the Serbian despotate, various members of the Branković family and others who had joined in the final succession wrangle also found a refuge in Hungary. In order to encourage his Serbian subjects in their resistance to the Turks, Matthias Corvinus granted the title of Despot of Serbia to Gregory the Blind, one of the claimants to the despotate after the death of George Branković, and also gave him large estates in southern Hungary, Croatis and Slavonia. The title continued to be bestowed until 1537; the last holder was Pavel Bakić, a Serb of exceptional military ability, but not in any way connected with the Branković family as previous holders of the title had been. When he was killed while fighting the Turks in 1537 the title fell into abeyance. By this time Hungary itself had been largely subjugated by the Turks, so that the fostering of Serbian national ambition in Hungary no longer had any practical value.

So far nothing has been said about Zeta, which had been an integral part of Serbia from the time of Nemanja to the death of Tsar Dušan. In the rapid disintegration of Tsar Dušan's Empire which followed his death, Zeta once more developed an independent political life. During the latter part of the fourteenth century and the first two decades of the fifteenth Zeta was dominated by various members of a powerful noble family named Balšić. The Balšići were typical feudal barons, concerned only to increase their own personal possessions and to avoid submission to any strong outside authority. The disturbed condition of the Balkan peninsula in the second half of the fourteenth century certainly favoured such aspirations, at least temporarily; but in fact Zeta, like the rest of south-eastern Europe was threatened by the Turks; and more immediately by Venice, who wished to extend her power on the Adriatic coast. In order to build up their local power, the Balšići maintained good relations with Venice; but this proved to be to the ultimate advantage of Venice, who, by an agreement concluded in 1423 gained possession of the chief coastal towns of Zeta: Ulcinj, Kotor and Pastrovice.

After the death of Balša III, the last member of the Balšić family, Zeta was once more incorporated into Serbia, now the Serbian despotate. But the connection with Serbia proved distasteful to many of the nobles of Zeta, who in fact preferred to acknowledge the suzerainty of Venice; and in 1455 all the Zeta feudatories west of the river Morača (a small river flowing into Lake Skadar) formally acknowledged Venetian overlordship. The most important among these pro-Venetian landowners was Stephen Crnojević, who was by that time the leading figure in Zeta.

Meanwhile the threat from the Turks was growing more acute. By 1479 they had overrun the whole of southern Zeta, and Ivan Crnojević (Stephen's son), who, with financial help from Venice, had tried to resist the Turkish advance, fled to Italy. But two years later he returned, when succession quarrels in Turkey following the death of Mehemet II offered a favourable opportunity for the recovery of the conquered territory. Venice refused to help him, being unwilling to provoke the hostility of the Turks against herself. The odds against him were overwhelming, and it was not long before he was once more obliged to recognise the sultan as overlord of Zeta. But though he had to accept the status of a tributary prince, he remained in control of the mountainous inner core of Zeta, the part later known as Montenegro – the Black Mountain.[1] Here he established a

---

[1] The name *Crna Gora* (= the Black Mountain) was first used in a treaty concluded in 1435 between George Branković and Venice. In this treaty it was used to denote only the mountainous region between Kotor and Budva; later it came to be applied to what had been the greater part of medieval Zeta.

miniature feudal state, with a fortified capital at Cetinje. It was a state with its own landowners – among whom the Crnojevići were the most important – and peasants, with their carefully defined feudal obligations and with its own religious foundations. The chief monastery was that of Cetinje, founded by Ivan Crnojević in 1485, which subsequently became the headquarters of the metropolitan of Zeta. Nor was cultural life forgotten; in 1493 a printing press (the first to exist in the whole territory included in present-day Yugoslavia) was set up in Cetinje by Ivan Crnojević's son, Đurad. Unfortunately family quarrels, which so often exercised a baleful effect on Balkan political life, weakened and divided the small principality, which was otherwise admirably fitted to be a spearhead of resistance against the Turks; Đurad Crnojević was virtually driven out of the country by his brother Stephen, who then ruled the country as a Turkish puppet. Before long Stephen fell into disfavour with his master and was imprisoned at Skadar. In 1499 Montenegro lost the last traces of its independence, and became part of the Turkish 'sanjak' of Skadar. However, although it was officially part of the Turkish Empire, Montenegro never came under effective Turkish control. Not only the memory but the reality of political freedom, albeit precarious and unacknowledged, remained alive there when it had been extinguished in all other parts of the Balkans.

The period from the late twelfth to the fifteenth century, which witnessed the political rise and decline of Serbia, was also a time of vigorous cultural activity among the South Slavs, notably in literature, painting and architecture. This cultural activity, at once Byzantine in its inspiration and national in its expression, is perhaps a better key to the understanding of the South Slavs than their stormy and chequered political history. It gives some idea of what their contribution to European civilisation might have been had their progress not been blighted by centuries of Turkish rule.

The Serbs and Macedonians shared with all the other Orthodox Slavs a very interesting and valuable literary heritage, namely the linguistic and literary work of the two brothers Constantine-Cyril and Methodius, sometimes known as the 'Apostles of the Slavs'. These two brothers lived in the ninth century, and were natives of the important Byzantine seaport of Salonika, second only to Constantinople itself in wealth and importance. As we have seen, in their migratory period the Slavs made many attempts to capture Salonika, and though they failed to do so, many individual Slavs penetrated into the town and settled there. Possibly Constantine and Methodius were partly Slav by descent; at any rate they grew up familiar with the form of Slavonic spoken by the Slavs living in Macedonia, though the language of their education was of course Greek. By temperament and education both were admirably fitted for missionary work among the barnarians living outside the imperial frontiers, by which successive Byzantine rulers sought to extend the political and cultural influence of the Empire.

In the year 863 an excellent opportunity for such activity offered itself. Prince Rastislav of Moravia, the ruler of a small Slavonic principality in what is now the western part of Czechoslovakia, sent to the Byzantine emperor Michael III with a request for missionaries who could instruct his subjects in the Christian faith in the Slavonic language.[1] Moravia was already nominally Christian, but the new religion was making slow progress because the Church services and religious books were all in Latin, which the people did not understand. The Emperor readily agreed to Rastislav's request, and entrusted the task of providing the necessary instruction to Constantine and Methodius.

Their first task was to provide a written alphabet into which the Church services, Gospels and other religious writings could be translated. This was done by Cyril (or Constantine, as he was known until shortly before his death, who invented a Slavonic alphabet known as the 'glagolitic' alphabet (from the Slavonic word *glagol* = a verb). There is a considerable volume of learned literature on the subject of the origins of this alphabet, which in fact was not used for very long. It consisted of letters which look rather like hooks and eyes combined into various shapes; each letter represented a sound in spoken Slavonic, so that the glagolitic alphabet was phonetic. Naturally Constantine

---

[1] Constantine had already undertaken an important mission to the Khazars who lived on the shores of the Caspian Sea, with a view to try and persuade them to accept Orthodox Christianity; without success, however.

based his alphabet on the form of Slavonic spoken in Macedonia, which he knew, but the spoken language of the whole Slav-inhabited area was at that time sufficiently undifferentiated for his written Slavonic to be understood by the Moravians. His next task was to translate the Liturgy and parts of the Gospels, and introduce these to Prince Rastislav's subjects.

The work of Constantine and Methodius and the few helpers who accompanied them to Moravia was at first warmly welcomed, and in 867 was given the official approval of the Pope when the two brothers visited Rome. Constantine stayed there, in order to take the highest monastic vows (at which time he assumed the name of Cyril), and died there in 869. Unfortunately Papal approval was not enough to protect the missionary work of the 'Apostles of the Slavs' from the jealousy of the local German-speaking bishops, and they soon had many enemies. Prince Rastislav was driven out of Moravia as a result of political quarrels, and without his support they found it impossible to continue their work there. Methodius and his fellow-workers then moved to Pannonia in the middle Danube, which was also inhabitated by Slavs, and Methodius worked there until his death in 885. After his death his disciples were forced to leave this field of work also. They then came to the Balkan peninsula, which was by that time mainly inhabited by Slavs, many of whom were nominally Christian by the end of the ninth century.

In Croatia they were at first welcomed, as they had been in Moravia, but the use of the 'Glagolitic' (i.e. Slavonic) Liturgy soon met with determined opposition on the part of the local 'Latin' clergy, and was eventually suppressed; though not without a struggle which produced at least one martyr.[1] But in the areas outside the jurisdiction of Rome the Slavonic Liturgy became firmly established, especially in Macedonia. This was largely due to the energetic work of Clement, Bishop of Ochrid, a devoted disciple of Methodius. Clement not only

---

[1] The Slavonic Liturgy was officially condemned in Croatia at an ecclesiastical council held at Split in 1060. Even the ordination of Slavonic priests was forbidden if they did not know Latin. There was strong local opposition to this decree especially in the island of Krk (in northern Dalmatia) under the leadership of a priest named Vulfa who was in 1063 condemned at a council specially convened by a Papal Legate, unfrocked, cruelly beaten, branded and sentenced to life imprisonment.

established the Slavonic Liturgy in his see, but considerably extended the scope of translations into Slavonic, and thus provided the Slavs with the beginnings of a literature.

In the course of the tenth century the rather clumsy glagolitic alphabet was replaced by a more convenient one known as 'Cyrillic' in honour of Constantine-Cyril, though it was not of course his work. Modified forms of this alphabet are still used in Russia, Bulgaria and parts of Yugoslavia (where it is known as *ćirilica*). Most surviving Old Slavonic manuscripts are written in the Cyrillic alphabet, though there are a few in the glagolitic. In the course of time linguistic variations developed, and by the middle of the twelfth century a distinctive type of written Slavonic had developed among the Serbs, which is usually known as the Serbian redaction of Old Slavonic.

The first works to be written in Old Slavonic were translations from Greek, mainly but not exclusively ecclesiastical. The scope of this translated literature gradually widened, although old favourites continued to be copied until the end of the Middle Ages. A study of the titles of these translated works affords an interesting glimpse of popular ecclesiastical (and secular) taste among the Orthodox Slavs. Apocryphal texts, for example, *The Book of Adam and Eve*, *The Virgin's Descent in Hell*, *The Book of Enoch*, *The Gospel of Thomas* and *The Gospel of Nicodemus* were very popular, judging from the number of manuscripts which have survived. They also had their favourite stories, such as *The Trojan War*, *Barlaam and Joasphat* and *Alexander the Great*. The latter, which would probably now be described as romantic biography, was particularly popular with the Serbs, so much so that Russian scribes who copied it from Serbian manuscripts called it the *Serbian Alexandrid*. This story of Alexander the Great was evidently regarded not only as light literature, but as a practical guide to the behaviour of nobles and rulers, and many motifs from it passed into popular traditional literature.

One of the first original works written in Slavonic was the *Sermon against the Heretics*, written towards the end of the tenth century by a Bulgarian priest named Cosmas. The heretics indicated in the title were the Bogomils, who were already active in Bulgaria and Macedonia at that time (see Chapter 1, p. 48). This sermon was a polemical treatise, written for a limited, practical purpose – the extirpation of the Bogomil heresy – and can hardly be considered as a work of literature in the usual sense of the word.

In Serbia, as practically everywhere in medieval Europe, the monasteries were the nurseries of the earliest literature. The earliest original Serbian literature appeared early in the thirteenth century, contemporaneous with the political development of the Serbian state, and was in fact the work of two of Nemanja's sons: Sava, the organiser of the independent Serbian church and Stephen the First-crowned. Both of them wrote biographies of their father. St. Sava's is quite short, and in fact was not composed as an independent work but as part of a foundation charter for the monastery at Studenica founded by Nemanja; that of Stephen the First-crowned is longer, and covers most of his father's life. Both works are strikingly mature. Their writers were clearly influenced by the form and style of the numerous translated Lives of Saints; but within this stereotyped framework they introduced a considerable amount of factual information, and were clearly concerned to draw a convincing (though possibly idealised) portrait of Nemanja as a successful ruler. Thus their works approach a little nearer to the modern conception of biography, in spirit if not in form, than the usual medieval Lives of Saints. This tradition of biographical writing spread and developed rapidly among the Serbs. St. Sava himself was the subject of a biography written in the thirteenth century by a monk named Domentian, a member of the monastery of Hilendar, the Serbian house on Mount Athos; the same monk also wrote a life of Nemanja under his monastic name of Symeon. The fourteenth century also produced a work which was encyclopaedic in conception, a *Collection of the Lives of the Serbian Kings and Archbishops*, written by Archbishop Danilo (*d.* 1338), which included accounts of the lives of the kings Uroš, Dragutin, Milutin, Stephen Dečanski, Tsar Dušan and his wife Helen, and of several archbishops. Finally, one notable work was produced in the tragic period of Serbia's political decline – a detailed biography of the Despot Stephen Lazarević, written by a layman known as Constantine the Philosopher. Naturally not all these works are of equal historical and literary value; but their very number testifies to a significant literary vitality, and by reason of the originality of their approach they virtually constitute a new 'genre' in medieval literature.

Other kinds of original works were also produced in medieval Serbia between the death of Nemanja and the Turkish conquest: chronicles, genealogies, chronogaphs (chronicle compilations of the 'digest' type), and eulogies of prominent individuals. One of these is of particular interest because of the manner and the circumstances of its composition: a eulogy of Prince Lazar written by his relative Jefimija (Euphemia) the wife of Despot Uglješ (see p. 61). The circumstances of Jefimija's life were very sad. Her parents died shortly after her marriage to Despot Uglješ, her husband was killed in the battle of Marica in 1371, and she had no children; so after her husband's death she was practically alone in the world. Macedonia was ravaged by the Turks after their victory at Marica, so Jefimija fled to Serbia, where she found a refuge at the court of Prince Lazar, to whom she was distantly related. Later, he too was killed while fighting the Turks, at the battle of Kosovo. Jefimija then sought shelter in a convent and became a nun. There she composed a eulogy of her kinsman and protector, Prince Lazar; this was not written on parchment or paper, but embroidered on silk with fine gold thread. It must surely be one of the saddest and most moving samplers ever produced:

'Now that thou hast departed to eternal joy,' run the princess's stitches, 'thy children are sunk in pain and sorrow; for they live under the rule of the infidel, and all need thy help. So we pray thee to offer thy prayers to the Almighty Ruler for thy children, and for all who serve them with love and faith; for they are cast down in great affliction. Those who eat their bread have plotted against them, and thy good deeds are forgotten, thou holy martyr. If thou hast passed beyond this life, yet thou knowest the pain and misery of thy children, and as a holy martyr thou hast free access to the Lord.'[1]

This extract shows that the unusual method of composition in no way lessened the princess's intensity of feeling or powers of expression.

[1] Translated from the modern Serbian translation of the eulogy in *Iz Naše Književnosti feudalnog doba* (Extracts from our Literature of the Feudal Period) ed. Dragoljub Pavlović, Sarajevo, 1954.

This short sketch gives some idea, though only a superficial one, of the scope of creative activity in medieval Serbia in the domain of literature. The same spirit is also present in painting and architecture, where the Serbian achievement is, perhaps, even more striking.

The visual arts, like literature, developed in the monasteries. As we have seen, all the important Serbian rulers, Nemanja, Stephen the First-crowned, Milutin, and Stephen Dečanski were very lavish in the building and endowment of monasteries, and it is in their foundations that the development of Serbian medieval art must be studied. The earliest architectural styles, as might be expected, show a strong Byzantine influence; but the monastic church at Studenica, built by Nemanja towards the end of the twelfth century, already shows distinctive features, produced by the blending of Byzantine and 'Roman' elements. This mixed style, which predominated in the buildings of the thirteenth century, has been described as the 'Raška School' (from the name 'Rascia' which formed the nucleus of the medieval Serbian state). The churches at Peć, Sopočani and Mileševo are examples of this style; the main characteristics are the square ground plan, surmounted by a single dome; the space to the north and south of the dome is usually occupied by low vestibules. The architects of the earliest buildings appear to have been Byzantines; but before the end of the thirteenth century 'primorci' (i.e. people from the coast) are mentioned as builders of Serbian churches.

Perhaps more impressive (at any rate to the non-specialist) than the architectural features of these churches are the paintings with which their interiors are decorated. The most sumptuously decorated Byzantine churches (and also those of Kievan Russia, which, like medieval Serbia, was strongly influenced by Byzantine culture) had their walls and domes covered with mosaics; but this appears to have been too expensive for the Serbian rulers, whose churches were decorated with frescoes. A happy result of this was the production, in a relatively small area, of an enormous amount and variety of wall-painting. No less fortunately, a considerable amount of this has survived, despite the wars and invasions which the Balkan peninsula has suffered; the preservation of the existing frescoes is now the object of the zealous care of the Yugoslav Government, and many different kinds of specialists are employed on this work.

The subject matter of these frescoes, as might be expected, is mainly Biblical. The general scheme of decoration was fairly stereotyped: the main dome is usually covered with a large head-and-shoulders figure of 'Christos Pantocrator', with the four apostles looking towards him from the pendentives; in the apse is the figure of the *Bogorodica* (= Mother of God), while the scene portraying the Assumption of the *Bogorodica* occupies the west wall. On the other walls are characters from the Old and New Testament, Fathers of the Church, 'Warrior Saints' and others portrayed in rows, varied sometimes by scenes from Biblical Stories. Within this scheme, however, there is a great variety of detail, style and treatment.

In the thirteenth century the 'monumental style' predominated. Both compositions and figures were large, stately and impressive. The finest examples of this style are to be seen at Sopočani, which some authorities regard as the greatest masterpiece of Serbian medieval art,[1] not only because of the splendour of its compositions and the execution of individual forms and faces, but also because of the originality of the colours – a blend of purples, greens, blues and ochre. Another original feature of the frescoes at Sopočani is the use of gold backgrounds criss-crossed with black lines to imitate mosaic cubes.

The fourteenth century saw changes in the styles of both architecture and painting.[2] In architecture the development was chiefly in greater plasticity of line and elaboration of detail; King Milutin's church at Gračanica, with its five domes and many-arched façade is an excellent example of this style. Painting became, in one sense, more naturalistic; portraits were frequent, and more attention was paid to depicting the inner life and feelings of the subject. Detail becomes more interesting, but some of the grandeur of the earlier painting was inevitably lost. The frescoes of this period were clearly influenced by developments in Macedonian art, which in itself reflected more

[1] See D. Talbot Rice, *The Beginnings of Christian Art*, London, 1958, p. 183.

[2] *Istorija Naroda Jugoslavije* (History of the Peoples of Yugoslavia), Zagreb, 1953, pp. 528–9.

intensely the humanistic trend which was one of the characteristics of the twelfth-century renascence in Byzantine art.

In the fifteenth century, the period of Serbia's prolonged and
finally unsuccessful resistance to the Turks, there was intense
activity in architecture and painting, as in literature; almost as
though the people knew that they were living on 'borrowed
time'. It was in this period that the most characteristically
'national' style of architecture developed, the so-called Morava
School. The characteristic feature of this style is the cruciform
design of the churches, the predominance of straight vertical
lines, and the richness of the decoration. Changes can also be
seen in the style of fresco painting, which became more refined
and delicate, but less vigorous – perhaps escapist in spirit.[1] The
best examples of this style of painting are to be found in the
churches at Ravanica, Ljubostinja, Kalenić, Rudenica and
Manassija.

See Talbot Rice, *op. cit.*, p. 187.

Chapter 3

The South Slavs under Foreign Rule

'FOR MORE than three centuries and a half, the South Slavs disappear from the pages of history.' So writes Sir John Marriott in his masterly work on *The Eastern Question*,[1] after describing the final conquest of the Serbian despotate, and Bosnia and Hercegovina by the Turks. Like most dramatic and over-simplified statements, it proves misleading under close examination; it would be truer to say that this particular page of the history of the South Slavs becomes difficult to read. The fact is that the historian is faced with the difficult task of deciphering two pages simultaneously: on the one hand, the part played by the territory occupied by the South Slavs in the diplomatic relations of the powers interested in that area – that is, Turkey, Austria and later Russia; and on the other hand, the changing social and economic conditions, and the pattern of the dormant and later resurgent national feeling among the South Slav peoples. The first of these, usually designated the 'Eastern Question' has now been relatively clearly charted by French, German and English historians; the second is in the process of being thoroughly investigated by Yugoslav historians. Although much valuable pioneer research has already been completed,[2] no work of synthesis in this field has yet been published; and it is very probable that as a result of further work, accounts of the internal history of the South Slavs during this period will have to be modified.

The Turkish conquest of Hercegovina destroyed the last remnants of political independence among the South Slavs,

---

[1] *The Eastern Question*, Cambridge University Press, p. 80. Actually Marriott qualifies his statement by adding that the Serbs of Montenegro were never effectually subdued by the Turks. 'Only in the region of the Black Mountain,' he writes, 'did a remnant of the race maintain their independence; but until the nineteenth century the gallant resistance of Montenegro was devoid of political significance.'

[2] See Wayne S. Vuchinich, 'Post-war Yugoslav Historiography', *Journal of Modern History*, XXIII, pp. 41–57.

apart from the inhabitants of Montenegro, but it did not mark the limit of Turkish aggression in Eastern Europe. During the latter part of the fifteenth century and the early sixteenth century, the sultans Mehemet the Conqueror and his successor Bayazit II were engaged in a protracted struggle with the Venetian Republic for the possession of the Morea and the Aegean Islands, and were also at war with Persia. Both these wars resulted in further extensions of Turkish territory, so that Suleiman the Lawgiver, who became sultan in 1520, inherited an empire stretching from the Danube to the Euphrates. But it did not include the important fortress of Belgrade, strategically situated at the confluence of the Danube and Sava rivers, which was still in Hungarian hands. Suleiman, a vigorous and capable ruler, determined to rectify this weak point on his northern frontier, and prepared a large-scale campaign against Hungary, just as his ancestor Murad I had done against Serbia nearly a century and a half earlier. Belgrade was captured in 1521; and five years later Suleiman, whose diplomatic position was now strengthened by an alliance with France, launched another offensive against Hungary and in 1526 inflicted a crushing defeat on a Hungarian army at the battle of Mohacs. The Hungarians never really recovered from this, and by the middle of the sixteenth century the whole of medieval Hungary, except a small strip of territory retained by Ferdinand of Habsburg,[1] was incorporated into the Turkish Empire as the *pashalik* of Buda.

Encouraged by the capture of Belgrade and the victory of Mohacs, Suleiman made an attempt on Vienna in 1529. However, although his army far outnumbered the garrison defending the city, he was unable to capture it, and after a siege of twenty-four days he retired. No further attempt on Vienna was made by any Turkish ruler until 1683, and then again without success. In fact the conquest of the greater part of Hungary represented the limit of Turkish power in Europe.[2]

During the latter part of the sixteenth century the situation in the Balkan peninsula was relatively stable, as regards inter-

[1] Ferdinand agreed to pay the sultan an annual tribute of 30,000 ducats for the possession of this territory.

[2] i.e. on the mainland of Europe. The capture of Crete in 1669 may be considered as an epilogue to the history of Turkish conquest.

national conflict, though there was considerable skirmishing near the Turkish-Hapsburg frontier. In 1606 the two powers concluded a treaty at Sitvatorck, in which the existing boundaries were formally recognised; but the sultan (Ahmed I) renounced his claim to suzerainty over Transylvania and agreed to accept a lump sum in place of the annual tribute paid by Ferdinand of Habsburg (see p. 78 note 1) for the strip of Hungarian territory under his rule. This treaty can hardly be described as a sign of the beginning of the decline of Turkish power in Europe, but it does show that it was no longer so confidently on the offensive.

In the first part of the seventeenth century, the power of Turkey was seriously weakened by a succession of degenerate and incapable rulers; for as absolute power was vested in the sultan, a weak sultan represented a danger to the state as a whole. Indeed the decline of Turkish power might have been much more rapid if the weakness of the rulers had not been counterbalanced, in the latter part of the century, by a series of able and vigorous Grand Viziers drawn from an Albanian Moslem family named Köprülü. This explains why no sultan took advantage of the Thirty Years War in Europe in order to improve the Turkish position in the Balkans, at a time when the Hapsburgs were fully occupied with other foes, whereas in the latter part of the seventeenth century Turkey was once more on the offensive.

The first sign of renewed vigour was a campaign in Transylvania in 1658, personally led by the Grand Vizier Mehemet Köprülü, then a man of over seventy years of age. The object of this campaign was the deposition of a hostile *voyvode* (= duke) George Rakoczy. This objective was achieved, but unrest in Transylvania continued and in 1663 Mehemet Köprülü's successor Ahmed organised and led a larger expedition. But this time the Austrian emperor Leopold I intervened, and the Austrian army, assisted by French contingents, decisively defeated the Turkish army at St. Gotthard. The moral effect of this victory was considerable, since it was the first time that a Turkish army had been defeated in the field by a European force. Events were to show that it was not to be the last.

Before long the internal situation in the Habsburg Empire provided the Turks with an opportunity for launching another

F

offensive in Eastern Europe. Now that the threat of further Turkish advances was no longer immediate, some of the Hungarian and Croatian landowners under Habsburg rule had become discontented, and a conspiracy was formed with the object of breaking away from the Habsburgs. The leaders of this movement appealed to various European rulers for help, including Louis XIV, but without success; so they then appealed to the sultan. The conspirators agreed to accept Turkish suzerainty if the sultan would give them military help against their Habsburg ruler. The sultan agreed in principle, but was unable to intervene in Hungary just then as Turkey was at war with Poland. However by 1681 Turkey was free from other entanglements, and the Grand Vizier then in power, Kara Mustapha Köprülü, prepared an expedition against the Habsburg Empire, not indeed with the object of helping the Hungarian malcontents, but with the more ambitious plan of attacking Vienna.

But once more, as in 1529, the Turkish attempt to capture Vienna failed. The city was saved by the heroism of its garrison, and the timely intervention of a Polish army led by the Polish king John Sobieski. He first decisively defeated the besieging army just outside Vienna, and finally drove the Turks out of Hungary (1683).

The relief of Vienna was both a dramatic and a significant event; but it did not end the war between the Turkish and Habsburg Empires, which continued for another fifteen years, during which time the Habsburg armies steadily advanced into Turkish territory. In 1686 Buda, the former capital of Hungary, was captured from the Turks, and the Hungarian crown declared henceforth elective in the House of Habsburg; and in 1687 the Turks were defeated on the very field of Mohacs where Suleiman the Lawgiver had been victorious over a century and a half before. The victory was followed by the occupation of Croatia and Slavonia by the Habsburg armies. Finally in 1688 Belgrade was captured, after which the Habsburg forces advanced as far south as Niš in central Serbia.

However, this proved to be the limit of the Austrian advance. In 1691 a Turkish army led by the Grand Vizier Mustapha Köprülü III recaptured Niš and Belgrade, though shortly after this his army was defeated and he himself killed in a battle with the Austrians. For some years after this there was no decisive action until 1697, when a Habsburg army under the command of Prince Eugene of Savoy inflicted a crushing defeat on the Turkish army at Zenta (on the river Tisa). The Turks did not recover from the effects of this defeat and at the beginning of 1699 concluded the Treaty of Karlowitz with the Habsburg Empire. By this treaty the whole of Hungary (except the *banat* of Temešvar) and the greater part of Croatia and Slavonia were transferred from the Turkish to the Austrian Empire.[1]

The Treaty of Karlowitz (now called Karlovci) is important from several points of view. In the first place, it was a sign of the beginning of the disintegration of the Turkish Empire in Europe, since it was the first time that Turkey had surrendered any territory to another power; secondly, it marked the beginning of Austrian ambitions and influence in the Balkan peninsula, which was to be a major factor in the diplomatic situation in Eastern Europe until the outbreak of the First World War; and thirdly, for a number of the South Slavs it meant a change of masters, a factor which was to exercise considerable influence on the future Yugoslav state. For in Croatia and Slavonia Austria acquired territory inhabited by South Slavs, and there were also many Slavs in southern Hungary, the numbers of which had recently been increased by the 'migration' led by Patriarch Arsenius *c.* 1990 (see below p. 88).

Austria and Turkey remained at peace until 1716. By that time Turkey was at war with Venice, from whom she wished to wrest the Morea, which had been in Venetian hands since 1699. Austria, fearing further Turkish aggression in the Balkan peninsula, made an alliance with Venice. Once more the Austrian forces under the command of Prince Eugene won several victories against the Turks, including the capture of Belgrade. Prince Eugene invited the Serbs to join his forces as volunteers, and a considerable number responded. This was a fact of greater significance than the Austrian commander probably realised at the time. It is true the Serbs were fighting as auxiliaries in a foreign army, but nevertheless they were fighting, and fighting against the Turks. In thus availing himself of the fighting spirit

[1] The treaty also included terms relating to Venice and Poland, which are not relevant to the history of Yugoslavia.

of the Serbs, which had never become completely dormant under centuries of Turkish rule, Prince Eugene no doubt helped (although indirectly and unconsciously) to prepare the ground for the Serbian revolt at the beginning of the nineteenth century.

In 1718, thirty years after the capture of Belgrade, Austria concluded a very favourable treaty with Turkey, the Treaty of Passarowitz. (Požarevac in modern Serbia.) By this she acquired the rest of Hungary (the *banat* of Temešvar), the region known as Little Wallachia on the lower Danube, Belgrade, together with a considerable part of Serbia, and part of Bosnia.[1] But just over twenty years later all this territory except Temešvar was restored to Turkey by the Treaty of Belgrade in 1739. This rapid reversal of the territorial situation in the Balkan peninsula was partly due to a display of vigour on the part of the Turkish army, which captured Niš in central Serbia and then advanced to Belgrade; but a more important factor was French diplomatic action in favour of Turkey.[2]

Meanwhile a new factor had developed in the Eastern Question: Russo-Turkish rivalry. At this time (i.e. the end of the seventeenth and the beginning of the eighteenth century), Russia, that is her dynamic and ambitious ruler Peter the Great, was not directly interested in acquiring Turkish territory in the Balkan peninsula, but in controlling the Black Sea in order to have free access to the Mediterranean, which was essential for Russia's future economic and political development. Hence from the time of Peter the Great (1689–1725) onwards, Russia was frequently at war with Turkey in the Black Sea and the Danubian principalities of Moldavia and Wallachia. It was clearly in Russia's interest to co-operate with Austria, and an alliance was concluded between the two countries in 1726, which lasted for more than a century.

Russia's interest in the Eastern Question introduced a new,

[1] Venice, on the other hand, was the loser by this treaty, as she had to surrender the Morea and the Greek archipelago to Turkey.

[2] It lies outside the scope of this brief sketch to discuss the Franco-Turkish alliance, which was an important element in the political and diplomatic situation in the Balkan peninsula from the sixteenth century onwards. A detailed discussion of its origins and influence can be found in D. M. Vaughan, *Europe and the Turk*, 1300–1700.

emotional factor into the situation; for Russia was a Slav and
Orthodox country, and after the Treaty of Karlowitz practically all the Christian subjects of the Turkish Empire were
Orthodox and many of them were Slavs. They were therefore
inclined to regard Russia rather than Austria as their natural
'liberator' and Russia lost no opportunity of taking advantage
of this belief. Throughout the eighteenth century Russian
agents were active among the Slavs in the Balkan peninsula,
especially among the Montenegrins, and also in Greece and the
Danubian principalities (whose inhabitants were Orthodox
though not Slav). The activities of these agents, together with
French diplomatic pressure on the sultan, were the real reasons
for the outbreak of war between Russia and Turkey in 1768,
though a pretext was found in the violation of Turkish territory
by Russia. In this war Russia won both military and naval
successes against Turkey, and also succeeded in inciting the
Greeks in the Morea to revolt, though this revolt proved
abortive. Indeed so striking were the Russian victories that
Austria became alarmed and in 1771 signed a secret treaty with
Turkey in which she promised to give her military help if
Russian troops crossed the Danube. At this point Frederick II
of Prussia intervened and suggested that both Austria and
Russia should divert their attention from Turkey and join with
him in the dismemberment of Poland. This suggestion was
acceptable to the Russian empress, Catherine II, who, in view
of the territorial compensation provided by the First Partition of
Poland (in 1772) agreed to surrender the territory she had occupied on the river Pruth and on the Danube, and thus placated
Austria. But the war between Russia and Turkey continued
until 1774, by which time Catherine II was anxious to end it
because of disturbances at home (an outbreak of revolt among
the Don Cossaks).

The Treaty of Kutchuk-Kainardji, which concluded this war,
was very favourable to Russia. Not least among the gains
secured by Russia was the right to 'protect' the Orthodox subjects of the sultan. The exact nature of this protection was not
clearly defined, for which reason it was greatly to Russia's
diplomatic advantage, as it could be invoked whenever it suited
her political interests. 'De là,' writes M. Sorel in his work on the
Eastern Question, '*pour la Russie l'obligation de s'immiscer dans*

les affaires intérieurs de la Turquie, chaque fois que les intérêts des chrétiens l'exige.'[1]

The next development in the Eastern Question was a scheme for the partition of the Turkish Empire, suggested by Catherine II to the Austrian emperor Joseph II in 1782. (Although Austria had taken no active part in the Russo-Turkish war of 1768–1774, the alliance between Austria and Russia was still in existence, and indeed grew stronger after Joseph II became sole ruler of the Austrian Empire after 1780.) This scheme of course was theoretical, but is of considerable interest for the light it throws on the political conceptions and dynastic ambitions of the interested parties. Its main provisions were as follows: the Danubian principalities of Moldavia and Wallachia were to be transformed into an independent kingdom of Dacia (the name of the Roman imperial province in that area) to be ruled by Catherine's minister and favourite Potemkin; Austria was to receive Serbia, Bosnia, Hercegovina and Dalmatia, Venice being compensated for the loss of Dalmatia by the acquisition of the Morea, Cyprus and Crete. Finally, the former 'Greek Empire', i.e. Constantinople, together with Thrace, Macedonia, northern Greece, Bulgaria and Albania, was to be revived, with Catherine's second grandson as emperor; this child had been appropriately christened Constantine. Catherine was prepared to offer satisfactory safeguards against the eventual reunion of the Greek and Russian Empires.

In fact Catherine's next move was something much more modest and practical than anything suggested in this grandiose paper scheme, namely the annexation of the Crimea in 1783. Four years later she demanded the cession of the Danubian territory of Bessarabia and the establishment of hereditary governors in Moldavia and Wallachia – perhaps as a first step in the formation of an independent kingdom of Dacia. This caused another Russo-Turkish war, in which Austria supported Russia. By the end of 1788 Russian forces had captured the fortress of Oczakov on the Black Sea, and the next year Austrian troops advanced into the Balkan peninsula, captured Belgrade, and then advanced into Bosnia. Once more Serb volunteers fought in the Austrian armies.

[1] A. Sorel, *La Question d'Orient au XVIII siècle*, p. 263 (quoted by Marriott, *op. cit.*, p. 153).

In spite of these military successes, both Austria and Russia made peace with Turkey, Austria by the Treaty of Sistova in 1791 and Russia by the Treaty of Jassy in the following year. Russia retained Oczakov, her most important acquisition during the war, but Austria surrendered Belgrade and the territory she had occupied in Serbia and Bosnia – to the great disappointment and indignation of the Serbs.

These treaties have an interest quite apart from their territorial provisions (which, as far as the South Slavs were concerned, simply restored the *status quo*), in that they were the last international agreements relating to the Turkish Empire to be signed before the Serbian Rising, which began in 1804. This introduced into the Eastern Question a new factor, to which the European Powers had as yet paid very inadequate attention: the nationalist feelings of the Balkan peoples themselves.

It is now necessary to try and examine the history of the South Slavs during this period from the inside. Until the Treaty of Karlowitz (1699) the greater part of present-day Yugoslavia was under Turkish rule. For administrative purposes the Turkish Empire was divided into districts known as *sanjaks*; each *sanjak* supported one unit of cavalry troops known as *spahis*. In the sixteenth century the practice was adopted of grouping together a number of *sanjaks* into a larger unit known as a *beglerbegluk* (later known as a pashalik); each *beglerbegluk* was administered by a *Beglerbeg* (later Pasha) who had his own *Divan*, or advisory council. For judicial purposes there were special divisions known as *kadiluks*.

However the real basis of the sultan's authority was his military power. The two most important elements of this were the *spahis*, already mentioned, and the Janissaries, an infantry force formed by forcibly abducting healthy male children from the families of the sultan's Christian subjects, then bringing them up as Mohammedans and training them as soldiers. During the fifteenth and sixteenth centuries the Janissaries were a highly disciplined and very efficient fighting instrument; later they were allowed to marry, after which they developed into a hereditary caste, more concerned to perpetuate their own considerable privileges than to serve the sultan. Both the *spahis* and the Janissaries were, directly or indirectly, maintained at the expense of the subject peoples of the Turkish Empire; in fact the position of the *spahis*, who were settled on estates in the conquered territory in the Balkan peninsula, was not unlike that of feudal landowners in medieval Europe, in that they held their lands in return for military service. They were not allowed to engage in either trade or agriculture; their lands were culti-vated, on a share-cropping basis, by the Slav peasants living on them, and they themselves were usually absentee landlords, living in the towns. Each *spahi*, whatever the size of his estate,[1] was the direct vassal of the sultan. The *spahis* were not here-ditary owners of their estates, although in practice the military duties and economic privileges of a *spahiluk* passed from father to son.

The Orthodox Church was tolerated, subject to its members paying a special tax. At first the Orthodox Serbs were under the ecclesiastical jurisdiction of the Archbishop of Ochrid. However, in 1557 an independent Serbian Patriarchate was once more established, with its headquarters at Peć. By this step the sultan hoped to strengthen the corporate feeling of the Serbian Church, use it as a link between the Government and the people, and thus strengthen his own power. But the Church proved to be an inadequate instrument for this purpose. In the first place, it was too weak and impoverished, and its leaders were frequently on bad terms with the Turkish authorities. As time went on, first the parish priests and later the higher clergy identified themselves more and more closely with the mass of the people, and indeed did much to keep alive the spirit of national self-consciousness, and ultimately to prepare the way for revolt.

Although the Christian subjects of the Turkish Empire were subject to heavy taxation, and to the inhuman method of recruiting the Janissaries, known as the 'tribute of blood' (abolished in 1638), it would seem that at first Turkish rule was not so oppressive as it became later. In the early days there seems to have been a small measure of local autonomy: native officials known as *bashi-knezevi* were responsible for the collec-tion of taxes and other administrative duties.

In the latter part of the seventeenth century, as we have seen,

---

[1] Estates with an annual income of over 400 ducats were known as *zijamets* while those with an income less than 400 ducats were known as *timares*.

Serbia became the battleground of the Turkish and Habsburg armies, and some Serbs fought with the latter. Hence it is not surprising to find that after the Treaty of Karlowitz Turkish rule became much more oppressive. The Danubian region was considered a dangerous frontier province and treated accordingly. The office of *bashi-knez* was abolished and all administration placed in the hands of Turkish officials. The number of *spahis* was increased and for the first time the Janissaries were introduced into Serbia. Consequently the financial burdens imposed on the Serbian peasantry became much heavier, especially as they had to satisfy the private greed and rapacity of the Turkish officials and troops, as well as fulfilling their legal obligations.

From the latter part of the sixteenth century onwards, the Turks were opposed by bands of outlaws known as *haiduks*. From the Turkish point of view, the *haiduks* were just professional brigands. To the Serbs and Bosnians they were heroes, and their natural protectors, since in fact they attacked and robbed only those who oppressed the common people and supported the Turkish authorities – tax collectors, rich merchants, etc. – and in this way sought the redress that the people were powerless to obtain by other means. Naturally the Turks tried by various methods to liquidate the *haiduks*; but it was not easy to run them to earth in their hide-outs in the forests and mountains, especially as they were almost invariably helped by the local population.[1] In the seventeenth and eighteenth centuries the number of *haiduks* increased considerably.

Perhaps the most negative aspect of Turkish rule in Serbia, as one looks back, was the strangulation of the country's economic and cultural life, both of which had been so vigorous and promising in medieval Serbia. Even in the early fifteenth century, as we have seen, the French traveller Bertrandon de la Broquière considered that Serbia was a prosperous country; and even allowing for the fact that he had not observed or was not considering the conditions of the poorer sections of the community (such as the workers in the mines), it is clear that the economic condition of Serbia declined considerably after two centuries of Turkish rule. Similarly with the cultural life. In the

---

[1] There is a good picture of the life and dangers of *haiduk* life in a short story by Ivo Andrić, *Žedj* (Thirst).

few monasteries that had escaped destruction during the wars
with the Turks, the old Byzantine-Slavonic ecclesiastical culture
still lingered; but it was sterile and without creative vitality.
Among the mass of the people, the orally-transmitted folk-
poetry (*narodne pesme*) kept alive the traditions of the past; but
no new secular culture developed.

A sufficiently striking indication of the discontent felt by many
Serbs was the great migration to Austrian (or rather Hungarian) territory under the leadership of Patriarch Arsenius III at
the end of the seventeenth century. In 1690, in the course of the
war between Austria and Turkey which was concluded by the
Treaty of Karlowitz, the Austrian army was forced to retreat
after being defeated in battle by the Turks, and between 30,000
and 40,000 Serbs followed them. Before crossing the frontier
into Habsburg territory the Serbs sent an envoy to the Emperor
Leopold I asking for land on which to settle with their families
and an assurance of religious toleration. Leopold was very glad
to receive them, since he realised that they would be a valuable
source of military strength in the defence of the frontier and in
future struggles with the Turks. So they were promised freedom
of worship and invited to settle in the district of Bačka north of
the river Sava (now part of the Autonomous Province of
Vojvodina). Actually the promised religious toleration was only
grudgingly observed, and the settlers and their descendants
were in many ways unfairly and even contemptuously treated
by their new rulers. The conditions of the peasantry were particularly bad, and in 1735 there was a peasants' revolt in this
region, which was, however, ineffective. Nevertheless the
descendants of these emigrants were better off materially than
they would have been under Turkish rule, and in touch with a
developing cultural life. Both these facts were to be of some
significance in the future history of Serbia; for when the Serbs
in the Turkish Empire revolted at the beginning of the nineteenth century, their compatriots in the Austrian Empire helped
them with volunteers, arms and money, and later provided the
nucleus of an educated professional class which helped to
establish the new state.[1]

---

[1] It was among these Serbs-in-exile that the oldest Serbian literary
society was founded, the *Matica Srpska* (the Serbian Queen-Bee), founded
in Novi Sad in 1826.

The situation in Bosnia under Turkish rule was somewhat different from that in Serbia, the chief difference being that a considerable number of Bosnians became converts to Islam, whereas in Serbia there were very few. Most of these were probably former members of the 'Bosnian Church' (see above, p. 49); many of them were landowners, but the converts also included some small peasant-proprietors (known as *kmetovi*) and landless peasants. Those who possessed lands retained their economic and social privileges, and had in fact, stronger common interests with their Turkish rulers than with their Christian fellow-Slavs; they were even referred to as 'Turks'. Hence in Bosnia there was a cleavage in the Slav population: the Moslem upper class had a strong vested interest in the maintenance of Turkish rule, while the Christians were in an even worse position than in Serbia since they were exploited as a subject people on both religious and political grounds. It is, therefore, not surprising that Bosnia proved more quiescent under Turkish rule than Serbia and Montenegro, since one section of the population had no reason to be discontented, and the rest were too weak to voice their discontent in any effective way.

The economic and cultural condition of Bosnia under the Turks was wretchedly low. An interesting first-hand account of this has been preserved by an Englishwoman, Miss Adelina Pauline Irby, writing as late as 1877. Miss Irby spent some years travelling in the European provinces of Turkey and recording her impressions. Finally she settled in Sarajevo and devoted her life to educational work among Bosnian girls, especially those orphaned or left destitute as a result of the Bosnian rising of 1875.[1]

'The soil of Bosnia,' she writes, 'teems with various and valuable minerals, her hills abound in splendid forests, her well-watered plains are fertile and productive, her race, under culture, proves exceptionally gifted. Yet her commerce is contemptible "plums", to quote the report of Mr. Consul Holmes for 1873, "being the most valuable article of trade in the province". Her population is uneducated, not one man in a

[1] Her work has been generously recognised and appreciated: her photograph is displayed in the Town Museum of Sarajevo, together with that of other educational pioneers, and a street in Sarajevo has been named 'Mis Irbina Ulica' (*ulica* = street) in her honour.

hundred knowing how to read, and the chief town Serajevo, which contains from forty to fifty thousand inhabitants, possessing not a single bookshop . . . With the exception of a few merchants the Pravoslav (Orthodox) population is miserably poor. There has been no development of the immense material resources of the country, no means of employment and occupation which might enable the poor to meet the ever-increasing taxation, the extortions of the officials and the heavy exactions of their own clergy. But in spite of all hindrances the Serb[1] merchants of Bosnia have advanced steadily, though slowly, in wealth and position.'[2]

Sarajevo, the present capital of Bosnia and Hercegovina, is a vivid legacy from the period of Turkish rule. The capital of the medieval kingdom of Bosnia was Jajce, and the Turkish administrative centre, after the conquest, was established at Travnik, not far away. Sarajevo was founded in the middle of the fifteenth century by Moslem Slavs, and for a long time they comprised the majority of its population. Their predominance explains the oriental appearance of the city: its mosques and minarets, the picturesque *Baš-čarsija* (= Old Market) and the *Kujundjija*, or 'Metal Workers' street', which still resounds with hammers beating on copper and silver coffee-cups and other metal objects. All these things, together with the magnificent surrounding scenery, make Sarajevo a popular tourist centre.

By the end of the eighteenth century Sarajevo was a relatively prosperous commercial centre with many domestic industries. Modern Sarajevo, in appearance at least, owes much to the period of Austrian administration (1878–1914): Austrian influence is particularly apparent in some of the public buildings and in the general appearance of the modern part of the town. It is now a developing industrial centre as well as an administrative capital, and in contrast to the backward town described by Miss Irby, it possesses a university, a National Theatre and some excellent museums as well as other cultural institutions.

[1] The word 'Serb' is used here to denote an Orthodox Bosnian as distinct from a Moslem or Roman Catholic.

[2] G. Muir-Mackenzie and A. P. Irby, *Travels in the Slavonic Provinces of Turkey-in-Europe*, 2 vols., 1877, pp. 1, 14.

The history of Montenegro during this period presents a still different picture. Montenegro, as we have seen, was the last refuge of the fighting Serbs; but in spite of their determined resistance under Ivan Crnojević the whole of medieval Zeta except the inner knot of mountains – Montenegro proper – was occupied by the Turks. But the interior was never brought under effective Turkish control, although nominally it formed part of the Turkish Empire. Its history for the next three centuries was that of a protracted Resistance Movement, although during the sixteenth and early seventeenth centuries there appears to have been little organised fighting. Twice at least the Turks made a serious attempt to subdue Montenegro: in 1690 (when the Montenegrins were supporting Venice in a war against Turkey) and again in 1713 (this time as a reprisal for help given by the Montenegrins to Russia in the Russo-Turkish War of 1710–11). In 1690 the Turks penetrated to Cetinje, burnt the palace built by Ivanbeg (see above, p. 67–68), and for some years maintained a garrison which managed to collect the tax payable by the Christian subjects of the sultan. On the second occasion the Turks sent an army estimated at 120,000 men to subdue a population of approximately 30,000. The whole country was ravaged, and thirty-seven Montenegrin chiefs were treacherously murdered after being invited to visit the Grand Vizier to discuss terms. But on neither occasion did the Turks succeed in establishing themselves permanently in the country.

As yet little is known about the internal conditions in Montenegro at this time. The chief social unit appears to have been the *bratstvo* (brotherhood) with an elected chief at its head. There was a strong obligation for members of each 'brotherhood' to protect its members and to avenge any injury done to any of them, and blood feuds were frequent. The people seem to have made a precarious living by stock-rearing, supplemented by plundering the estates of Turkish *spahis* in the more fertile neighbouring regions since the land was on the whole unsuitable for agriculture. The only unifying force in the community was the church, so that it is not surprising to find that the bishops – who were elected by leading members of the 'brotherhoods' – acquired political as well as ecclesiastical functions; the bishop was in fact the natural leader of the people.

From 1696–1735 the office of *vladika* or bishop was held by a man of considerable administrative talent, Danilo Petrović-Njegoš. He performed valuable services to Montenegro by reducing blood-feuds (it proved impossible to eliminate them entirely) and ridding the country of its Moslem converts, who, though few in number, presented an obstacle in the way of complete liberation from the Turks. He also did much to promote greater co-operation among the 'brotherhoods' in their anti-Turkish activities. After his death the office of *vladika* became hereditary in the Petrović-Njegoš family.

It was in the time of Danilo Petrović-Njegoš that the first contacts were made between Montenegro and Russia. As we have seen, Russian agents had been active in the Turkish Empire from the time of Peter the Great onwards; and in 1711 a Russian envoy arrived in Cetinje. The object of his visit was to persuade the Montenegrins to attack the Turks, with whom Russia was then at war (the Russo-Turkish War of 1710–1711). The Montenegrins readily responded, though after the Russian defeat on the river Pruth in 1711 they paid dearly for their action (see above). In fact this visit proved to be the beginning of a long and close association between Montenegro and Russia. From then on Russian subsidies helped to support Montenegrin 'resistance', and many boys from leading Montenegrin families were sent to Russia to be educated.

An interesting result of this association was the appearance in Montenegro in 1766 of a 'pretender' named Šćepan Mali who claimed to be Peter III of Russia, the husband of Catherine II. He was enthusiastically received by the Montenegrins, and in 1768 proclaimed 'gospodar', or ruler, of the country. Naturally this incensed the sultan who sent a large force to invade Montenegro; however, it was repulsed. But some years later, in 1774, Sćepan Mali was killed by a hired assassin in the pay of the Pasha of Skadar.

Unfortunately conditions in Montenegro were not favourable to the development of the gentler arts of civilised life. Evidence is not lacking that the Montenegrins inherited the cultural tradition of medieval Serbia; for it was in Cetinje that one of the earliest printing presses to be used in the Balkan peninsula was set up, in 1493; and this at a time when the people were fighting the Turks for their very existence. And they have pro-

duced one poet of outstanding calibre: Peter Petrović-Njegoš
(1813–51); unfortunately his work is not well-known outside
Yugoslavia because of the difficulties it presents to its trans-
lators. Thus we have some idea of what the cultural life of
Montenegro might have been had suitable conditions for its
normal development prevailed.

Croatia, as we have seen, formed part of the medieval kingdom of Hungary after 1102; consequently most of it came under
Turkish rule between the middle of the sixteenth century (when
the Turks overran Hungary) and the Treaty of Karlowitz in
1699. Meanwhile the nobles in that part of Croatia which had
escaped Turkish conquest decided that their best chance of
preserving their lands and social privileges was union with the
Habsburg Empire. Accordingly in 1527 the Croatian Diet
offered the crown of what was left of Croatia to Ferdinand of
Habsburg, on condition that he guaranteed their rights and
possessions and undertook to defend their lands against the
Turks, to which he agreed. However the majority of the
Hungarian nobles in the region that had escaped Turkish conquest, together with some Croatian landowners in Slavonia,
preferred as their king a Hungarian noble named Ivan Zapolje.
The result was a prolonged civil war in the former Hungarian-
Croatian state, of which the chief beneficiaries were the Turks.
Finally the supporters of the Habsburgs proved stronger, and
after 1540 what remained of medieval Hungary-Croatia was
finally incorporated into the Habsburg Empire.

In the following century certain Croatian nobles took part in
an unsuccessful attempt to break away from the Habsburg connection (see above, p. 80). This movement was in no sense a
national one, supported by the mass of the people; the conspirators relied on foreign help to achieve their object, and in
fact their rebellion was used to the advantage of Turkey under
the energetic leadership of the Grand Vizier Ahmed Köprülü.
Meanwhile the conspiracy became known in Vienna; an imperial army intervened, the conspiracy was crushed and its
leaders sentenced to death. So ended the attempt to break
away from the Habsburgs.

The future was to show that the discontent which had inspired this conspiracy was not lasting or deep-seated. Before

half a century had elapsed, there was a serious dynastic crisis in the Habsburg Empire. The Emperor Charles VI (1711–1740) had no male heir to succeed him; and, being very anxious that the hereditary dominions of his family should not pass to strangers, he wished the various parts of his empire to accept as his successor his daughter Maria Theresa. One of the first to agree to this was Croatia, in a document known as the Croatian Pragmatic Sanction, promulgated in 1712. This decision was very significant, since it showed that the Croatian Diet still exercised the right to make independent decisions about the political future of Croatia; and also that at this time there was no strong desire among the Croatian nobility to break away from the Austrian Empire.[1]

The sixteenth century was a time of serious social unrest in Croatia. The position of the peasants was indeed wretched, since in addition to the normal burdens imposed on them under the feudal system they had to bear the brunt of the wars against the Turks and civil war among the landowners in the middle of the sixteenth century. Finally in 1573 a large-scale revolt was organised under the leadership of a certain Matthew Gubec. The programme of the rebels was radical and comprehensive: the reduction of the economic privileges of the landowners, political rights for the peasants and the abolition of internal customs' duties in the interest of trade. A concerted attack on Zagreb was planned, and at first the rising had some success. But the organising ability of the leaders was not adequate for such large-scale operations; and before long the landowners got the upper hand and the rising was crushed with great severity. Its only result was a negative one: a long legacy of bitterness and hostility between landowners and peasants in Croatia.

The condition of the peasantry remained very depressed until towards the end of the eighteenth century, when important social reforms were introduced by the emperor Joseph II, one of the most energetic of the 'Enlightened Despots'. The most important of these was the abolition of serfdom; i.e. henceforward the peasants were no longer to be tied to the estates of their landowners, but were free to leave the land and live and

---

[1] The Emperor attached more importance to the support of the Hungarian nobles; but it was not until ten years later, in 1722, that the Hungarian Pragmatic Sanction was issued.

work where they chose. This reform, and also the decrees of religious toleration issued by the same emperor and the secularisation of monastic property to finance education were progressive in spirit and had a positive influence on the social and cultural development of all parts of his dominions including Croatia. However certain other aspects of 'Enlightened Despotism' had a less favourable influence there, notably the increased centralisation of the administration, and the attempts to force the use of the German language throughout the Empire.

By the beginning of the sixteenth century practically the whole of modern Slovenia (except the hinterland of the Istrian ports Koper and Piran, which belonged to Venice) had become part of the Habsburg Empire. In fact the Habsburgs had had covetous eyes on this 'East Alpine' region from the time of the rise of their house in the thirteenth century, and had succeeded in acquiring and consolidating territory there by lucky inheritances in a characteristic fashion. During the later Middle Ages there was considerable infiltration of Germans into Slovenia (mostly from Bavaria): the majority of these immigrants belonged to the landowning class but they included some peasants and townspeople.

After the conquest of Serbia and Bosnia by the Turks, Slovenia was also seriously threatened. Between 1469 and 1483 Turkish armies raided Slovenian territory every year; but these were in fact plundering expeditions and the Turks never tried to conquer Slovenia.[1] Nevertheless, they were very destructive, especially to the peasants; and discontent at the failure of the ruling class to protect them against the Turks was one of the causes of a peasants' revolt that broke out in 1478. Ironically enough, it was Turkish troops rather than those of the local landowners that crushed the revolt. Quite apart from the effects of Turkish raids, the condition of the peasantry was very bad in Slovenia, as it was in Croatia; and in 1515 there was another revolt, on a larger scale than the previous one. Many feudal estates were plundered and their owners driven out; and it took a pitched battle to subdue the peasants. Though numerous, determined and not without organisation, the rebels were no

[1] A number of Slovene churches still have round them the high protective walls which were built to afford shelter to the villagers during the Turkish raids.

G

match for the more experienced and better-armed troops of the nobles. After a battle at Celje the revolt was crushed with great severity, some of the leaders being broken on the wheel. But nothing was done to improve social conditions and discontent continued to smoulder, as can be seen from the fact that parts of Slovenia were involved in the great Croatian peasant rising of 1573.

An interesting feature of Slovenian history in the sixteenth century was the influence of the Protestant Reformation. It was not until then that Protestant ideas began to gain ground among the South Slavs; some of the supporters of Protestantism were landowners who were no doubt partly influenced by the hope of enlarging their estates from secularised church lands; but the movement also found adherents among the townspeople and even among the peasantry towards the end of the sixteenth century. The most important individual figure among the Slovenian Protestants was a clergyman named Primož Trubar (1508–86), who translated the New Testament and other religious works into Slovenian and thus helped the development of Slovenian as a literary language. However, the force of Protestantism were not strong enough to withstand the forces of the Counter-Reformation, and especially the activities of the Jesuits. By the beginning of the seventeenth century the Slovenian Protestants had been forced either to conform to Roman Catholicism or go into exile.

It remains only to consider the Dalmatian coast during this period. During the Middle Ages this region had been divided between Croatia (and together with it incorporated into the kingdom of Hungary after 1102) and Zeta, which for some time was part of Serbia. But it had always been very jealously regarded by Venice. The internal troubles of the South Slavs, and also of Hungary, in the fifteenth century, gave Venice an excellent opportunity to satisfy her ambition. Early in the fifteenth century King Ladislav of Hungary sold his Dalmatian territory to Venice; Venetian control was formally established in 1420 and extended over the whole of the Dalmatian coast except Dubrovnik. At first the area under Venetian control was confined to a narrow coastal strip, but it was extended as a result of the treaties of Karlowitz and Passarowitz.

The sixteenth century was a period of social and political unrest in Dalmatia, as in the Habsburg Empire. The Dalmatian towns continued to enjoy varying degrees of municipal self government which they had had during the Middle Ages; but for the most part these were exercised by a small, economically privileged class. Consequently there was discontent among the more numerous class of artisans, small tradesmen and farmers; and the situation was made worse by the fact that the commerce of the Dalmatian towns was in any case exploited in the interests of Venice.[1] In the second decade of the sixteenth century the prevailing discontent caused a revolt on the island of Hvar. The programme of the rebels was partly economic and partly political: among their principal demands were the reduction of taxes and more democratic municipal government. The revolt dragged on inconclusively for some years before it was finally crushed by Venetian naval and military power.

At the time of the Turkish conquest of the Balkan peninsula many Slavs from the interior fled to the coast and settled there, especially in the region between Knin and Skradin in northern Dalmatia. One group of these refugees settled in the town of Senj, opposite the island of Krk in the northern Adriatic; and for nearly two centuries their descendants maintained themselves by preying on both Venetian and Turkish shipping. Because of the damage they did to Venetian commerce, the Uskoks (as they were called) were unofficially encouraged by successive Habsburg rulers; this actually led to a war between Venice and the Austrian Empire in the early seventeenth century. This war was concluded by the Treaty of Madrid (1617) by which the Uskoks were to be deported from Senj. But piracy in the Adriatic still continued, though not on the same scale as before.

Dubrovnik did not come under the rule of Venice, but remained an independent city-state, subject to the payment of an annual tribute to Turkey. However in return for this Dubrovnik enjoyed considerable commercial privileges throughout the Turkish Empire, and had her agents in practically every important town in the Balkan peninsula. During the fifteenth

---

[1] e.g. All merchandise exported from or imported into Dalmatian towns had to pass through Venice, where it was subjected to customs duties.

and early sixteenth century the commerce of Dubrovnik was very flourishing, but later her prosperity declined to some extent, as did that of the Italian trading cities, after the discovery of the New World and the Cape route to the east and the consequent re-orientation of world commerce. But even in the period of its decline Dubrovnik was both more prosperous materially and more advanced culturally than those parts of the Balkan peninsula under foreign rule, especially the regions under the Turks. In 1667 the city was badly damaged by a serious earthquake, from which it never recovered completely; in the eighteenth century it was further weakened by social dissensions. In 1806 it was occupied by French forces then operating in the Adriatic (in the course of the Napoleonic War) and never recovered its independence; in 1815 it was transferred to Austria and remained part of the Austrian Empire until 1918.

From this brief sketch it can be seen that during the period when the inhabitants of present-day Yugoslavia 'had no history' as an independent state (or group of states) they were subject to very varied political, social and cultural influences, all of which were destined to leave some mark on their future development. The following chapters will show how, under the dynamic force of national feeling, helped by changes in the political and diplomatic situation in Europe, first Serbia, and then other parts of modern Yugoslavia regained political independence and began the task of creating a new state.

Chapter 4

The Serbian Rising

THE SERBIAN RISING is naturally one of the most important landmarks in the history of Serbia, and indirectly in that of modern Yugoslavia too, since the small independent state of Serbia which emerged from the Rising was destined to be the nucleus of the future Yugoslavia. The rebirth of Serbia was also an event of major international importance. Because of the geographical position of Serbia, and the state of the Eastern Question at the end of the eighteenth century and the beginning of the nineteenth, neither Austria nor Russia could be indifferent to the progress of the Serbian Rising, and were in fact constantly in touch with its leaders. Indeed in studying the history of the Rising, it is impossible to isolate entirely its national and diplomatic aspects; it is the interplay of the one upon the other which gives the movement its special character.

In order to understand the immediate causes of the Rising, it is necessary to consider briefly the state of the Turkish Empire at the end of the eighteenth century. It was clear at that time that Turkish power was steadily declining, and that the Empire's military system had become obsolete. One important reason for this was the change that had taken place in the character of the Janissaries: from being the most dynamic and effective element in the Turkish army they had become, especially in the course of the eighteenth century, an undisciplined and self-seeking body (see above, Chapter III, p. 85–87). Realising that they were now a source of weakness rather than strength, the reforming sultan Selim III (1789–1805) resolved to reduce their power, and, if possible, to eliminate them altogether; as a preliminary step in this policy in 1793 (after Turkey had made peace with Austria and Russia (see above, Chapter III, p. 85) the Janissaries were forbidden to return to the pashalik of Belgrade. This was naturally welcomed by the Serbs, who at that time were especially afraid of the vengeance which was likely to be exacted by the

Janissaries for the part played by Serbian volunteers in the
Austrian army during the recent Austro-Turkish war. Immediately after this the sultan took another step more directly
designed to win the loyalty of those of his subjects who lived
near the Austrian frontier: in 1793-4 he issued two decrees
granting the Serbs certain privileges. They were to be allowed
once again to elect their own *knezovi* (an office abolished in
Serbia under the Treaty of Karlowitz in 1699); Turks were forbidden to settle in districts already occupied by Serbs, or to
confiscate their property; the amount of direct and indirect
taxation was formally defined; and finally an assurance was
given that no obstacles would be placed in the way of building
new Orthodox churches and monasteries in Serbia. As an
earnest of his sincerity in issuing these decrees, in 1793 the
sultan appointed as pasha of Serbia Hadji Mustapha Pasha,
who was known to be a champion of reform in the Turkish
Empire.

Unfortunately the more favourable conditions created by the
sultan's reforms and the enlightened administration of Hadji
Mustapha Pasha did not last long. The new situation was very
distasteful to the Janissaries, who made determined efforts to
force their way back into Serbia and in October 1801 succeeded
in capturing Belgrade. One of their first actions after they had
entered the town was the murder of Hadji Mustapha Pasha.[1]
Then a group of four leading Jannissaries, known as the *Dahis*,
took over the administrative power, and the next vizier was
their puppet.

Under the new régime the privileges granted to the Serbs by
the sultan were abolished, and Serbia was ruled simply in the
interests of the Janissaries. The new régime was not only
intolerable to the Serbs, but also unpopular with many of the
Turkish *spahis*. Discontent among the Serbs became so acute
that a small group of them staged an abortive revolt in 1802.
The Janissaries, feeling their position insecure, resolved on a
desperate step to try and keep themselves in power: the massacre
of all prominent Serb patriots who had fought as volunteers in
the Austrian army in the last war between Austria and Turkey.

[1] Mustapha Pasha had realised that he could expect trouble with the
Janissaries after their expulsion from Serbia, and had therefore established
an armed bodyguard of 1,500 men to protect himself, two-thirds of whom
were Serbs.

By thus depriving the people of their natural leaders, the Janissaries hoped to cow them into submission.

Their plan had the opposite effect of stirring the Serbs into open revolt. Some of the Serbs earmarked for extermination managed to escape, but there were many victims, including two prominent patriots, Ilija Birčanin and Aleksa Nenadović, both *knezovi* in the Valjevo district near the Bosnian border. Meanwhile there was a spontaneous movement 'to the woods', and a considerable increase in the ranks of the *haiduks*; many Turkish homes were burnt and the Janissaries were driven out of many villages where they had installed themselves. This was the beginning of the revolt.

It was not long before this spontaneous movement began to acquire the rudiments of organisation and a policy. At the beginning of the year 1804 (the date taken to mark the beginning of the rising) the rebels in the district of Šumadija[1] (='Woodland') to the south of Belgrade elected as their leader a pig-farmer named George Petrović, better known as Karageorge (= Black George). He had served as a volunteer in the Austrian army, and was on the Janissaries' black-list, but had managed to escape.

It is important to note that the rising was directed not against the sultan, but against the tyrannical rule of the Janissaries, who were in any case usurpers; and in the course of 1804 representatives of the rebels had a meeting with those of the sultan (at Ostrižnica near Belgrade) to discuss a settlement, with Austria acting as mediator. The requirements of the rebels were moderate and reasonable: in the main the restoration of the privileges granted in 1793 and 1794. The Turks agreed that the Serbs had cause to be discontented, and gave vague assurances that they would not be ill-treated in the future. But they refused to promise that the Janissaries – the cause of the trouble – would be expelled from Serbia, and were in fact unable to offer the Serbs any adequate guarantees of better conditions. So the negotiations were broken off without anything definite being achieved.

Meanwhile the leaders of the revolt, realising that their struggle was likely to be prolonged, and that some outside help

---

[1] Both Tito and Mihailović first raised their standards of revolt in the Šumadija. (See Part II, Chap. 3, p. 172.)

was desirable, sent a deputation to Russia. They had already approached Austria before the meeting with the sultan's representatives; but Austria, being then unwilling to incur the hostility of Turkey, could promise nothing but moral support and her good offices in negotiations with the sultan. The Russian ruler Alexander I was also anxious to keep on friendly terms with Turkey at that time; but he was also sympathetic towards the Serbian rebels and promised some financial help.

The Serbs now made another attempt to negotiate, this time by sending a deputation to Constantinople with two petitions to the sultan. The terms of these were much the same as those proposed in the earlier meeting with the sultan's representatives, though the functions of the *knezovi* were here defined in some detail. The sultan pretended to be willing to consider these petitions, but secretly began to make plans to crush the revolt.

From this point onwards (the summer of 1805) the rising began to acquire a new character and a more powerful momentum. From being a protest against the rule of the Janissaries, it became a struggle against the Turkish Government. The rebels, realising that they would get no satisfaction from the sultan without force of some kind, became more vigorous; on November 20th, 1805, they captured Smederovo, the capital of the former Serbian despotate, and also made further advances in the early months of 1806. But they did not stop sending petitions to the sultan, and to the rulers of Austria and Russia as well. Meanwhile the sultan planned a counter-attack from the pashalik of Bosnia.

These military measures proceeded against an increasingly complicated diplomatic background, in which a very active role was played by Alexander I's chief minister Čartoriski. He was in favour of giving the Serbs both diplomatic and financial support to prevent them from turning to France. A similar attitude was adopted by Austria.

The Turkish counter-attack proved unsuccessful. Karageorge in particular proved himself to be a brilliant general, and the Serbian forces three times defeated the Turks in battle. The culmination of their success was the capture of Belgrade in December 1806. This taste of victory naturally increased the self-confidence of the rebels, and their demands increased proportionately. Another mission was dispatched to Constantinople, this time asking for wide powers of self-government for Serbia. The sultan agreed in principle to this in a convention concluded with the Serbian deputies on January 25th, 1807. But this convention was almost immediately repudiated by the Serbian leaders; under Russian influence they were easily persuaded to renew their struggle against the Turks in alliance with Russia, who by the end of 1806 was at war with Turkey. Henceforth the fate of the Serbian Rising became much more closely bound up with Russian foreign policy, not only in relation to Turkey, but also in relation to the great European powers. Thus the history of the rising has to be studied against a wider European background. It was in fact indirectly affected by the Treaty of Tilsit concluded in July 1807 between Alexander I and Napoleon. Under this treaty the tsar agreed to make peace with Turkey, thus neutralising the alliance recently concluded between Russia and the Serbs. Although the treaty seemed a set-back to Serbian hopes, a secret article bound both Russia and France to work for the liberation of all Turkish territory in Europe except Rumelia and Constantinople.

In the ensuing peace negotiations with Turkey, Russia certainly did not neglect the interests of the Serbs, and suggested that Serbia should become a tributary principality of the Turkish Empire (like the Danubian provinces of Moldavia and Wallachia) under a prince to be chosen by the Serbs themselves, the settlement to be guaranteed by Russia and England. However, in the armistice concluded by Russia and Turkey in August 1807 there was no mention of the future status of Serbia. The most that the Russian representatives were able to secure was a promise that Turkey would take no military action on that part of the frontier where Russian and Serbian troops were stationed together.

In the period between the Treaty of Tilsit (1807) and the Treaty of Bucharest in 1812 (which concluded a renewed outbreak of war between Russia and Turkey) the situation in Serbia was very confused. The main theme which emerges from a study of the rapidly changing events of this time is the rivalry between Russia and Austria for the position of Serbia's protector and chief ally in the struggle against the Turkish Government. On the whole Russian influence prevailed and from 1807–9 there was a permanent Russian agent in Belgrade. It is true that the agent, Rodofinikin, was not very popular, and in 1809, at a time when anti-Russian feeling happened to have got the upper hand, he was obliged to leave Belgrade. A group among the Serbian leaders favoured a closer connection with Austria. Shortly after the Treaty of Tilsit, Austria offered her 'protection' to the Serbs. At first Karageorge himself was willing to accept this offer and to agree that Serbia should become part of the Austrian Empire, on certain conditions, the most important being that Serbia should not be subject to Hungary in any way, and that adequate guarantees of religious toleration should be given. On further consideration, no doubt influenced by Rodofinikin, the Serbs broke off the negotiations with Austria.

Meanwhile in March 1809 the sultan again began to take serious measures to crush the Serbs by military force. He also prepared to renew the war with Russia, since peace negotiations had broken down because of Russia's objections to an alliance which Turkey had recently concluded with England. Thus by the spring of 1809 the situation was very similar to that of 1807.

This time, although the Russians had some military successes against the Turks, the Serbs were less successful than they had been before. Without waiting for the Turks to attack, the Serbs opened an ambitious four-fold campaign in the directions of Vidin, Niš, the *sanjak* of Novipazar (which bordered on Montenegro), and Bosnia; this was intended to liberate south Serbia and to persuade the Montenegrins to join in the struggle against the Turks. This plan was frustrated by a decisive Turkish victory near Niš in the spring of 1809. The Serbs blamed the Russians for failing to co-operate with them at the right time, and anti-Russian feeling became so strong that Rodofinikin was obliged to flee from Belgrade. At the same time the Serbs made overtures both to France[1] and Austria, but nothing definite came of these. Russian prestige was soon restored by the expulsion of all Turkish troops from Serbian territory at the end of October 1810 and even more by a decisive victory won by the Russian general Kutuzov in 1811. After this Russia was anxious to make peace with Turkey, since her relations with France (with whom she had been at peace since

[1] Some Serbs were influenced in favour of a connection with France as a result of the creation of the Illyrian Provinces under French protection.

the conclusion of the Treaty of Tilsit in 1807) were now very strained and a renewal of the war with France seemed imminent.

The war between Russia and Turkey was concluded by the Treaty of Bucharest in 1812. Russia gained very favourable terms in this treaty, and extended her territory as far as the river Pruth and the Danube, and the Black Sea. But nothing definite was stated about the future of Serbia, except that the fortified centres which had existed before the rising were to be restored to the Turks, and those which had been established since were to be destroyed. It is true that the Turks promised to concede the Serbs certain rights of self-government, including the right to collect their own taxes (see above, p. 103); but the Serbs were left to make their own terms with the sultan; and once all fortresses were restored to the Turks they would be negotiating in a very weak position. Experience had already shown that Turkish promises without adequate guarantees that they would be observed were quite valueless.

The Serbs were naturally intensely disappointed by the terms of this treaty, since it seemed that they had gained practically nothing from their eight-year struggle. The only possible course for them in the circumstances was to prolong negotiations as long as possible in the hope that Russia would use her influence to secure them reasonable terms. Meanwhile, in order to delay the return of Turkish troops to their fortresses, they asked that some Russian troops should remain in Serbia as a guarantee that the Serbs should remain at peace while negotiations were in progress. To their consternation this request was refused by Russia, and Russian troops were withdrawn beyond the Danube.

However, this did not mean that Russia had lost all interest in the fate of the Serbs. In June 1812 a Russian envoy arrived in Belgrade to explain the difficulties of Russia's position at that time (Russia was then facing a French invasion) and to assure the Serbs of Russia's sympathy and diplomatic support in their negotiations with the sultan. But this was of little practical value, especially as the sultan decided to conduct these negotiations at Niš instead of Constantinople in order to avoid Russian interference.

At the outset the progress of these negotiations was discouraging and they ended in failure. Proposals and counterproposals were put forward, but without any real hope of achieving a settlement since the Turks insisted that the Serbs should return to their former state of subjection, and this they refused to do. At last the Serbs reduced their terms to two moderate demands. They asked that they should not be deprived of light arms such as guns and pistols, and that the Turks who had left Serbia should not be allowed to return, as it was feared that they would surely seek vengeance on their former subjects. Even these modest demands were refused, and the Serbs were left with the equally desperate alternatives of unconditional surrender without any guarantees against Turkish reprisals, and resistance, without outside help, to a numerically superior and determined enemy.

Although aware of these difficulties Karageorge nevertheless issued a proclamation urging the people to continue to resist.

'What have we to fear?' he said, 'Are these not the same people over whom we have been victorious right from the first day, when we had no means of resistance except our determination and our courage? Now we have 130 cannon 7 fortresses and 40 entrenched positions which the Turks have not been able to take away from us though they have shed much blood in the attempt. And in spite of our losses we are now more numerous than before, our brothers from the neighbouring regions have doubled our army. We shall defend ourselves for ten years without help, and before six months pass our allies will return to us . . . So I summon you to rise up and arm yourselves against the enemy who has attacked us . . . Better to die in our faith in our fatherland than to deny that faith, for in the Gospel it is written that he who has faith will be saved. Better, then, to die in our faith than to be punished before God and our people, and may Almighty God help us!'

Despite these brave words, and the heroic resistance they inspired, the Serbs were unable to withstand the large-scale counter-attack which they now had to face. In October 1813 Turkish troops entered Belgrade, by which time Karageorge and many other Serbian leaders who had managed to escape were refugees in Austrian territory. The First Serbian Rising had ended, and disastrously for the Serbs.

.   .   .   .   .

After the entry of Turkish troops into Belgrade, there followed a period of reprisals: the city was plundered, and the oppressive administration which had preceded the rising was restored. Then there followed a short period of peace, but only a peace of exhaustion as far as the Serbs were concerned. In fact their discontent with Turkish rule was now stronger than ever, and early in 1814 there was another abortive rising at Čačak in south Serbia, and an increase of haidukism everywhere. In the spring of 1815 a more serious rising broke out in Valjevo, near the Bosnian border, which had been the scene of one of the first outbreaks in the First Rising. The movement soon spread; and once more, as in the First Rising, the leaders met (in April 1815) and appointed a leader: this time Miloš Obrenović, who had played a prominent part in the latter part of the First Rising, and who, unlike Karageorge, had remained in Serbia and accepted temporary submission to the Turks in 1813.

The rebels had some military success against the Turks, including a victory in a pitched battle fought at Ljubića on June 10th under the leadership of Miloš Obrenović. This success was encouraging but the position of the Serbs remained very difficult. The Turks were preparing to counter-attack from Bosnia after the renewed outbreak of revolt, and Austria had closed the frontier bringing foreign trade practically to a standstill, so that the Serbs were threatened with a shortage of munitions and even of food. In these circumstances Miloš Obrenović considered it prudent to try and come to terms with the Turks, and therefore embarked on a period of negotiations, a field of activity in which he was to prove himself a master.

Then began a period of missions, proposals, counter-proposals, suggestions and compromises which lasted for fifteen years, and finally ended with the sultan's recognition of Serbia as a self-governing principality within the Turkish Empire, with Miloš Obrenović as hereditary prince.

Both the pattern of events in the Second Rising and their background were different from those of the First Rising, the most striking difference being that the First Rising was concerned more with fighting and the second with negotiation. Moreover, although Russia continued to give the Serbs diplomatic support,[1] the events of the Second Rising were not so directly bound up with the relations of the Great Powers.

A new and important background influence in the period of negotiation which followed the fighting at the beginning of the Second Rising was the unrest in the other parts of the sultan's European dominions. This unrest, which had its roots in the discontent felt by the peoples of Greece and the Balkan peninsula with Turkish rule, was fomented by a Greek secret society known as the *Heteria*, which had its headquarters at Odessa on the Black Sea. Representatives of this society entered into negotiations with Karageorge, who in 1817 was living in exile in Russia. The aim of the *Heteria* was to promote a general rising of all the Christian subjects of the sultan and their liberation from Turkish rule. Although at that time the Serbs were not actually fighting the Turks, but trying, under the leadership of Miloš Obrenović, to reach a settlement, Karageorge agreed to return secretly to Serbia to lead a new rising. In spite of the efforts of the Russian Government to detain him, he succeeded in crossing the frontier into Serbian territory on July 10th, 1817. Karageorge's arrival was in the highest degree distasteful to Miloš Obrenović, since it might have frustrated both the latter's personal ambitions for his own advancement, and his policy of coming to terms with the Turks by negotiation. Miloš therefore had Karageorge assassinated, an action which displayed the ruthlessness which was one of the features of his strong but somewhat repulsive character.

The assassination prevented a renewal of fighting against the Turks in Serbia, but in 1821 revolts broke out both in the Danubian principalities of Moldavia and Wallachia and in Greece. It so happened that at this time the Serbs had sent a special mission to the sultan. Their terms were reasonable. They simply sought the rights of self-government promised in the Treaty of Bucharest and made proposals concerning the boundaries of Serbia. The outbreak of revolt in Moldavia and Wallachia was at first to their advantage, since it made the sultan

---

[1] When the Second Rising broke out, the representatives of the Great Powers were at Vienna, discussing the peace treaty to end the Napoleonic War. When news of the rising reached Vienna none of the Powers expressed any sympathy with the Serbs except Russia. England's attitude was one of strict non-intervention because of her friendly relations with Turkey.

more inclined to accept their proposed terms. But the outbreak of the Greek Revolt a little later caused such a panic in Turkey that the Serbian deputies who had come to Constantinople were arrested and held as hostages. As a result nothing came of this mission.

It was not until five years later that the sultan agreed to a definite settlement with the Serbs. The immediate reason for this was a change of ruler followed by a change of policy in Russia. In 1825 Alexander I died and was succeeded by Nicholas I. He adopted a more energetic attitude towards the situation in the Balkan peninsula and Greece, and demanded that the sultan should make agreements with his rebellious subjects, including the Serbs who were not actually fighting at this time. To give more force to his words Nicholas moved Russian troops up to the frontier between Russia and Turkey.

Thus faced with external pressure and internal unrest, the sultan agreed to negotiate a settlement, and signed the Convention of Ackerman with Russia in October 1826. In Article V of this convention the sultan agreed to negotiate directly with the Serbs on the basis of the terms proposed by them in 1820; freedom of worship, internal self-government, the return of territory taken from Serbia in 1813; freedom of trade and permission for Serbian merchants to travel throughout Turkish territory; the right to build schools, hospitals and printing-presses; and a prohibition on Mohammedan settlement outside the towns in Serbia. The fulfilment of these terms was prevented by a crisis in the Greek Revolt; in order to prevent the massacre of the Greeks of the Morea by the troops of the sultan's vassal Ibrahim Pasha of Egypt, Britain, France and Russia signed the Treaty of London in 1827, in which they pledged themselves to compel the Sultan to make an armistice with the Greeks by all means short of open war. In fact it proved impossible to prevent military supplies from passing into Greece without hostilities, and in the summer of 1827 a naval engagement took place between English vessels stationed in the Levant and the Turkish navy, as a result of which the Turks were decisively defeated at the battle of Navarino. The sultan then repudiated the Convention of Ackerman, whereupon Russia declared war. Once again the Serbian deputies in Constantinople were arrested and held as hostages. However the war did not last long and in 1829 the sultan signed the Treaty of Adrianople with Russia. By this treaty Greece was to become a tributary principality of the Turkish Empire under a Christian prince, and Serbia was promised the fulfilment of the Convention of Ackerman.

The final settlement with the Serbs was made in a document known as a *Hatisherif*, solemnly proclaimed in Belgrade in December 1830. The previous year the sultan had reaffirmed the promises made in the Treaty of Bucharest and the Convention of Ackerman, and promised to restore to Serbia the territory taken from her at the end of the First Rising in 1813. In the *Hatisherif* of 1830, the terms made with the Serbs were defined in detail: they were to have complete religious freedom; Miloš Obrenović was recognised as prince of Serbia, the office to be hereditary in his family (by a separate *berat*); he was to be responsible for the internal administration of Serbia, in co-operation with an elected *skupština*, or assembly; a Russo-Turkish commission was to be appointed to fix the boundaries of the six *nahijas*, or districts, to be returned to Serbia; Miloš Obrenović as prince was to be allowed to keep a small military force for the maintenance of internal order, although the Turks were still to garrison the larger towns; the Serbs were to have the unrestricted right to build schools, hospitals and printing-presses throughout the principality; finally the rights of Turks resident in Serbia and the extent of their property was to be defined. The arrangement made with regard this last point was that Turks living in Belgrade were to be allowed to stay there, but those in smaller towns were to leave Serbia within a period of five years.

Thus Serbia finally became a tributary self-governing principality within the Turkish empire, after a military and diplomatic struggle lasting over a quarter of a century.

An important strand in the complex history of the second phase of the Serbian Rising was the personal career of Miloš Obrenović. He is the dominant personality in the second part of the story as Karageorge is in the first. Miloš's services to the cause of Serbian independence[1] were invaluable; no more suit-

---

[1] Serbia was still nominally a part of the Turkish Empire; but as a self-governing principality with a hereditary prince chosen from her own people, she was virtually independent as regards internal administration, although the Turks continued to garrison certain fortified centres in Serbia until 1867.

able person could have been found for the long, weary period of negotiation which followed the short period of fighting at the beginning of the Second Rising. He was a most astute diplomat, a tenacious negotiator, a man with an inborn sense of the political situation and he never lost his head. He was also very ruthless and ambitious, as can be seen from his prompt assassination of his personal and political rival Karageorge; and Karageorge was not the only opponent for whose death Miloš was responsible. Naturally such a man had his enemies both among his own compatriots and elsewhere. Nevertheless he achieved his objects, as determined and ruthless people usually do; not only was he the main architect of the virtually independent Serbia created by the *Hatisherif* of 1830; he was also formally acknowledged both by his compatriots and the sultan as the hereditary prince of Serbia. He was destined to have a long and stormy political career, including a forced abdication, and a triumphant return to power when he was nearly eighty years of age. A broad, tree-lined boulevard in Belgrade, in which many foreign embassies have their headquarters, commemorates his name.

H

Chapter 5

The South Slav Lands in the Nineteenth Century

HE SERBIAN revolt represents the first step along the
road to the creation of a South Slav state. By 1829
Miloš Obrenović was the ruler of a state which was
independent in all but name. During the nineteenth century
Serbia threw off the last shadowy traces of Turkish suzerainty.
Step by step she enlarged her territory, and emerged as the only
possible nucleus round which the new Yugoslav state could
grow.

Serbia's success encouraged the first stirrings of nationalism
amongst the Slavs who still bore the yoke of foreign occupation.
During the century which preceded the outbreak of the First
World War the national aspirations of many Croats, Slovenes,
Bosnians and Montenegrins came to be focused on the idea of a
Yugoslav state headed by Serbia. At first, however, the Slavs
within the Habsburg lands sought autonomy for themselves
within the Empire. The 'Yugoslav idea' was a dream in the
minds of a few writers and intellectuals, and the mass of the
people did not acquiesce in it until the end of the First World
War. Many of them did not really accept it until the Second
World War.

The history of the Balkans during the nineteenth century is
intimately bound up with the destinies of the Turkish and
Austrian Empires, and with the rivalries of the big powers. The
Turkish Empire was obviously in the last stages of decay. As the
Sultan relaxed his grip on the Balkans, the Habsburgs stretched
out their hands to seize the vital lands which lay between the
Austro-Hungarian borders and the Aegean Sea. Russia, playing the role of big brother to the Slav-speaking peoples, and
especially to the Orthodox Serbs and Bulgarians, was trying
desperately to find a way out to the warm waters of the Mediterranean by establishing a bridge-head in command of the

Dardanelles. Britain sought to prevent the inevitable squabble between the powers over the disposal of Turkey's effects in Europe by keeping the 'sick man' alive as long as possible. The attempts of British Governments to inject new life into Turkey conflicted with the generous sympathies of many of her people concerning the fate of the subject nationalities in the Balkans. These subject peoples found that their national struggle was not solely a matter of settling accounts between themselves and their foreign masters. Every move which they made was watched by the great powers, every action judged in the light of the wider struggle for influence in the Balkans which was being waged in the Chancelleries and on the battle-fields of Europe. The South Slavs suffered the fate of all peoples whose struggle for independence is fought out in the geographical setting of an area of great strategic interest. The peoples of the Middle East and South East Asia are learning in the twentieth century what the Yugoslavs learned in the nineteenth century – namely that they cannot escape from outside interference in their attempts to solve their problems in their own way. They are like men walking across an unmapped minefield, where every step invites an explosion which may destroy them, and may even shake the foundations of the international order. It is against this background that we should examine the history of the South Slavs during the nineteenth century.

There are two main strands in the story: the development of Serbia and Montenegro as independent states, and the growth of national feeling amongst the Slavs under foreign rule. These two strands are of course connected, notably in 1848, the 'year of revolutions' and in the Balkan Wars of 1912. Serbian foreign policy was always influenced and at times dominated by the nationalist aspirations of the South Slavs under foreign rule; and in many ways Serbia was fitted to play the same role in the political unification of Yugoslavia as Piedmont did in that of Italy. Unfortunately Serbia had no Cavour; though Ilija Garašanin, one of the outstanding figures in Serbian political life in the middle years of the nineteenth century, can be compared with the great Italian statesman. Perhaps if Garašanin had had the support of a ruler such as Victor Emmanuel II he might have accomplished more, and possibly accelerated the union of Yugoslavia.

Serbia in the Nineteenth Century

The history of Serbia after 1816 makes depressing reading when compared with the story of the heroic struggle for liberation with which the century opens. It is, for the most part, a story of intrigues, assassinations, shifts of policy, and attempts, mainly ineffective, to establish some kind of constitutional government. The unsatisfactory nature of Serbian political life at this time can be largely attributed to two factors: the lack of strong, constructive leadership at the time of the consolidation of the new state, and the vitiating influence of the feud between the descendants of the two leaders of the Rising, Karageorge and Miloš Obrenović. There was also a more healthy influence at work: the freedom-loving spirit of the Serbian people, who had to learn the difference between submission to tyranny and submission to authority. And this is a lesson which can only be learnt by experience. The disorderly scenes which sometimes took place in the Serbian assemblies might compare unfavourably with the behaviour of Victorian parliaments, but if they are compared with English parliaments of the late sixteenth and early seventeenth century the difference is not so great.

From 1816 to 1839 Serbia was under the personal rule of Miloš Obrenović. He gained some support among the peasants by dividing among them lands which had been confiscated from Turkish landowners in order to prevent the consolidation of big estates. Naturally those who had been thus prevented from enriching themselves were against Miloš from the start; and even the peasants felt no real security since they were subjected to arbitrary taxation, were often exploited by unscrupulous moneylenders and were constantly in fear of eviction either for debt or at the dictates of their autocratic Prince.[1]

By 1834 Miloš's despotic rule had proved so unpopular that he was opposed by an armed rising, known as the Miletin Rising after its leader Mileta Radojković. As a result of this

---

[1] The moneylenders borrowed from the Government at 6 per cent and loaned to the peasants at rates varying from 12 per cent to 120 per cent: Miloš made efforts to compel the Serbian peasants to leave their scattered farmsteads and settle in nucleated villages. See Ruth Trouton *Peasant Renaissance in Yugoslavia*, Routledge 1956, and Djordević *Srbija pre sto godina* (Serbia a hundred years ago), Belgrade. 1946.

rising Miloš, agreed to the Sretenje Constitution.[1] This constitution reflected the liberal ideas then in vogue in Europe, and gave considerable powers, including that of drafting the laws, to an elected assembly: it also guaranteed the peasants in possession of their lands. It was too liberal for Miloš's taste, and also for that of Russia and Turkey, who, under the terms of the Treaty of Adrianople and the *Hatisherif* of 1830, held a watching brief for the administration of Serbia. (It must be remembered that Serbia was still nominally part of the Turkish Empire, though a self-governing unit within it.) Miloš was therefore able to suspend the constitution one month after its promulgation, being assured of the support of Russia and Turkey in this action. Three years later a new constitution was issued, known as the 'Turkish Constitution'. This document, as its name suggests, was drawn up in Constantinople, after a diplomatic battle between England and France on the one hand, and Austria and Russia on the other.

The new constitution was much less liberal than the old one. The Prince was to rule with the advice of a Senate of seventeen members appointed by him, but removable only by the Sultan. The opposition groups in Serbia forced Miloš to accept their nominees to the Council. Miloš attempted to defeat them by encouraging a rising in his favour, but this failed, and under increasing pressure from Russia Miloš abdicated in favour of his son, Milan, and retired to his Rumanian estates. Milan, a young man of twenty, was incurably ill when he succeeded his father. After a few weeks he died, and his younger brother, Michael, then seventeen years old, became the new ruler. The Sultan insisted on appointing advisers, and three years later, one of these Vučić,[2] carried out a *coup d'état* in favour of Alexander Karageorge, son of the Karageorge who had led the First Rising.

Unfortunately the change of dynasty did not have a stabilising influence on Serbian political life. From the start the new régime was weakened by the opposition of Obrenović

---

[1] Sretenje = meeting. When used, as it is here, as a proper name, it refers to a traditional 'festival' in the later part of February, supposed to be the meeting-point of summer and winter.

[2] Vučić belonged to a group known as the 'Ustavobranitelji' (Defenders of the Constitution).

supporters, which in 1844 found expression in an abortive rising. In addition – and more serious – the prince and the leaders of the Constitutional 'party' were no better able to work together than in the previous reign, and there were perpetual quarrels between the Constitutionalists and the 'Prince's Party', as the personal supporters of the prince were known. To make matters worse the Constitutionalists were not even united among themselves, especially after 1848. These internal dissensions were fostered by Austrian and Russian agents, who preferred to see Serbia weak and divided than strong and independent; and also by those of Miloš Obrenović, who had not given up hope of becoming Prince of Serbia once more. After the Crimean War (1854–6) the political situation in Serbia deteriorated to something like chaos, in which the one clear element appeared to be the dissatisfaction of all groups with the existing régime. In 1857 there was a plot (with the connivance of Miloš Obrenović) to kill Alexander Karageorge and restore Miloš. This plot was detected and the conspirators arrested. Public opinion was at first against the conspirators, but turned in their favour when they were badly treated in prison. The situation was so disturbed that the sultan sent a special representative to investigate. Meanwhile certain leaders of the Constitutionalists began an intensive propaganda to demand the summoning of a *Skupština* (the Serbian word for an assembly, and still used to describe the Yugoslav Federal Parliament). Prince Alexander reluctantly agreed. This assembly (known as the *St. Andrew's Skupština* because it met on St. Andrew's Day, 1858), consisted of locally elected representatives and certain officials. Its first action was to depose Alexander Karageorge and invite Miloš Obrenović to become prince of Serbia once more.

The most outstanding personality who emerges from this chequered and unsatisfactory period of Serbian history is Ilija Garašanin, who until 1854 directed Serbia's foreign policy. He was a man of strong character and statesmanlike vision, the first clear protagonist of the 'Yugoslav Idea', that is, the eventual political unification of all the South Slavs regardless of historical and cultural background. He believed that it was Serbia's mission to take the lead in turning this idea into reality. In 1848 he had great hopes of achieving some part of this plan, but in this he was disappointed, since the events of that year were followed by the restoration of the *status quo ante* as regards the political situation of the South Slavs living in the Habsburg Empire. In 1854 he was dismissed from his post as a result of Russian pressure but after the Crimean War he returned to office, and his ideas continued to dominate Serbian foreign policy right up to 1918.

The restoration of Miloš in 1858 can be attributed to two factors: a general feeling that a strong hand was needed to counteract the chaos of the preceding two or three years (and Miloš had shown that he had this!); and also a hope that he might be able to secure the complete formal independence of Serbia from the Turkish Empire, as he had been instrumental in securing her self-government after the Second Rising. Serbia was still, in 1858, part of the Turkish Empire, though some change in her situation had been made at the Treaty of Paris in 1856, whereby the Russo-Turkish guarantee of her privileges of self-government was replaced by the collective guarantee of all the European Great Powers. Actually, it was not until 1868, after Miloš's death, that Turkish garrisons were finally withdrawn from Serbia.[1]

Miloš's second period as prince of Serbia was short, and, it need hardly be mentioned, autocratic. In 1860 he died, and was succeeded by his son Michael, recalled, like his father, after a long period of exile. In 1861 Prince Michael summoned a *Skupština* and organised a new system of government. According to this the *Skupština* was to be summoned only once every three years, and its functions were to be advisory; in fact the prince ruled with the help of a council whose members were responsible to him. Not unnaturally, such a system was unpopular with many sections of the people and in 1868 its author was struck down by an unknown assassin.

The *Skupština* then chose Michael's fourteen-year-old cousin Milan. For four years, until he became of age, Milan's royal functions were carried out by a Regency Council. The Regency Council summoned a *Skupština* to frame a new constitution.

---

[1] The circumstances leading to this withdrawal took place some years earlier. In 1862 a Serbian youth was killed in the small town of Čukur-Česmi; this caused a clash between groups of Serbs and Turks, and as reprisals for this incident the Turkish garrison in Belgrade bombarded the city. The Serbs protested and eventually the Turkish garrison was withdrawn altogether, at the request of the Great Powers.

According to this the *Skupština* was to be in permanent session, but would still have no control of legislation or finance, and the prince was to have the right to nominate one-third of the members. This 'Regency Constitution', despite its limitations, represented some advance on the 'Turkish Constitution' and the system of government organised by Prince Michael. The internal political life of Serbia became more tranquil than it had been for some time, perhaps partly because of the pressing importance of foreign affairs, particularly at the time of the Bosnian Rising in 1875. By the 1880s there were at least three clearly defined political parties in Serbia: Radicals, Progressives and Liberals, as well as an embryonic Socialist group based on the ideas of the energetic publicist Svetozar Marković who died in 1875.[1] It was a sign of some progress towards greater political maturity that these parties had clearly differentiated policies based on more positive principles than mutual antagonism and opposition to the government.[2]

During the 1880s Milan's unpopularity grew. He was a pleasure-loving Prince, whose private life frequently brought scandal on the name of the Royal Family. In 1882 his Principality became a Kingdom, but the new dignity of Kingship did little to improve Milan's authority in the eyes of his people. In 1883 an attempt to collect arms from the peasants was met with open revolt. There were other reasons for the unpopularity of the Government at that time – notably its Austrophil attitude,[3] and the strong suspicion that prominent Ministers were guilty of peculation in connection with the construction of the Belgrade-Niš railway.[4]

Many prominent Radicals were sentenced to death for alleged complicity in these outbreaks. Some of them managed to

[1] As well as being one of the pioneers of Socialism in Serbia, Svetozar Marković was also an advocate of a federation of Balkan republics.

[2] The Radicals followed the political principles of Svetozar Marković, but not his social and economic programme, and had considerable support among the peasants; the Progressives were on the whole conservative in spirit, and supported Prince Milan's regime while the Liberals, supported mainly by the middle class, represented a 'middle way' between the Radicals and the Progressives.

[3] For details of Milan's secret agreement with Austria-Hungary, see page 127–8.

[4] Completed in 1884.

escape, but the Radical Party as a whole was seriously weakened. In 1888 Milan, now King of Serbia, issued a new constitution which introduced secret voting and also organs of local self-government. After the promulgation of the constitution he abdicated in favour of his son Alexander.

The reign of Alexander Obrenović (1888–1903) marks the nadir of Serbian political life. It was not long before the new king had alienated almost all sections of his people by his attempts to limit or abolish their cherished political privileges; by his foolish decision to allow his father to return to Serbia and even to become commander-in-chief of the army; and by his marriage to the unpopular Draga Mašin in 1900. In the fevered atmosphere created by his intense unpopularity it is hardly surprising that there were plots against him, and in 1903 he and his wife were brutally murdered as a result of a conspiracy organised by a group of army officers.[1] His assassination marked the end of Obrenović rule in Serbia, and he was succeeded by Peter Karageorge, the son of the Prince Alexander Karageorge who had been deposed in 1858.

Peter Karageorge promised to rule in accordance with the 1888 constitution and kept his promise. The result was a period of orderly rule in Serbia, for practically the first time in her history as a modern state. This proved to be of great benefit, both to the economic development of the country and to the pursuit of a vigorous foreign policy, and undoubtedly helped to prepare Serbia for the ordeal she was to endure in the First World War.

MONTENEGRO IN THE NINETEENTH CENTURY

The nineteenth century is important in the history of Montenegro since it saw the first stirrings away from the bad old traditions of savagery and corruption which had for centuries

---

[1] There is a vivid and detailed account of this event in Rebecca West's *Black Lamb and Grey Falcon*: in addition it has recently served as the subject of a play called *Konak* by Miloš Crnanski, which was recently performed in Belgrade. The organiser of the crime was Colonel Mašin, brother of Queen Draga's first husband. Dragutin Dimitrijević (later known as 'Apis') was one of the conspirators. 'Apis' is thought to have planned the murder of the Archduke at Sarajevo in 1914. He was shot after a court-martial at Salonika in 1917, after being found guilty of the attempted murder of Crown Prince Alexander (see part II, page 139).

defaced the way of life of this medieval survival.[1] Actually this
process began in the late eighteenth century, under the rule of
the *vladika* Peter I Njegoš (1781–1830). He made a modest
beginning by trying to reduce blood-feuds and promote greater
co-operation among the tribes; he also planned to introduce a
written legal code and encouraged road-building. His policy
was continued by his successor Peter II, who established a
senate of twelve members with legislative, executive and judicial functions; but the *vladika* remained in effect an absolute
ruler since he dismissed any members of the senate who disagreed with him. As might be expected from a ruler who was also
a poet, Peter II did not neglect culture: schools were founded,
and for the second time in Montenegro a printing press was set
up in Cetinje; the one set up in 1493 by Đurad Crnojević had
been melted down for bullets.

After the death of Peter II in 1851 quarrels broke out between
the supporters of his nominated successor Danilo and certain
members of the senate led by the late ruler's brother Pero.
Danilo proved to have stronger support among the people and
was finally elected *vladika* in 1852 by an assembly of tribal
chiefs. His first action as ruler was to secularise his position
by proclaiming himself Prince of Montenegro.[2] He then proceeded to establish a centralised, autocratic form of government
and introduced regular taxation – which was extremely unpopular with his subjects! He also strove to extend the frontiers
of his state by intervening in the frequent local risings which
occurred in the neighbouring Turkish territory of Bosnia and
Hercegovina in the middle of the nineteenth century. This
involved him in a war with Turkey, and in 1852 Turkish troops
invaded Montenegro, but withdrew as a result of the intervention of Austria; five years later the Turks again attacked
Montenegro and were defeated. At this point the Great Powers
intervened and a commission was appointed to define the
boundary between Turkish and Montenegrin territory. This
action is significant as a tacit recognition of the independence of

[1] There is a vivid account of the brutality of life in Montenegro in
Land Without Justice by Milovan Djilas.

[2] Certain members of the Petrović-Njegoš family, and also the rulers of
Austria and Turkey opposed this change, but Russia supported it and her
influence was still strong in Montenegro.

Montenegro, which had long been a reality, but had never been formally acknowledged; in fact it was not officially proclaimed until the Congress of Berlin in 1878 (when Serbia also was proclaimed an independent state).

During the Crimean War Prince Danilo introduced a modified constitution, which, though reactionary in spirit, did represent some advance on his previous personal autocracy. He also organised a census (for taxation purposes), which revealed that Montenegro had 80,000 inhabitants and no towns! In fact Prince Danilo rendered considerable services to his small state, but his autocratic rule was unpopular and in 1860 it was terminated by a method all too common in the Balkan peninsula in the nineteenth century – assassination. He was succeeded by his nephew Nicholas, who, on the occasion of his Golden Jubilee in 1910, proclaimed himself King of Montenegro.

Nicholas continued the policy of his predecessor in both domestic and foreign policy. Montenegro helped a rising of Hercegovnian rebels in 1861, and like Serbia, declared war on Turkey after the outbreak of the Bosnian Rising in 1875; on this occasion she occupied a considerable amount of neighbouring Turkish territory. At the Congress of Berlin Montenegro was handsomely rewarded. Its area was doubled by accessions of territory, which included a strip of coastline, and some fertile agricultural land. As a result the economic life of Montenegro developed considerably; even industry was introduced in the shape of a textile factory at Podgorica (now Titograd, the capital of the People's Republic of Montenegro). Roads were built and telephone and telegraph services established.[1]

To meet the needs of his expanded state, Prince Nicholas introduced a new system of government based on the principle of the 'separation of powers': a State Council with legislative functions, a group of ministers to be responsible for the executive powers and a supreme judicial organ known as the *Veliki Sud* (High Court). Nevertheless the effective power of government continued to be concentrated in his own hands. In 1905, under pressure from the growing middle class he introduced a National Assembly, but refused to allow it to control either legislation or finance (cf. the Serbian constitution introduced by

[1] A considerable amount of foreign capital was invested in these developments, mainly Italian after the beginning of the twentieth century.

Prince Milan in 1869). The members soon divided into two groups, one supporting the prince and the other demanding greater powers for the assembly; the latter were known as *Klubaši* ('Clubbists') because they called themselves the 'Club of the National Party'.

During the later part of his reign Nicholas was unpopular with many sections of his people both because of his autocratic government and his increasingly Austrophil foreign policy. Two attempts to assassinate him failed, and he was still ruler of Montenegro at the outbreak of the First World War.

South Slavs under Foreign Occupation

Apart from Serbia and Montenegro, all the territory comprising present-day Yugoslavia was under foreign rule during the nineteenth century: Slovenia, Croatia and Vojvodina (now an autonomous province of the People's Republic of Serbia) were part of the Habsburg Empire, and Macedonia and Bosnia and Hercegovina were part of the Turkish Empire.[1] In all these regions the spirit of nationalism was a vital force during this period, working like a ferment beneath the surface of everyday life, occasionally finding violent expression, as in the Bosnian Rising of 1875. The forms in which this national feeling expressed itself and the aims of its different exponents, were very varied. The Illyrian Movement which flourished in Croatia and Slovenia in the early nineteenth century; the influence of the Slovenian poet France Prešeren and of the Macedonian patriot Dmitar Mladinov who, together with his brother, strove to awaken and intensify Macedonian feeling by publishing collections of folk poetry and compiling a dictionary and grammar of the Macedonian language; the Internal Macedonian Revolutionary Organisation and the 'Young Bosnia' movement – all these, though widely diverse in both aims and methods were expressions of a single spirit. It would be a fascinating task to analyse and compare these, and other, expressions of national feeling among the South Slavs, and to trace the development of the 'Yugoslav Idea' which became a political fact after the First World War; but such a task would require a book to itself. But

---

[1] Bosnia-Hercegovina were nominally Turkish up to 1908, when they were formally annexed by Austria. They had in fact been under Austrian administration since 1878.

one striking fact emerges from even a casual study of the areas under consideration: in those under Habsburg rule, nationalism expressed itself mainly in cultural activities and the more orthodox forms of political agitation, and showed itself on the whole politically conservative, even in 1848, whereas in the Turkish provinces it found expression in repeated risings and revolutionary propaganda. It would seem that the cause of this difference should be sought in the different circumstances under which the people lived. The vitiating influence of Turkish rule, which never succeeded in offering its subjects any positive benefits, cultural or material, produced a mood of despair which could only result in either apathy or violence. The South Slavs living in the Habsburg Empire, on the other hand, were members of a civilised European society; and though many of them were, with good reason, dissatisfied with their position in that society, they shrank on the whole from violent action which might destroy much that was good. This, at any rate, was the prevailing attitude among the middle class, who provided most of the exponents and leaders of nationalism.

As it is impossible, in this brief survey, to deal adequately with all aspects of the history of the South Slavs under foreign rule, it is proposed to concentrate on certain outstanding expressions of nationalist feeling which were directly or in-directly responsible for the creation of Yugoslavia: the Illyrian Movement, the events of 1848, the Bosnian Rising and the events leading up to the Balkan Wars of 1912.

The Illyrian Movement, which was confined to Croatia and Slovenia, derived its name from the Illyrian Provinces estab-lished by Napoleon; these included the whole of medieval Croatia, from the Adriatic Sea to the river Sava, and also Slovenia. French administration was enlightened and pro-gressive, and the use of native languages was encouraged; more-over the mere fact of being part of a single administrative unit had the effect of stimulating the national self-consciousness of those who lived in it. The Illyrian Provinces lasted only from 1809 until 1813, but their influence was felt long after that, and in the thirties of the nineteenth century produced something like an organised movement, known as the Illyrian Movement. In Croatia its leaders were mainly intellectuals, the most prominent

being the philologist Ludovit Gaj. Their immediate aim was
the reduction of Hungarian cultural influence, which had
increased in the late eighteenth and early nineteenth centuries[1]
but they also had the wider one of uniting all the South Slavs
into one political unit. There was nothing revolutionary in
either their programme or their methods, and their practical
activities were mainly cultural. Among other things they
worked for the establishment of a common language for all the
South Slavs; founded reading rooms, discussion groups and
newspapers and had their own publishing house, the 'Matica
Ilirska' (the Illyrian Queen Bee). They also formed a political
party known first as the 'Illyrian Party' and later as the
'National Party'; the object of this was to counteract the
influence of the so-called 'Magyar Party', supported mainly by
landowners and the petty bourgeoisie, which favoured Hungarian influence. In time a Radical wing developed in the Illyrian,
or National Party, whose members demanded the reform of the
Croatian Diet along democratic lines, separate government for
Croatia and freedom of the Press. This Radical section, as might
be expected, appealed particularly to young people. Feeling
ran high in both the National and Magyar Parties, and sometimes street clashes occurred between their respective supporters; but until 1848 there was nothing that could be
described as organised revolt.

In Slovenia the Illyrian Movement followed a similar course.
But whereas in Croatia it was the main vehicle of nationalist
feeling in the first half of the nineteenth century, in Slovenia
there was another parallel trend whose adherents advocated not
only self-government for Slovenia but also social and economic
reforms, notably the abolition of surviving elements of feud-
alism. The supporters of the Illyrian Movement, on the other
hand, tended to be conservative in their attitude to social and
economic questions, and to concentrate more on the fostering of
the 'Yugoslav Idea'.

The events of the year 1848 are particularly confusing in the
parts of the Habsburg Empire inhabited by South Slavs. In
Croatia, Slovenia and Vojvodina, attempts were made to secure

---

[1] For example in 1825 Hungarian was made a compulsory subject in all
Croatian schools.

some degree of political autonomy, in all cases without lasting success. The complicating factor was the nationalist movement in Hungary. Both Croatia and Vojvodina were nominally part of Hungary, though Croatia had its own diet and a certain measure of autonomy. In 1848 the Hungarians, under the leadership of Louis Kossuth, made a determined attempt to break the connection with Austria and establish an independent state. However, as well as being anti-Austrian, they were also anti-Slav, and not at all willing to concede to the South Slavs who lived within the borders of what had been the medieval kingdom of Hungary the same concessions as they themselves demanded from the Austrian Emperor. The nationalists of Croatia and Vojvodina therefore found themselves in the ironic position of indirectly helping the Austrian emperor Franz Josef by proceeding against their more immediate opponents, the Hungarian nationalists. The ultimate beneficiary in this confused situation was the Emperor, who welcomed the support of the Croats while he was seriously threatened by the Hungarian rebels, but refused to consider their claims once the Hungarians had been effectively defeated, with Russian help.

In Slovenia the situation was somewhat simpler. There were revolutionary demonstrations in Ljubljana in March 1848, and also some local risings among the peasants; these were chiefly concerned with abolishing the remaining feudal privileges of the landlords. The middle class, however, were anxious to prevent violence and formed a National Guard for the protection of property. But even the more conservative Nationalists were driven by the pressure of popular opinion to put forward a constructive political programme, the main point of which was internal self-government for Slovenia within the Habsburg Empire. But they were not willing to use violent revolutionary methods to attain this end.

Naturally these events caused great interest in Serbia. The official Serbian attitude was one of non-intervention, since the reigning prince, Alexander Karageorge, did not want to incur the hostility of Austria. Nevertheless the foreign minister, Garašanin had some hopes that the Serbian nationalist movement in Vojvodina would lead to the incorporation of this region into Serbia; and volunteers from Serbia went to the help of the rebels in Vojvodina, just as volunteers from

Vojvodina had taken part in the Serbian Rising nearly half a century before. But with the defeat of the Hungarian rebels the Serbian movement in Vojvodina also collapsed, and it was not until 1918 that the region became part of Serbia.

As we have seen in Chapter III, the situation in Bosnia and Hercegovina was particularly gloomy for the Christian Slavs, since they were oppressed not only by the representatives of their foreign rulers, but also by the native Moslem landowners. Throughout the nineteenth century Bosnia-Hercegovina was in a state of continual unrest which found expression in frequent local risings, and finally flared up on a bigger scale in 1875. The immediate cause of the Bosnian Rising – or rather series of risings – of that year was shortage of food, following a bad harvest in 1874. The rising began when the Christian peasants of a village near Mostar rose against the local Turkish bureaucrats. Soon there was trouble for the Turkish officials throughout Bosnia and Hercegovina.

The flames which burst out in the little village of Nevesinje in July 1875 soon got out of control, and engulfed the whole of the Balkans. Milan, under pressure from Serbian public opinion, declared war in 1876. Nicholas of Montenegro, who had given open support to the rebels in collaboration with the deposed Serbian king's son, Peter Karageorge, now joined Milan in declaring war on Turkey. The Montenegrin troops had a number of successes, but the Serbian forces were soon in retreat. Russia intervened to prevent a débâcle, and a temporary armistice was signed. Abdul Hamid (Abdul the Damned) gave out the routine promises of better treatment for the Christian subjects of the Porte, but it soon became apparent that once again these gestures were of no value. In May 1877 Russia abandoned the attempt to persuade Abdul Hamid to agree to a scheme of reform, and in concert with Rumania, Serbia and Montenegro she marched against the Turks. This time the Turkish forces were defeated. Russian troops pushed as far south as Thrace, and the Serbs captured Niš, in the Morava valley. The Russians forced on Turkey the Treaty of San Stefano, which would have created a Bulgarian state stretching from the Aegean to the Danube, and from Macedonia to the Black Sea. Serbia and Montenegro were to be given territory at the expense of Turkey, and Bosnia was to be given autonomy within the Turkish Empire, under a Christian Governor. Austria-Hungary feared that the autonomy of Bosnia would be the first step towards the annexation of the province by Serbia whenever the next crisis occurred in the Balkans. Already the Austro-Hungarian Ministers were coming to regard Serbia as their chief enemy. In addition they distrusted the intentions of the Russian Government, for under the Secret Treaty of Reichstadt (January 1877) Russia had promised that Austria should be the inheritor of Turkish power in Bosnia and Hercegovina in the event of any changes being made in that area. Britain and France were more concerned about Russia's control of the Straits, and saw in the 'Big Bulgaria' a Russian satellite giving the Tsar access to the outlet from the Black Sea. All the powers therefore combined to prevent Russia from carrying out the Treaty of San Stefano. Under the 'honest brokership' of Bismarck, a Congress was held in Berlin, and the map of the Balkans was redrawn in the light of the conflicting interests of the powers. No one thought of consulting the peoples or governments of the Balkans. Their fate was settled for them in their absence. The Ministers at Berlin refused to hear the Serbian Premier, Ristić, and they contemptuously swept aside the warnings of Bishop Strossmayer of Slavonia concerning the policy which they proposed to follow in Bosnia.

Serbia gained something from the Treaty of Berlin. Her complete independence was at last recognised, and she acquired territory in the Pirot region, and along the S. Morava valley between Niš and Vranje. Montenegro also gained some territory. Austria was given the right to occupy Bosnia and Hercegovina, and also the Sanjak of Novi Pazar. By occupying the Sanjak she drove a wedge between the two young Slav states, and ensured that Serbia would have no access to the sea through the territory of a friendly Slav neighbour. Ristić reported from Berlin that the Russians were unwilling to support Serbia in any resistance to the Austrian demands. Milan's reaction to this situation was to make himself the client of the Habsburgs.[1] He made no further attempts to resist Austrian encirclement – in fact he secretly accepted it. By a secret agreement

[1] B. H. Sumner, *Russia and the Balkans 1870–1880*, O.U.P. 1937. Chapter XVIII.

in 1881 he promised that he would 'tolerate no political, religious or other intrigues which, taking Serbian territory as a point of departure, might be directed against the Austro-Hungarian Monarchy; including therein Bosnia, Hercegovina and the Sanjak of Novi Pazar'. Milan promised to maintain a friendly neutrality in the event of Austria being involved in war, and promised that Serbia would not admit foreign troops without Austrian permission. In return Austria-Hungary promised to give diplomatic support to any Serbian expansion into Macedonia.

Milan struggled on for a few years with Austrian support. He was hated by his people for his dissoluteness, his public quarrels with his pro-Russian wife, Natalie,[1] his savagery against the Radical opposition, and his obvious partiality for the Dual Monarchy. His last act of folly was his attempt in 1885 to seize part of Macedonia from Bulgaria as 'compensation' for the union of Eastern Rumelia with Bulgaria. He was defeated at the Battle of Slivnica[2] and his attempt to recover favour by offering the *Skupština* a liberal constitution was unsuccessful. Realising that his position was untenable he abdicated in 1889 in favour of his thirteen-year-old son, Alexander. He and Natalie (now divorced from him) continued their squalid intrigues during the period of the Regency which administered the country during Alexander's minority. Eventually Milan was induced to gratify his dissolute tastes in Vienna, the capital of his former masters, and Natalie then made her way to Biarritz.

Serbia's policy in connection with the Bosnian Rising can be regarded as the first stage in the successful realisation of the ideas of Garašanin: the acquisition of territory inhabited by fellow Slavs under alien rule. It was a modest, but nevertheless significant step in the creation of the future Yugoslavia. The formation of the Balkan League in 1912, and the subsequent war between the Balkan powers and Turkey represents another aspect of the same policy. As early as the 1860's Garašanin, once more Foreign Minister in the reign of Michael Obrenović, was making tentative agreements with Montenegro, Greece and Rumania, and even with groups of Bulgarian *émigrés*

---

[1] Natalie was the daughter of a Bessarabian landowner. At the wedding in 1875 the Tsar had acted as proxy for her father. Her uncle, Catargi, was Serbian representative in Bucharest for a time during the 1870's.

[2] This is the battle referred to in Bernard Shaw's *Arms and the Man*.

(Bulgaria was still part of the Turkish Empire) and Croats. At that time these bore no special fruit, but they can be regarded as foreshadowing the Balkan League concluded in 1912: a series of agreements between Serbia and Bulgaria, Bulgaria and Greece, and Serbia and Montenegro.

THE BALKAN LEAGUE

The first step towards the creation of the Balkan League was taken in March 1912 when Russian initiative brought about a temporary alliance between Serbia and Bulgaria. These two states had a long-standing dispute over Macedonia, the origins of which lie buried deep in the history of the Balkans. The historic land of Macedonia lies across the neck of the Greek peninsula, and through it runs a route of great strategic and commercial importance. This route, which is now followed by the main railway from Belgrade to Salonika, affords access from the plains of the Middle Danube to the Aegean Sea. It was the route by which the Turks advanced to batter at the gates of Christendom, and by which the Habsburgs hoped to move forward as the Turkish Empire slowly crumbled during the nineteenth century. The area inhabited by the Macedonians extends from the Aegean to the Vardar-Morava watershed in the north, and from Lakes Prespa and Ochrid in the west to the Rhodope mountains in the east. At present it is divided between Greece, Bulgaria and Yugoslavia, the largest portion being that held by Yugoslavia. Although the Macedonians have a distinct culture and language, they have never been united under a government of their own since the time of Alexander the Great. For over 2,000 years they have been subjected to one foreign occupation after another, and during the greater part of this period of alien rule they have evinced little interest in the idea of political independence. For a period in the fourteenth century Skopje was the capital of the Serbian Empire, and most of Macedonia was under the rule of Tsar Dušan. Dušan's Empire broke up under the Turkish attacks which culminated in the epic battle of Kosovo Polje, and for six centuries Macedonia formed part of the Turkish Empire. During this period the Turks used the religious differences amongst their Christian subjects as an instrument in their policy of *divide et impera*. At one period they would favour the Bulgarian Church, and allow its clerics special privileges in civil as well as ecclesiastical matters. At another time the Greek clergy would be favoured, whilst for two centuries after 1557 the Serbian Patriarchate was supreme. During the late nineteenth century Bulgaria, the protégé of Russia, secured a dominant position for herself through the activities of the Bulgarian Exarchate. Another instrument of Bulgarian influence was IMRO (the Internal Macedonian Revolutionary Organisation), an extreme nationalist body which was created in 1895. The peak of Bulgaria's success came in 1878, when the Treaty of San Stefano gave her control of the whole of Macedonia. This was a short-lived victory, however, for the prize was snatched from her by the great powers at the Congress of Berlin. Bulgaria continued to dream of recovering the frontiers of San Stefano, and she used IMRO to promote her claims amongst the Slav-speaking Macedonians. In 1903 IMRO was encouraged to organise a rising against the Turks. The Turks successfully repressed the outbreak and burned down 10,000 Macedonian homes. As a result of this outrage, the powers forced the Turks to accept an international police force. The powers hoped to proceed from this point to put pressure on Turkey for further reforms, but their plans were thwarted by the Young Turk Revolution of 1908. In the same year Ferdinand of Bulgaria declared his complete independence from Turkey, and Austria-Hungary annexed the Balkan provinces of Bosnia-Hercegovina. The final result of all these developments in 1908 was to create a climate of opinion favourable to a rapprochement between Bulgaria and Serbia. For a brief period both saw the opportunity to realise part of their ambitions by acting together against Turkey. Serbia was interested in acquiring territory in Macedonia from Turkey. Bulgaria also wanted territory in Macedonia, but she was prepared to wait before pressing her full claim if she could first obtain a frontage along the Aegean by seizing Turkish Thrace. In March 1912 Russia brought the two states together to sign the first of the series of alliances which constituted the Balkan League. Sazanov, the Russian Foreign Minister, saw the alliance as a bulwark against Austro-Hungarian ambitions. 'Well, this is perfect,' he told his Ambassador in Sofia. 'Five hundred thousand bayonets to guard the Balkans – this would bar the road for ever to German penetration, Austrian invasion'. The treaty was seen in a different light by the Serbs and Bulgars. It was an offensive alliance against Turkey, not a defensive pact against Austria-Hungary. Serbia may have hoped that if she helped Bulgaria in a war with Turkey, she might count on Bulgarian support if she became involved with the Dual Monarchy later on. The main object, however, was to take advantage of Turkish weakness and seize as much as possible whilst conditions were favourable. The treaty awarded Serbia all the territory north and west of the Šar Planina, whilst Bulgaria took the Struma valley and all the land to the east of the Rhodope Mountains. The future of the rest of the country was to be decided by the arbitration of the Tsar of Russia if the signatories could not agree between themselves. A military convention laid down the contributions which both states promised to make towards the defeat of Turkey in Europe. In May 1912 Greece joined the alliance by signing a treaty with Bulgaria. Venizelos, the Greek Premier, hoped to win Salonika and part of Thrace for his country, but no attempt was made in the Treaty to define the territorial gains which would pass to Greece, and in fact Greek desires clashed with the secret intentions of Bulgaria. The membership of the League was completed by the adherence of Montenegro in September 1912. The four Balkan powers were now ready to present their demands to Turkey. Their ultimatum demanded autonomy for all the European provinces of Turkey, under the protection of the Great Powers. Montenegro had already declared war on Turkey before the note was sent, and the other three soon found themselves in the same position when Turkey rejected their demands. To the surprise of the powers the Turks were thrown back to the gates of Constantinople within a few weeks. The Bulgarians were so successful in Thrace that the Russians mobilised their Black Sea fleet as a warning to their protégés lest they should go too far and take the Turkish capital. Whilst the Bulgarians were thus occupied in the east, their allies were able to consolidate their position in the disputed areas where their ambitions clashed with those of the Bulgarians. Serbia occupied most of the Slav-speaking areas of Macedonia. The Greeks took Salonika. Even Montenegro, whose troops made the worst showing of any of the members of the League, was able to occupy Scutari in Albania,

and Peć and Djaković in the Upper Drina valley. But the
Powers were not content to look on whilst the new nations of the
Balkans drove the 'Sick man' from Europe. The whole point of
the Eastern Question which had disturbed the peace of Europe
for nearly a century was that all the Powers wished to stake out
their claims to the territory which the Turk would leave behind
when he finally decamped from Europe.

The Powers therefore called a meeting in London and drew
up the terms of the settlement. Turkey ceded all her territory in
Europe except Albania and a small region between Constantinople and Adrianople to the Balkan League. Austria-Hungary
insisted that Serbia should be denied an outlet to the Adriatic,
and persuaded the Powers to agree that Albania should be given
its independence. The Montenegrins were forced to evacuate
Scutari. Greece was given Salonika and part of Thrace, and
Serbia was allowed to keep most of Macedonia. The Bulgarians
had borne the brunt of the fighting, but they felt that they had
been cheated of the spoils of victory. Excited by the success of
their campaign against the Turks, they felt they could easily
overcome their former allies, so in June 1913 they attacked
Greece and Serbia. But Bulgaria's plans sadly misfired. Not
only did Greece and Serbia stand firm but Turkey moved in to
reoccupy Adrianople, and Rumania invaded Bulgaria in order
to take the Dobrudja region from her. The Second Balkan war
ended in the Treaty of Bucharest (August 1913) by which
Bulgaria was forced to recognise Serbian occupation of the
disputed areas in Macedonia and Greek occupation of Salonika.
For once the Powers did not intervene. 'That old phrase "the
Balkans for the Balkan peoples" had come true. All the great
Powers except Austria-Hungary accepted this outcome.'[1]

The virile nationalism of the Balkan peoples had shattered one
Empire. Austria-Hungary was to be the next victim. Within a
year Serbia and Montenegro were once again fighting side by
side against their last enemy. By the Treaty of Bucharest Serbia
had more than doubled her size, and was the obvious leader of
the South Slav peoples still under foreign occupation. Nevertheless, Nicholas of Montenegro still aspired to the role of Saviour
of the South Slavs.

[1] A. J. P. Taylor *Struggle for the Mastery of Europe*, p. 498.

After Bosnia and Hercegovina came under Austrian administration, there was considerable economic progress; both industry and transport were developed, especially mining and the production of timber. An inevitable accompaniment of these developments was a change in the social structure, i.e. the emergence of a middle and working class. This in turn was accompanied by social unrest, which in 1906 found expression in a General Strike.[1] Despite economic progress and the generally efficient character of Austrian administration when compared with that of the Turks, Austrian rule was not popular, and from the beginning there were various movements against it. One of the first of these was the struggle for *crkveno-školska autonomija*, or freedom of religious instruction, which was finally granted to the Serbs (as the Orthodox Bosnians were called) in 1905 and the Moslems in 1909. Later the dominant influence in nationalist agitation was that of the young intellectuals who formed the 'Serbian Nationalist Organisation', and also a 'Moslem Nationalist Organisation' and a 'Croatian Nationalist Organisation'. After the annexation of Bosnia-Hercegovina in 1908 anti-Austrian feeling became more intense. It was at that time that the organisation 'Young Bosnia' (= *Mlada Bosna*) was formed – a movement revolutionary in spirit with a policy based mainly on isolated acts of terrorism, including assassination. Against such a background it is hardly surprising that Sarajevo was the scene of the murder of the Austrian archduke Franz Ferdinand in 1914, which proved to be the immediate cause of the First World War.

[1] The immediate cause of this was the imprisonment of a group of delegates representing the workers in tobacco factories who were seeking higher pay. The strike achieved some gains for the workers as a whole, including shorter hours, higher wages and more freedom of activity for trade unions.

PART TWO

The Birth of Yugoslavia and the Modern State

by F. B. SINGLETON, M.A.

Chapter 1

The First World War and the Birth of Yugoslavia

THE TREATY OF BUCHAREST did not give Serbia the outlet to the sea which she coveted. In Macedonia her frontier ran fifty miles inland from the Aegean port of Salonika: in the west the newly-created State of Albania barred the way to the Adriatic. Nevertheless, Serbian gains as a result of the Balkan Wars represented a great victory for Slav nationalism and an equally severe blow to the multi-national Empire of the Habsburgs. The Austro-Hungarian *Drang nach osten* had been halted. There was now no hope of building the projected Sanjak railway from Sarajevo to Salonika as long as a truculent Serbia controlled Macedonia and the Sanjak of Novi Pazar. Serbia was no longer afraid of economic sanctions directed against her by Austria-Hungary. In the 'pig war' of 1906, when the Monarchy had placed a crippling duty on Serbian exports of livestock, the Serbs had found other outlets for their trade after Turkey had given her permission to use Salonika. Now that Salonika was in friendly hands, she was confident that she could stand up to economic pressure, and saw no reason to moderate her hostility to the Monarchy.

The rulers of Austria-Hungary realised that there would be no peace for them as long as the Slavs within the Empire continued to receive encouragement for their national aspirations from the militant and successful Serbs. One group in Vienna, led by the Chief of Staff Conrad von Hötzendorf, believed that the only hope for the Monarchy lay in the destruction of Serbia as an independent state. A more moderate policy was advocated by Archduke Franz Ferdinand, nephew of the old Emperor, Franz Joseph, and heir to the throne. Ferdinand favoured the creation of a semi-autonomous Slav unit within the Empire, enjoying a position of equality with the Austrian and Hungarian units. By this scheme the Dual Monarchy would become the Triple Monarchy. Franz Ferdinand's ideas were most unwelcome to the rulers of Austria and Hungary, and there is no doubt that the news of his assassination in June 1914 was received with some relief in high circles in Vienna and Budapest. Count Stephen Tisza, Premier of Hungary, is reported to have said 'The Lord God has willed it so, and we must be grateful to the Lord God for everything'.[1] The Archduke's so-called 'Trialist' solution to the Empire's nationality problem was also unpopular with the Serbs. They feared that the Croats and Slovenes might be seduced from the idea of an independent Slav State, headed by Serbia, by the promise of equality of status within the Empire. Thus the Serbs had no reason to mourn the loss of Franz Ferdinand, although there is no proof that the Serbian Government actively participated in the plot which led to his murder in Sarajevo.

In June 1914 Franz Ferdinand and his wife visited the annexed provinces of Bosnia and Hercegovina. After witnessing the Army's summer manœuvres they were to make a State visit to Sarajevo, capital of Bosnia. The visit was timed for June 28th – Vidovdan – the anniversary of Serbia's defeat at Kosovo Polje. A. J. P. Taylor has likened this to a visit by a British monarch to Ireland on St. Patrick's Day at the height of the troubles. It has also been suggested that the Austrian authorities were well aware of the risks which they were taking. There is no doubt that Serbian officials sent warnings to Vienna, for these were later mentioned by the Austrians as proof that the Serbian Government was privy to the murder plot. There is no evidence to suggest that the Archduke's enemies within the Austrian Government deliberately sacrificed the heir to the throne in order to remove an obstacle to their plans for war with Serbia.[2] On the other hand, there is no convincing explanation of the extraordinary laxness of the security arrangements. It may simply have been the monumental inefficiency of the Habsburg security arrangements which prevented the adoption of the most elementary precautions.

The conspirators were members of one of the many extreme nationalist organisations which flourished in the Balkans at

---

[1] This remark has also been attributed to the Emperor.

[2] Wickham Steed suggests Austrian complicity in the murder in *Through Thirty Years*. Heinemann. 1924. Vol. 1. p. 394, *et seq*.

this time. Their leaders, as is the wont of professional patriots, despised the governments and politicians whose patriotic pretensions they felt to be lukewarm and insincere. One of the less irresponsible of these organisations was '*Narodna Odbrana*'.[1] It had been formed in 1908 with the purpose of defending the interests of the Slavs living in the annexed territories of Bosnia and Hercegovina, and its overt activities were limited to culture and sport. Some of its members, however, belonged to the revolutionary group '*Mlada Bosna*' (Young Bosnia), the aims of which were directed towards the violent overthrow of the Austro-Hungarian régime in the annexed provinces. Both *Mlada Bosna* and *Narodna Odbrana* were under the influence of a Serbian underground movement called '*Ujedinjenje ili Smrt*' (Union or Death).[2] *Ujedinjenje ili Smrt* aimed at the union of all the South Slavs under Serbian leadership. Its methods can be deduced from the heraldry of its emblem – the death's head, the dagger, the bomb and the poison bottle. The Secretary of *Narodna Odbrana* and the leader of *Mlada Bosna* were both members of the inner circle of *Ujedinjenje ili Smrt*. The relationships between these organisations was known to the Serbian authorities, and it is probable that a number of Serbian officials and army officers were members of *Ujedinjenje ili Smrt*. It has been shown that Colonel Dimitrijević, Chief of Staff to the Serbian Secret Service, actually planned the assassination of the Archduke in collaboration with the terrorists.[3] It seems certain the *Ujedinjenje ili Smrt* directed the operation which was carried out by members of *Mlada Bosna*, but no one has successfully disentangled the web of deceit and conspiracy which surrounds the relationships of these organisations.

The attempt nearly failed. As the Royal pair drove to the Town Hall in Sarajevo one of the conspirators, Čabrinović, hurled a bomb at their car. The Archduke and his wife were unhurt, but an officer in the next vehicle was injured. After the ceremonies at the Town Hall the Archduke decided that he would visit the injured officer in hospital, but the change of plan

---

[1] 'National Defence.'

[2] Also known as the 'Black Hand'.

[3] See Joachim Remak, *Sarajevo*. Weidenfeld and Nicolson. 1959.

was not communicated to the chauffeurs. The procession moved off along the embankment by the side of the Miljačka river, and had passed the street corner where Gavrilo Princip waited with his revolver. Princip thought he had failed, but to his surprise a second opportunity was offered to him. The cars halted and reversed on to the embankment near the little bridge over the river which is now known as 'Princip's bridge'. In the confusion Princip was able to take aim and to kill both the Archduke and his wife before being arrested. The spot where the assassin is supposed to have stood is now marked by a pair of footprints set in concrete, and near by the 'Mlada Bosna' museum displays relics of the successful assassin and his fellow-conspirators. Princip is now a national hero, but at the time the Serbian Government disowned him, and disclaimed all knowledge of the plot. When the Government heard the news from Sarajevo, the Vidovdan ceremonies were suspended and a notice in the official Belgrade newspaper denounced the murderers.

Conrad von Hötzendorf and the war party in Vienna saw the Sarajevo incident as a great opportunity. They now had an excuse for eliminating Serbia from the map of Europe. There were, however, two points of resistance to their plans. Count Tisza, Premier of Hungary, was not prepared to support a war with Serbia, and the old Emperor, Franz Josef, now near the end of his long reign, wished to end his days in peace. It was a month before these obstacles could be overcome, and meanwhile the Government went through the motions of an investigation which they hoped would show that the Serbian Government was implicated in the plot. No such evidence was found, but it was shown that the inspiration for the murder came from organisations with headquarters on Serbian territory. The Austria authorities, perhaps understandably, found great difficulty in defining the relationships between these organisations, and wrongly accused *Narodna Odbrana*. On July 23rd an ultimatum was sent to Serbia, containing the following demands:

1. To suppress any publication directed against Austria-Hungary.
2. To dissolve the *Narodna Odbrana* and to suppress similar societies in future.

3. To eliminate anti-Austrian propaganda from the public schools.
4. To remove army officers and civil functionaries guilty of propaganda against the Monarchy.
5. To accept the collaboration of Austrian representatives for the suppression of the subversive movement.
6. To take judicial proceedings against accessories to the Sarajevo plot, with Austrian delegates participating in the investigation.
7. To arrest Tankošić and Čiganović.[1]
8. To prevent the illicit traffic in arms and to punish the officials who helped the conspirators to cross the frontier.
9. To explain hostile utterances of Serbian officials.
10. To notify the Austro-Hungarian Government of the execution of these measures.

The Serbian reply was conciliatory, and accepted almost all the points of substance in the Austrian note. This can be seen from the following summary of their reply:

1. Yes; will suppress all anti-Austrian publications.
2. Yes; will suppress the *Narodna Odbrana* and similar societies.
3. Yes; will expel all anti-Austrian teachers and teaching as soon as evidence given.
4. Yes; will expel all anti-Austrian officers and officials, if Austria will furnish names and acts of guilty persons.
5. Yes; will accept collaboration of Austrian representatives in these proceedings, as far as consonant with principles of international law and criminal procedure and neighbourly relations.
6. Yes; will take the judicial proceedings; will also keep Austria informed, but cannot admit the participation of Austrians in the judicial investigations, as this would be a violation of the Constitution.
7. Yes; have arrested Tankošić; ordered arrest of Čiganović.

[1] The men referred to here are Major Voja Tankošić, assistant to Colonel (Apis) Dimitrijević, and Milan Čiganović, an employee of the Serbian State Railways, and agent of the Black Hand.

8. Yes; will suppress and punish traffic in arms and explosives.

9. Yes; will deal with the said high officials, if Austria will supply evidence.

10. Yes; will notify without delay.[1]

Even the Kaiser had to admit that the Serbian reply met all the Austrian demands. He is reported as saying: 'This is more than one could have expected . . . With it every reason for war disappears . . . I am convinced that, on the whole, the wishes of the Dual Monarchy have been acceded to.' Nevertheless, on July 26th the German Ambassador in Vienna declared that 'The Serbian concessions are all a sham'. Sir Edward Grey, the British Foreign Secretary, urged the German Government to intervene in order to restrain the militarists in Vienna. He considered that 'the Serbian reply involved the greatest humiliation to Serbia that I have ever seen a country undergo, and it was very disappointing . . . that it was treated by Austria as a blank negative'. Grey's efforts were in vain. The Austrians were determined to go to war, and the German Government was not disposed to stop them. Austria would never have attempted war unless she had been sure of German support. Both Governments assumed that Russia would not carry out her threat to mobilise if Serbia was attacked, and they seemed surprised when the Tsar ordered the mobilisation. By July 27th the opposition of Count Tisza and the Emperor had been overcome[2] but the Austro-Hungarian army was not yet ready. Despite this, the attack was launched on July 28th, because Berchtold, the Chancellor, calculated that the favourable diplomatic situation would not last until August 12th, the date set by the military leaders. Within two weeks of the Austrian attack on Serbia, Russia, Germany, France, Belgium, Montenegro and Britain had all been drawn into the war.

When the attack came the Serbian commander, Vojvoda Putnik[3] was at a holiday resort in Austria, recuperating from his

[1] See Gilbert Murray, *The Foreign Policy of Sir Edward Grey*. London. 1915.

[2] See A. J. P. Taylor, *The struggle for the Mastery of Europe*, p. 522, Oxford University Press. 1954.

[3] Vojvoda – the term originally meant 'Duke', but was later awarded to military leaders, as a courtesy title.

exertions during the Balkan wars of the previous year. The Austrians allowed him to return home to defend his country against their attack – a gesture of diplomatic courtesy which would have been unthinkable a generation later. The Serbs knew that they could not hold out indefinitely against the weight of the Empire, but they hoped to delay the enemy long enough to allow their allies time to send help. If necessary they would abandon Belgrade and the plains and retreat into the hills of Southern Serbia.[1] (The Government was moved to Niš a few days before the war actually started.) The Austrians wanted a quick victory, and on August 11th they attacked in force across the rivers Sava and Drina. Within a few days they were in command of the town of Šabac and the whole of the Mačva plain which lies in the angle between the two rivers. Putnik was taken by surprise, as he expected the first attack to be made across the Danube, with Belgrade as the first objective. His forces soon recovered, however, and within two weeks the Austrians were thrown back across the Sava, and the Serbs were even able to pursue the enemy into the plains of Srem on the opposite bank of the river. One reason for the success of the Serbian counter-attack was that Potiorek, the Austrian commander, was unable to use part of his forces, as they were being held in readiness for the Galician front, where the Russians were making headway against the Austrians. In his second attempt, in September, Potiorek was more successful. They again crossed the Sava and the Drina near Šabac, and advanced to the Kolubara River, which enters the Sava twenty miles west of Belgrade. The Serbs held them here for over a month, but eventually the weight of numbers told against them, and they were pushed back to their former capital.

December 2nd was the Emperor's eighty-fourth birthday, and also the sixty-sixth anniversary of his accession. Potiorek was able to present Franz Josef with the city of Belgrade as a birthday present. A fortnight later, however, the Serbs had successfully counter-attacked, and the Austrians were back where they had started, but with a quarter of a million fewer men. The Serbs had lost heavily in battle, but their casualties from disease during the next few months were even more

---

[1] See *A Short History of World War I*, Sir J. E. Edmonds, Cambridge University Press, 1951. pp. 20–21.

serious. Their roads were littered with rotting corpses, their towns bursting with homeless refugees, and there were over 70,000 wretched Austrian prisoners held in makeshift camps under appalling conditions. It is not surprising, therefore, that a plague of typhus swept the country carrying off over 150,000 during the winter of 1914–15.

For several months there was a lull on the front. The Serbian 'swineherds' had shown the Austrians that they could fight heroically in the defence of their homeland. The plans of the Central Powers required the elimination of Serbia, however, and the Germans came into the Balkans to help their allies as soon as the situation in Poland made a diversion of resources possible. In April 1915 von Mackensen effected a break-through in Galicia and pushed the Russians back nearly 200 miles. After this victory the Germans were able to concentrate on the situation in South Eastern Europe, where their attention was urgently required. In October 1914 Turkey had joined the war as the ally of Austria and Germany, and it was vital that direct communications should be opened up between Vienna and Istanbul. The only way that this could be achieved was by seizing control of Serbia and Bulgaria. Bulgaria could be won over by diplomacy, but Serbia had to be crushed by force.

The Allied landing at Gallipoli in February 1915 called for an immediate reply, and it was impossible to send help to the Turks unless overland communications across the Balkan Peninsula could be secured. Whilst the Central Powers were making their plans for an attack on Serbia, the Allies were discussing the possibility of a landing at Salonika. An Allied advance along the Vardar-Morava corridor would bring relief to Serbia, and might also draw Rumania into the war on the side of the Allies, and deter Bulgaria from joining the Central Powers. The landing was made on October 3rd. Three days later von Mackensen ordered the bombardment of Belgrade, and by the middle of October the Bulgarians were moving into Macedonia in accordance with a secret agreement with Germany. There was little hope that the Allies could bring help to the Serbs in time. 'The first practical difficulties were that Salonika was only a small port, and that the railway running north . . . was only a single line of rails. At an Allied War Council on January 8th, 1915, it was admitted that this single line . . . could not support a large army.'[1] There were also political difficulties. Constantine the pro-German King of Greece, dismissed his Prime Minister, Venizelos because of the latter's support for the landing. A screen of neutral Greek troops was thrown between the Anglo-French forces in Salonika and the Bulgarians in the interior of Macedonia. For three years a large Allied force was held prisoner in Salonika, unable to make contact with the enemy. Malaria took a heavier toll of casualties than enemy action. During the summer of 1916, for example, 35,000 French troops were admitted to hospital, of whom only 700 were suffering from war wounds. As the British Official History comments, the situation 'would have been ludicrous had it been less tragic. Britain was sending troops only to help Greece to fulfil her obligations and now it was almost certain that Greece did not intend to fulfil them . . . To crown all, it was probable that the landing had in any case been made too late to save Serbia'. Whilst the British and French commanders quarrelled about the desirability of maintaining the Salonika bridgehead, an ill-equipped army of Serbian peasants fought an heroic rearguard action against overwhelming odds.

Von Mackensen's attack began with the bombardment of Belgrade. Soon he had forced a crossing of the Sava and the Danube and was advancing into Northern Serbia. Belgrade fell on October 9th, and the fortress of Smederovo was taken on the 11th. On October 10th, Bulgarian troops had begun to move into Macedonia. By the end of October the Serbian army was concentrated around the munitions centre of Kragujevac, sixty miles south-east of Belgrade in the Šumadija region. This position soon became untenable, and in order to avoid encirclement Putnik ordered a retreat to the south, along the Ibar valley to Kosovo. For the second time in Serbian history Kosovo Polje was to witness the destruction of Serbian independence. When it became clear that there was no hope of an Allied advance northward from Salonika the Serbian High Command was faced with three possibilities. They could stand and fight, with the certainty of defeat as the enemy bore down upon them from the surrounding hills; they could surrender; or they could break out to the west across the wild mountains of Montenegro and Albania, preserving as much as they could from the ruins,

[1] Edmonds, *op. cit.*, p. 125.

in the hope that somehow, at some time, they could fight their way back to Belgrade. The last possibility was the only one which was seriously considered.

As the first snows of winter were falling the tattered remnants of the peasant army began its weary trek to the Adriatic. They took with them thousands of civilians, especially young boys, who would provide the recruits for the reborn army when they reached the safety of allied occupied territory. Many of these boys died of cold, hunger and exhaustion on the way across the mountains. Thousands more died within sight of the Adriatic, before the allies agreed to evacuate the survivors to Corfu. Two thousand alone died whilst waiting for the Italian commander at Valona to give them permission to enter the town. Throughout the long journey their privations were made all the more terrible by the malevolence and treachery of the Montenegrins and Albanians over whose land they were forced to cross. As they struggled through the snows of Montenegro, reduced to eating the corpses of their dead horses, the bark of trees, even the leather of their boots, they were refused supplies by the local population. Although Nicholas of Montenegro liked to pose as the champion of the South Slavs, he was constantly intriguing with the enemy. Whilst issuing his windy manifestoes and proclaiming his loyalty to the cause, he reinsured himself by betraying Serbian plans to the Austrians. After a token resistance he allowed his country to be taken, and as he fled abroad to Paris he attempted to lay the blame for his defeat at the door of the Serbs. One of the last acts of this unworthy king was to order his troops and police to prevent his subjects from either giving or selling food to the wretched Serbian troops as they struggled across the wintry mountains.

The tribulations of the Serbs were not over when they came to the borders of Albania. After the sullen hostility of the Montenegrins, they now had to face the ambushes of armed Moslem bands who roamed across the mountains of Albania. On one occasion a large group of Serbs was forced to buy its way out of an ambush, as they lacked the strength to put up a fight. Eventually, by January 1916, most of the survivors had reached the Scutari (Shkoder) district of Northern Albania, and plans were made for an evacuation from the port of Shëngjin (San Giovanni di Medua). The Italians refused to send relief ships from Brindisi, on the grounds that Austrian submarines based at Kotor might attack them. About this time, Nicholas of Montenegro had surrendered the Lovčen bastion to the Austrians, and was on his way into exile. After the collapse of Montenegro the Austrians were able to invade Northern Albania, and both Scutari and Shëngjin were taken. The indomitable Serbs set off to walk to Durazzo (Durrës), but even here they were not safe from the advancing Austrians. After a further trek of 130 miles through the coastal marshes of Albania they reached the outskirts of Valona. After a delay occasioned by the petty vindictiveness of the local Italian authorities who commanded the port, all that remained of the Serbian army was evacuated to the French held island of Corfu. By April 1916, 155,000 Serbs were safely quartered in Corfu. Many of them never recovered from the after-effects of months of forced marching in the bitter cold of a Balkan winter. By July, however, three-quarters of them had recovered sufficiently to be ready for service again. They were taken by sea to Salonika, the Greeks having refused them permission to travel overland. In a short time they had made their presence felt by capturing 400 square miles of Serbian soil from the Bulgarians.

This little corner of Serbia cost them 27,000 casualties, and it was two years before they were able to advance any farther into their homeland. The fact that they were waiting on their own territory may have made the long period of inactivity more bearable. Certainly the fact that they had a fighting force of over 100,000 men back on their own soil within a year of the retreat from Kosovo Polje set the seal on Serbian claims to leadership of the South Slavs.

In 1916, however, the prospects for the South Slavs looked black indeed. Apart from the tiny foothold around Bitolj, which the Serbs had recaptured in November, all the lands which now form Yugoslavia were under foreign rule. Macedonia lay under the brutal occupation régime of Bulgaria; Montenegro had capitulated to the Austrians; and Austro-German troops strutted through the streets of Belgrade. In the Slav provinces of the Empire many Slovenes and Croats seemed to be reconciled to the rule of the Habsburgs. In London, a Yugoslav Committee, representing a number of *émigrés* from the Habsburg provinces, was barely tolerated by the British authorities. Early in 1916 this committee had published a map which purported to show the territorial gains which had been promised to Italy under the secret Treaty of London signed in April 1915. The map later proved to be based on accurate information. When the war started in 1914 Italy was a member of the Triple Alliance, but she did not go to war on the side of Germany and Austria-Hungary. She decided instead to sell herself to the highest bidder, the price of her support being the acquisition of territory at the expense of Austria-Hungary. Italian leaders dignified this policy with the name 'Sacro egoismo'. In April 1915 a series of private talks between Russia and Italy culminated in the signature of a treaty to which all the allied powers except Serbia were participants. Italy was promised Istria and large areas in the Julian region and in Dalmatia which were inhabited by Slovenes and Croats. Russia had been consulted in the first instance because of her self-appointed role as protector of the Slavs. It was felt that if Russian agreement could be obtained to the cession of territory inhabited by Slavs, then the opposition of the Serbs could be discounted. Rumours of this Treaty caused dismay amongst the Slovenes and Croats in the Austrian occupied provinces, and many of them joined the Austrian army in desperation, determined to resist any Italian advance into the Julian region. During the battles on the Isonzo front the Slav-speaking 'frontiersmen' under the command of General Boroević fought valiantly against the Italian invaders.

During 1917 events moved in favour of the Yugoslavs and as the war drew to a close the Allies began to look with more interest on the idea of a South Slav state. President Wilson's 'Fourteen Points' gave American blessing to the principle of self-determination as applied to the subject nationalities of the Monarchy. Russia's withdrawal from the war after the Revolution removed one of the major obstacles to a union between the Orthodox Serbs and the Roman Catholic Croats and Slovenes. The Slovene and Croatian Deputies in the Reichsrat in Vienna issued a manifesto in May 1917 calling for 'the unification of all the territories of the Monarchy inhabited by Slovenes, Croats and Serbs in one independent political body, free from all foreign domination and founded on a democratic basis, under the sceptre of the Habsburg dynasty'. This was as far as they dared go at the time, but it was generally understood that the reference to the Habsburg sceptre was purely tactical. Meanwhile the Serbian *Skupština* in Corfu had received the representatives of the Yugoslav Committee and had proclaimed a 'Kingdom of Serbs, Croats and Slovenes which would be a democratic and parliamentary monarchy under the Karageorgević dynasty'.

The hope expressed in the Pact of Corfu became a reality when the Serbian army marched triumphantly back to Belgrade in November 1918. As the Austrians retreated from Bosnia, Croatia and Slovenia local committees took up the reins of government and declared their support for a South Slav state. In Montenegro, a hastily convened assembly deposed the exiled Nicholas, and voted for a union with Serbia. Yugoslavia, the land of the South Slavs, thus emerged from the ruins of the Habsburg Empire.

Chapter 2

'Old Yugoslavia'

TERRITORY AND PEOPLE

WHEN THE First World War began, Yugoslavia did not exist. In her place were several provinces of the Habsburg Empire, and two independent states – Serbia and Montenegro. Both Serbia and Montenegro had recently enlarged their territories at the expense of Turkey. Both sought the leadership of the Slavs who lived under the Austro-Hungarian rule, and they looked forward to the creation of a South Slav state after the expulsion of the Habsburgs from the Balkans. Only Serbia had any hope of leading a South Slav alliance, but many of the Slavs within the Empire preferred Habsburg to Serbian domination. The Slovene and Croat leaders, Western in culture and Catholic in religion, looked with distaste upon the Orthodox Serbs, whom they considered to be uncivilised. They preferred the Trialist solution to the nationality problems of the Empire – a solution which envisaged the creation of an autonomous Slav unit, equal in status to Austria and Hungary, thus turning the Dual into a Triple Monarchy. The events of 1917 and 1918 sealed the fate of the Empire and so made the Trialist position untenable. The '*prečani*'[1] Slavs had no alternative but to accept the Yugoslav idea. Some of them had already done so with enthusiasm, but many were reluctantly converted by the pressure of circumstances. Their main task then became the winning of as much autonomy as possible for their people in the face of the hegemonistic tendencies of Serbia.

The collapse of Austria-Hungary also forced the Allied Powers to think again about the future of Central Europe. In 1914 they had thought in terms of territorial adjustments at the

[1] Prečani – Serbian word. Literally people from 'the other side' – i.e. of the Danube and the Sava. Used in a restricted sense to refer to the people of Vojvodina and Srem, but more generally to include the Slavs living in the former Austro-Hungarian provinces.

expense of the Habsburgs; they had not envisaged the necessity of redrawing the political map of Europe. In the arrangements which they had made in the early part of the war, they had assumed that both the Austro-Hungarian and the Tsarist Russian Empires would remain substantially intact. These assumptions were invalidated by the events of 1917 and 1918 but the agreements based upon them created major problems at the Versailles Peace Conference. One such agreement was the secret Treaty of London (1915), which promised Italy the Istrian peninsula, the Isonzo (Soča) valley, and large areas of Dalmatia, in return for Italian participation in the war on the side of the Allies. When Italy presented her bill to the conference, the account had to be met at the expense of the new South Slav state, the original victim having passed away.

The Yugoslavs thus found that their new state was beset from birth by problems which arose out of historical circumstances over which they had no control. The legacies of the past worked against the hopes of the future. The generation of 1918 was unable to kindle a loyalty to Yugoslavia in the hearts of the Slavs who came together out of the ruins of the Habsburg Empire. The Kingdom of the Serbs, Croats and Slovenes never achieved real unity. It required another baptism of fire before the mass of its people could free themselves from the bitter internal feuds of the inter-war period, and stand together as Yugoslavs.

Merely to list the elements which constituted the new state at its proclamation in December 1918 will give some idea of the magnitude of the task of welding the South Slavs into a nation. At the head of the list would be the independent Kingdom of Serbia, with a population of four and a half millions. The Serbs had wrested their independence from Turkey in the nineteenth century, and had always looked upon themselves as the champions of the Balkan Slavs against both Turkey and Austria-Hungary. Serbia's position had been ineffectually challenged by Nicholas of Montenegro, a petty prince in every sense of the word. In November, 1918, the Montenegrins deposed Nicholas and voted for union with Serbia. Most of the original inhabitants of Montenegro were akin to the Serbs in speech and religion, although the acquisitions of 1913 had added a number of Moslems from the former Turkish Empire.

Of the provinces of the Habsburg Empire, the most important was Croatia-Slovenia, an area which reached from the Adriatic coast near Fiume to the plains of the Sava and Drava valleys. The Croats enjoyed a limited autonomy under their Ban, or Governor, who was responsible to a Hungarian Minister. The agreement under which the Hungarians held the sovereignty over Croatia, the 'Nagoda' of 1869, recognised the Croat nation as 'a political nation possessing a special territory of its own'. Such limited regional autonomy was a far cry from the glories of the medieval kingdom of Croatia, but it was sufficient to make many Croats cling to the pale shadow of their former (and greatly exaggerated) greatness, rather than to risk losing their identity in a Serbian-dominated Yugoslavia. Other territories which were under the administration of the Hungarians were the Vojvodina, a southern extension of the great Hungarian Plain, which was mainly inhabited by a Serbian-speaking people; and the small areas along the river Mur (Prekomurje and Medjumurje), both with a mixed Slovene and Hungarian population. The Austrian-controlled parts of the Empire which passed to Yugoslavia were Dalmatia, Carniola and parts of Styria and Carinthia. The last three were inhabited by Slovene-speaking people, the first by a mixed Slav and Italian population. Finally, there was Bosnia-Hercegovina, which had been snatched from Turkey in 1878 and formally annexed by the Dual Monarchy in 1908. A third of the two million inhabitants of the annexed territory professed the Moslem faith.

Within the lands mentioned above are fragments of two great multi-national Empires. The peoples of these Empires had inherited from their masters customs, ways of life, methods of administration, legal codes – even religious beliefs and languages. The new state contained Orthodox, and Roman Catholic Christians, and over one and a half million Moslems. There are three South Slav languages – Serbo-Croat, Slovene and Macedonian, as well as several non-Slav languages, e.g. Albanian, Magyar and Turkish. Even Serbo-Croat, the official language of the state, has two systems of orthography, and many quite different dialects. When the new state began there were six legal codes in force, and the task of reconciling them was never completed during the twenty-three years of independent existence of the Yugoslav kingdom.

The idea that the peoples of these territories should come together into one nation had only begun to make an appeal to the mass of the South Slavs when the First World War began. It was something talked about by professional politicians, intellectuals, lawyers and artists, but it meant little to the Moslem shepherds of Bosnia, the Catholic fishermen of Dalmatia, the Orthodox peasants of remote Macedonia, or the Slovene soldiers of the Habsburg army. The Yugoslav Committee in exile had won acceptance for the idea from the liberal politicians in Western Europe and America, but they still had to convince many of their own people. The nation did not consist only of men like Meštrović, the Croat sculptor, Mgr. Korošeć, the Slovene priest, Trumbić, the former mayor of Split, or Pašić, the domineering Premier of Serbia. The fact that these men could work out a scheme on paper for a South Slav state did not ensure that the people would accept the idea without question.

These problems were sufficient to ensure that the birth of Yugoslavia would be difficult and painful, but there were further dangerous complications. Mention has already been made of the attitude of Italy at Versailles. The Italians, having fought on the side of the victorious Allies, were in a strong position to press their territorial claims, and they eventually obtained their demands. During the long-drawn-out negotiations at the Peace Conference, Britain and France had little option but to support Italian claims to territory which was not theirs to give, but which they had nevertheless promised to Italy by the Treaty of London. Woodrow Wilson, on behalf of the U.S.A., refused to support the provisions of the secret treaty, and sought to modify the Italian demands. The Italians stood firm until the American electorate removed Wilson from the international scene. The disillusioned Yugoslavs then reached an agreement with the Italians at Rapallo in November, 1920. The Rapallo Treaty gave Italy the town of Zara in Dalmatia, the island of Lagosta, the whole of Istria and the Julian region as far as the watershed between the Adriatic and the Black Sea. In this area there were over half a million Croats and Slovenes. At this stage, the Yugoslavs still refused to abandon their rights in Fiume. The Peace Conference had accepted a French suggestion that Fiume should become a Free City State, to which both Italy and Yugoslavia would have access, but the city had been seized by a band of Italian adventurers, under the leadership of the poet D'Annunzio. The Allies had tamely ignored this defiance of their orders, and D'Annunzio remained in Fiume, issuing his grandiose manifestoes until the idea of a Free State was officially dropped. In 1924, by the Rome Treaty, Yugoslavia accepted the *fait accompli* and recognised Fiume as an Italian port.

In order to reach agreement about Yugoslavia's frontier with Austria, it was necessary for the Allies to hold a plebiscite in the area of Carinthia between the Drava and the Karawanken mountains. In this area, most of the peasantry spoke Slovene, but the townsfolk were German-speaking. The plebiscite of October 1920 gave a 60/40 majority to Austria, and as a result the new frontier was fixed to run along the crest line of the Karawanken Alps. Nevertheless, some 30,000 Slovenes were left on the Austrian side of the frontier, and Yugoslavia continues to lay claim to 'Slovene Carinthia'.

Along the Hungarian frontier Yugoslavia fared better. Although she was forced to withdraw from Pecs, the coal-mining district of southern Hungary, she obtained the city of Subotica and a large part of the plains of Banat, Bačka and Baranja, all of which contained many people of Magyar speech. In the whole area of this former Hungarian territory awarded to Yugoslavia (i.e. the Vojvodina) there were in 1921 376,000 Magyars, and 316,000 Germans in a total population of 1,346,000. These minorities proved to be a source of weakness in the new state, especially in the 1930's, when their minority grievances were exploited by the German Nazis and the Hungarian Fascists. Hungary's bitterness against Yugoslavia prevented any co-operation between the two countries in the face of the Nazi pressure which finally destroyed both states.

Yugoslavia acquired the lion's share of the Banat from Hungary. The rest went to Rumania, a member of the alliance which had overthrown the Central Powers. Rumania had claimed the whole of the Banat as the price of her adherence to the Allied cause in 1916, but, unlike Italy she was unable to force the Peace Conference to pay her claim in full. There is no doubt that the rejection of the full Rumanian claim was not based purely upon ethnic considerations. Seventy thousand

Rumanians were left within the borders of Yugoslavia, but this price was considered necessary in order to give Belgrade the security which Rumanian occupation of the whole Banat would have jeopardised.

Strategic considerations also affected the drawing of the new boundary with Bulgaria. A number of minor rectifications were made, to the advantage of Yugoslavia, and the gains which Serbia had made in the Balkan wars were confirmed by the Treaty of Neuilly (November, 1919). The number of Bulgarian-speaking people who remained in Yugoslav Macedonia was under 50,000. A far larger number of Turks also remained in Macedonia. They were the survivors of the centuries of Turkish occupation in the Balkans. Although originally coming as soldiers, administrators and overlords, many of them chose to settle down as merchants and farmers, and declined to avail themselves of the opportunity to return to Turkey. Since 1925 the Turkish Government has disowned them, and, unlike many of the other minorities they have never become a source of embarrassment to Yugoslav-Turkish relations.

One of the largest non-Slav groups to be found in Yugoslavia is the Albanian minority, which is found all along the borders of the two countries, but especially in the Kosovo-Metohia region. These Albanians (known as Shqiptars) are descended from the pre-Slav inhabitants of the Balkans who were driven to their present homeland by the pressure of the Slav invaders. During the period of Turkish rule they accepted Islam, and under the benevolent eye of their Turkish masters they began to infiltrate into parts of Serbia. During the Balkan wars of 1912 and 1913 they embarrassed the Serbs by invading Macedonia. After the war the powers insisted on the creation of an autonomous state of Albania, but the frontiers were drawn so as to leave over half a million Shqiptars in Yugoslavia. This turbulent minority frequently petitioned the League of Nations for redress of its grievances, demanding as a minimum concession that they should be allowed to have their own schools and a fair share of the administrative posts in their part of Serbia. After the Italian occupation of Albania, propaganda for the incorporation of the Kosovo-Metohia area in Albania was encouraged, and in 1941 the frontiers of that state were redrawn to achieve that aim.

The minorities mentioned above constituted 17 per cent of

the total population of Yugoslavia in 1921 – a total of nearly two million people. On the other hand, nearly a million people of Yugoslav origin were left outside the boundaries of the state, most of these in Italian occupied Dalmatia, Istria and the Julian region. Most of the minorities were dissatisfied with their lot, some violently opposed to the new dispensation and often willing to receive help from abroad in order to disrupt the settlement which they so heartily detested. It was therefore to be expected that Yugoslavia's relations with her neighbours prevented any sort of political or economic co-operation between the succession states of the former Habsburg Empire. It has been truly said of these nations that they were 'societies united by a common error as to their origins and a common aversion to their neighbours'.

Having spoken of the territories and peoples who came together to constitute the Yugoslav state, we must now turn to an examination of the efforts made to solve internal problems during the early years of its existence. The new state was at first called 'The Kingdom of Serbs, Croats and Slovenes'. It might well have been called the Kingdom of Greater Serbia, for the other peoples – the *prečani* of the former Austro-Hungarian provinces and the depressed non-Slav minorities – had no say in the government of the country.

THE KINGDOM OF SERBS, CROATS AND SLOVENES

The Declaration of the Kingdom of Serbs, Croats and Slovenes was made in December 1918, but it was not until St. Vitus' Day (June 28th), 1921, that the Constituent Assembly had completed its work of producing a new Constitution. The date of the promulgation of the Constitution was significant. 'Vidovdan' was the Serbian National Day, when parades and services were traditionally held to commemorate the tragedy of Kosovo Polje (1389) when the Serbian army was defeated by the Turks. On the same date in 1914 the Serbian inspired assassin, Gavrilo Princip, shot Archduke Franz Ferdinand in Sarajevo. Thus the symbolism of Vidovdan served to emphasise Serbia's leading position in the new state, and an examination of the provisions of the Vidovdan constitution confirms this impression. It could hardly have been otherwise. Serbia had been independent for over a century; she had been the focus of opposition to the Turkish and Austro-Hungarian Empires, and had grown steadily throughout the nineteenth century at their expense; she had a parliament (the *Skupština*), a bureaucracy and a Royal House, and she was the ally of the victorious Western Powers. The real issue before the Yugoslavs was whether they were to have a state organised on federal lines, with Serbia as the most important of the federal units, or whether the 'Kingdom of Serbs, Croats and Slovenes' was to be an enlarged Serbia, with all power centralised in Belgrade. The Centralists, led by the Serbian Premier, Nikola Pašić, had their way in the Constituent assembly, but their victory was an empty one. Because they failed to respect the rights of the non-Serbs they ensured that Yugoslavia between the wars never enjoyed internal peace and often hovered on the brink of civil war and disintegration. The Vidovdan Constitution provided a framework which looked 'democratic' on paper. The King had more power than the constitutional monarchs of North-West Europe, but he was subject to the will of Parliament. The Council of Ministers was responsible both to King and Parliament. The Parliament was a single chamber legislature elected by universal manhood suffrage through a process of proportional representation similar to that at present in force in Finland. Local government followed the French pattern, with provincial prefects (*župani*) directly responsible to the central government, and lesser councils (*srezi* and *opštini*) responsible to the župan. Elections to the local councils were on the same basis as the parliamentary elections, but the central government had powers of veto over the election of mayors. But the spirit of democracy does not flourish as a result of paper constitutions, and Yugoslavia in the 1920's lacked many of the essential requirements of a healthy democracy. It has been said that the success of parliamentary government in Britain lies in the fact that the major parties agree upon the fundamental issues, and can therefore afford to bicker about the details without fear of overthrowing the established order. Such underlying agreement on fundamentals was lacking in Yugoslavia. Of the 419 members of the constituent assembly of 1920, 155 withdrew from its deliberations because their views were irreconcilably opposed to those of the Pan-Serb majority. These included 58

Communists, 50 Croat Peasants, 27 Slovene Populists and 10 Social Democrats. Within six months of the passing of the constitution all the Communist deputies were unseated by Government decree, whilst the Croat members maintained their boycott until 1924. For a brief period from 1924–6 the Croats co-operated with the Serbs, but by 1927 Radić, the Croat Peasant leader, was again leading the opposition against the corruption and self-seeking of the Serbian centralists and the sinister Čarsija clique of Belgrade businessmen. The scandals and crises of the 1920's, the squalid horse trading for votes, the corruption of the administration, the secret power of a clique of wealthy Serbs – all these had their roots in the unhealthy atmosphere of 1921 when a paper majority in the Constituent Assembly forced through a constitution which ignored the wishes of a substantial minority of the people. The death blow to the Vidovdan Constitution was struck by a Montenegrin deputy, Puniša Račić, who murdered the Croat Peasant leader, Radić, and two of his supporters in full view of the assembled members of the *Skupština* (June 1928)[1]. After this outrage which went virtually unpunished, the Croat parties withdrew to Zagreb, and there convened an 'anti-Parliament' consisting of deputies from the non-Serb areas. Yugoslavia was in danger of splitting up into its component parts, and perhaps would have done so but for the intervention of the King.

In January 1929 Alexander assumed responsibility for the government of the country, and dismissed the Skupština and the Council of Ministers. His avowed aim was to bring his people together, and to lay the foundations for democracy by removing some of the main causes of separatism. Nevertheless his new government, under General Živković, was dominated by Serbs. The few Croats who did co-operate were looked upon as traitors by many of their countrymen. Some of the Croat leaders fled abroad and attempted either by intrigue or propaganda to enlist the support of foreign powers in favour of Croat independence. Pavelić, the terrorist, went to Italy, Hungary and Bulgaria. Leaders of the official Peasant Party took their grievances to the League of Nations in Geneva, or to the liberal press of Britain and America.

Parliament was dissolved, the political parties banned, free-

---

[1] The shots were fired on June 20th, 1928. Radić died on August 8th.

dom of the Press and freedom of assembly were restricted by government decree, political trials were staged and any opposition to the King's government was rigorously suppressed. At first the opposition seemed to be taken by surprise. Perhaps the people were ready for a 'holiday' from politics after the scandals of the previous decade. Perhaps the King really intended to hold power only for a brief period in order to recreate the conditions under which democracy could work. One of the first acts of the royal dictator was to change the name of the state from the Kingdom of Serbs, Croats and Slovenes to the Kingdom of Yugoslavia. He also made serious attempts to reconcile the Croats. By a decree of 1929 the old provinces (*oblasti*) of the Vidovdan constitution were reduced to nine *banovina* which corresponded more closely to the historic provinces, especially as far as Croatia-Slavonia was concerned. In 1931 a new constitution was promulgated. A two-chamber parliament was set, up, with limited powers. The lower house (*Skupština*) was chosen by universal suffrage, but there was no secret ballot. The upper house, the Senate, consisted partly of official members chosen by the King. The powers of either house were limited, and the King was the active head of both the executive and the legislature. It was claimed by the King's supporters that the 1931 Constitution was but a first step on the road back to democracy, but the opposition saw it as a smoke screen to conceal the reality of Serbian hegemony and royal dictatorship. The opposition was no longer confined to the '*prečani*'; Serbian liberals opposed the autocratic tendencies of the King, and even members of the Serbian Radical Party, formerly the mainstay of centralism, circulated illicit pamphlets urging the people to boycott the elections under the new constitution. Up to 1932 the King had governed without the support of a political party. All the old parties had been dissolved, and as yet he had not thought it necessary to create a new party of national unity. After a futile bid for the support of Dr. Maček, the successor to Radić, as leader of the Croats, an attempt was made to form a national party which would rally to it the supporters of the old Serbian Radicals, the Democratic Party and the Peasants. The grotesque title of this new organisation was the Yugoslav Peasant Radical Democratic Party. Later the name was changed to the Yugoslav National Party. But titles and slogans

L

could not disguise the fact that it was in effect an instrument of the Serbian ruling groups, and its empty manifestoes produced no flicker of response from the mass of the people. Not so the Zagreb Manifesto, a document produced by the leaders of the opposition. This demanded a return to democratic procedures and a recognition of the rights of the non-Serbs. The Government's reaction was to imprison three of the most important non-Serb leaders – Mgr. Korošeć, of Slovenia, Dr. Spaho, the Moslem leader, and Dr. Maček. During 1932 and 1933, economic discontent was added to political opposition. The King had manifestly failed in all the objectives which he had set himself in 1929. After five years of dictatorship the country hovered on the brink of disaster. A ruined peasantry, a stagnant foreign trade, isolation in foreign affairs, an opposition turning more and more to methods of terrorism – these were the outstanding features of the Yugoslav scene in the autumn of 1934 when Alexander set off on his last journey to Marseilles. It is said that the King had already decided that the dictatorship had failed, and was preparing to introduce a democratic constitution on his return from France, but the opportunity was never afforded to him to repair the mistakes of the previous five years. As he rode through the streets of Marseilles with Mr. Barthou the French foreign minister, an assassin in the pay of a Croat terrorist group murdered both King and Minister. The outburst of indignation throughout Yugoslavia which followed this outrage showed that many who detested the King's policies still respected him as a courageous man who had sincerely, if mistakenly, attempted to force the diverse elements over which he ruled into a common Serbian mould.[1]

The Regency of Prince Paul

Alexander's son, Peter, was a boy of ten in an English preparatory school when his father was murdered. The extensive powers which the King had assumed during the period of royal dictatorship had, therefore, to be entrusted to a Regency Council until the young Peter was old enough to wield

---

[1] The Yugoslav Foreign Minister was able to show before the League of Nations that the Croat terrorists, led by Pavelić, who had planned the murder had been assisted and encouraged by agents of the Horthy régime in Hungary.

them for himself. In Yugoslavia, Kings reached their majority at the age of eighteen, so that the Regency was expected to be in control until the autumn of 1941.[1] There was an understanding amongst the leading figures in the political struggle in the country that no major constitutional changes would be enacted until Peter was old enough to play his full part in the decisions which had to be made. Until August 1939, the minority of the King was frequently used as an excuse for delaying the settlement of the Croat problem, but eventually the course of events in Europe forced the Regency to make a belated attempt to placate the restive Croats. The settlement was reluctantly accepted by the more moderate Croat leaders, but before its effects could have been judged old Yugoslavia had disappeared, engulfed by the tidal wave of Nazi power. This, in outline, is the history of the last years of old Yugoslavia.

The Regency Council was headed by Peter's uncle, Paul, a man of Western culture and supposed anglophile leanings. Paul was supported by two little-known Serbs, one a Professor of medicine, the other a minor official. These two co-Regents were of no importance in determining the future of Yugoslavia. Their very obscurity only emphasised the undisputed supremacy of Prince Paul. The first Regent, despite his English education and sympathies, showed no inclination towards constitutional monarchy, and when the crisis came in 1941 he showed that he feared German military power more than he respected Western democracy. In his internal policies he wore the mantle of Alexander's royal dictatorship; abroad he reversed his brother's policy of friendship with France and the Little Entente, and placed his trust in the big battalions. Both policies helped to seal the fate of the old régime.

One of the first acts of the new Government was to prepare for a general election. Some gestures were made to the opposition, notably by the release from prison of Dr. Maček, the Croat Peasant leader, and Dragoljub Jovanović, the Serbian liberal. Such acts of amnesty do not in themselves create the conditions for free political controversy. The Press was still subject to a censorship and rights of free speech and assembly were still denied to the opposition parties. Electoral laws still

---

[1] In fact Peter was declared of age in March 1941 after the *coup d'état* which overthrew the Cvetković government.

favoured the Government parties, and officials used their power to coerce and intimidate voters. For example, the Ban of Primorska (the coastal province) issued an instruction to his subordinate officials informing them that 'The official list must have a majority, and every official who does not vote for it will be held responsible and punished without mercy'. It is not surprising that the Government won the elections of March 1935. What is surprising is that, of 2,800,000 voters, over 1,000,000 voted for the opposition parties. When the seats were distributed however, the opposition's million votes gave them only 67 seats in a Parliament (*Skupština*) of 368. As in the Constituent Assembly of 1921, a paper victory had gone to the supporters of centralism and Serbian hegemony, but the problem which divided the nation and threatened its very existence was no nearer a solution. Immediately after the election, the Archbishop of Zagreb remonstrated with the Government about the scandalous conduct of the elections in his diocese, and the Opposition deputies once again assembled in a counter-Parliament in the Croatian capital. In an effort to prevent the complete disintegration of the state Paul persuaded a number of the leaders of non-Serb and *prečani* groups to join a government headed by a young Serbian financial expert, Dr. Milan Stojadinović. Dr. Maček was persuaded to give his blessing to the new government, and even to express approval for the idea of a new constitution, in which foreign affairs, the army and the currency would be under the control of the central government. Maček was also prepared to accept the Karageorgević dynasty. In return for these concessions the Regent promised that the new constitution would guarantee a wide degree of federal autonomy for Croatia. The Stojadinović government was to be a caretaker government, whose main task would be to prepare the way for the new dispensation. The Slovene Clericals, led by Mgr. Korošeć and the Bosnian Moslems led by Dr. Spaho, agreed to join the Government in the hope that they would be able to win concessions for the groups which they represented. Apart from these opportunists, the main parliamentary support for Stojadinović came from the newly formed Yugoslav Radical Union, a body created by the Premier after his expulsion from the Serbian Radical Party. The new party was as unrepresentative of the Yugoslav people as the Yugoslav National Party,

which King Alexander had created as a prop to his dictatorship. Curiously enough, the remnant of the National party
drifted into the ranks of the officially permitted Opposition,
perhaps out of chagrin that its leading members were not
offered places in the new government. Despite the promises to
Dr. Maček and the *prečani* leaders nothing was done to redeem
the pledges which both Regent and Premier had given concerning the granting of regional autonomy to Croatia. Between
1935 and the elections of 1938 the division at the heart of the
young state remained.

A far greater danger, however, to the integrity of Yugoslavia
than this unresolved bitterness between two groups of its citizens
came from abroad. Throughout the period of the Regency the
rising menace of German Nazism provides a sombre accompaniment to the shrill chorus of quarrelling and posturing Yugoslav
politicians. With the notable exception of Czechoslovakia, all
the succession states to the former Habsburg Empire appeared
to be hypnotised by the power of Germany. As Hitler emerged,
always stronger, from each of the crises which he had manu-
factured – the Rhineland, Austria, Sudetenland, Memel,
Poland – the nations of Central Europe hastened to attach
themselves to the war chariot of the victor. Alexander had
attempted to find security in the Little Entente of Rumania,
Czechoslovakia and Yugoslavia, which had been linked to
France, but this policy seemed futile in the face of the realities
of power in the 1930's. The democracies of Western Europe
seemed to be incapable of any resistance, physical or moral,
to the advancing tide of Nazism. Economically, Britain and
France had less to offer Yugoslavia than Germany. Although
French capital still financed the Bor copper mines, the largest in
Europe, and British capital controlled the lead and zinc mines
of Trepća, neither Britain nor France were able to provide
Yugoslavia with an outlet for her raw materials. Most of the
output of these mines went to Germany after 1935. Under the
guidance of Dr. Schacht, Germany succeeded in tying the
economies of a number of Central European states to those of
the Reich. Dr. Schacht's cunning was reinforced by the awe-
inspiring successes of his master, and the two combined to throw
countries like Yugoslavia in the orbit of the German economic
and military machine. Perhaps Paul had no choice in the

decision to tie the Yugoslav economy to that of Germany. Given that the Western democracies had nothing to offer, the only alternative to Germany was the U.S.S.R. To men like Paul, the internal consequences of an alliance with the 'red peril' ensured that the prospect of an alliance with the U.S.S.R. was not even considered.

In October 1938, the fate of Czechoslovakia confronted the smaller nations of Europe with a terrible example of the price which they would pay if they attempted to resist the Nazi onslaught. This was the time chosen by the Germans for an initiative on the economic front in the Balkans. Reichsminister Funk visited a number of Balkan countries and offered trade treaties. In Belgrade he offered to take the whole of Yugoslavia's export surplus and to supply her with all her needs. The treaty which he negotiated did not give him the whole of the Yugoslav foreign trade, but it did ensure that in the following year Germany was the largest trading partner of Yugoslavia. In 1939 Germany and the occupied regions of Moravia and Bohemia took 53 per cent of Yugoslavia's exports and supplied 54 per cent of her imports. Italy and Hungary, two of Germany's close friends at this time, were responsible for 19 per cent of the exports and 22 per cent of the imports. Britain and France together were only able to take 10 per cent of the exports and to supply less than 6 per cent of the imports.

The events of 1938 helped Germany to secure her position of supremacy in the Balkans. In March the occupation of Austria had brought the troops of the Reich to the north western borders of Yugoslavia. The failure of the Western democracies to prevent the occupation of Czech Sudetenland in the autumn of 1938 confirmed Stojadinović in his view that the only realistic policy for Yugoslavia was to ally herself with Germany. Hungary had been able to take parts of Slovakia, and Poland had obtained a portion of the Teschen region because they were willing to play the role of jackals when the German tiger began to devour Czechoslovakia. The Yugoslav people did not seem to be as complacent about these events as their leaders. Demonstrations in favour of the Czechs were a serious embarrassment to the Government during the winter of 1938-9. Whatever views may have been sincerely held in Western Europe, the peoples of Central Europe knew that the Munich settlement was but a prelude to the destruction of Czech independence. When the Nazis marched into Prague in the spring of 1939 Stojadinović was no longer Premier, but his successor, Cvetković continued his rival's foreign policy. The Yugoslavs joined the queue of Ministers and heads of state eager to pay their respects to Hitler and to assure him of their loyalty to the new order. Prince Paul and Princess Olga, accompanied by the new Foreign Minister, Cincar-Marković, made their journey in June. At a banquet in their honour the Führer referred to the 'common political, cultural and economic interest' of the two countries, and rather ominously mentioned that they now had a common frontier, a fact which set the final seal on their 'mutual confidence and respect'.

The drift away from the policy of the Little Entente and towards an alliance with Germany was reflected in Yugoslavia's relations with her neighbours. In 1937 a Pact had been signed with Italy which ended the long-standing dispute about the Italian treatment of Slovenes and Croats in Istria and the Julian region. The Pact gave the first official recognition by Fascist Italy of the existence of a minority problem. One immediate outcome was the release of a number of Slav-speaking political prisoners. It soon became apparent, however, that the Italians had no intention of reversing their policy of Italianisation. The cells which had lately been emptied were soon refilled with another batch of Slovenes and Croats who could not be persuaded to deny the language and customs of their forefathers.[1] The only difference in the situation caused by the signing of the Pact appeared to be that the Yugoslav Government was now more reluctant to protest to the Italian authorities. The Pact of 1937 was followed by a number of trade agreements which strengthened Yugoslavia's ties with the dictators. Another move by the Yugoslav Government during 1937 was designed to improve relations with Italy, but it was defeated by the opposition of the Orthodox hierarchy. Stojadinović proposed a Concordat with the Vatican, and took up the negotiations which had been suspended on the death of Alexander in 1934. The bill passed the *Skupština*, but following the decision of the Synod of the Orthodox Church to excommunicate the Ministers

---

[1] For an account of the treatment of the Yugoslavs in Italy *see* Lavo Čermelj, *Life and Death Struggle of a National Minority*. Ljubljana. 1945.

responsible, the Government dropped the proposal and the affair was soon forgotten. Further evidence of the drift away from the policies of the Little Entente was afforded by the improvement in relations between Yugoslavia and her two 'revisionist' neighbours, Hungary and Bulgaria. In 1937 the 'Treaty of Perpetual Friendship' with Bulgaria helped to ease tension in the disputed areas of Macedonia, but it caused some uneasiness amongst the liberal elements in Yugoslavia and amongst the other members of the Little Entente. In a speech at the time of the Munich crisis Stojadinović referred to the recent improvement in relations with Hungary, but it was not until 1940 that a 'Pact of lasting peace and eternal friendship' was concluded between the governments in Belgrade and Budapest.

Prince Paul must bear a large share of the responsibility for aligning his country with the dictatorships during the late 1930's. As Senior Regent he took an active part in shaping the foreign policy of his country, and although Ministers like Stojadinović and Cincar-Marković were nominally responsible, these men could not have pursued their policies without Paul's approval and encouragement. Paul no doubt believed that he could keep his country out of war, and that he would succeed in withdrawing his head from the mouth of the tiger where others had failed to accomplish this feat. Looking back on the events of 1937–41 we can see the steps by which he led the nation to the brink of the abyss, but perhaps to the men who were then so deeply enmeshed in the day-to-day affairs of a process whose outcome was enshrouded in the mists of the future, the pattern was less obvious. Nevertheless many Yugoslavs did oppose the dangerous tendencies which they saw in the policies of their Government. At the general election of November 1938 many of them voted for the opposition parties. The Government felt that the Munich settlement had justified their policy of 'realism' and that patriotic Croats would hesitate before splitting the country at a time when the international horizon was so dark. In the event the Government vote dropped by 100,000 from the 1935 figures, and the opposition increased their vote by 300,000 bringing it to 1,347,000 or 45 per cent of the total. Despite this increased vote the curious processes of Yugoslavia electoral arithmetic left the Government with 306 seats to the opposition's 67. The pro-Nazi, Ljotić, received only 1 per cent of the vote, and his Fascist 'Zbor' group had no seats in the *Skup-Ština*. After the elections Stojadinović remained Premier for a few months, but was forced to resign in the spring of 1939 because of a dispute with his non-Serbian colleagues over the violently pan-Serb sentiments of one of his ministers. Paul summoned Mr. Cvetković to succeed the former strong man. The new Government was charged with the urgent task of reaching a reconciliation with the Croats before the outbreak of the European war which everyone knew to be imminent. A settlement was reached in August 1939. The Croats received less than they had asked for, but an autonomous Croatia was created, under the governorship of a Ban appointed by the Regency, but governing with the advice of an elected Croat Assembly. Despite their reservations the Croats accepted the *Sporazum* of 1939 as the best offer they were likely to get. Maček and his followers were not disposed to weaken the country at a time when national unity was so vitally necessary. The new dispensation had come too late, however, to effect any radical improvement in the internal situation before old Yugoslavia disappeared in the flames of World War II. When the problem of the nationalities came to be tackled afresh after the war new men had seized the levers of power and new methods were used.

Chapter 3

Yugoslavia in the Second World War

IN MARCH 1941 it seemed as if Yugoslavia was slowly drifting into the Axis orbit. Cvetković and Cincar-Marković went to Vienna at the behest of the Führer, and returned having signed the Tripartite Pact, pledging support to Italy and Germany. But the Yugoslav people were not prepared to see their country tamely following in the path of Hungary, Rumania and Bulgaria. They rose in spontaneous anger against their rulers. The shame of the betrayal brought together a coalition of army officers, students, politicians and orthodox priests,[1] and a government representative of all sections of the community was formed, pledged to defend the country's independence.

Prince Paul was deposed and sent into exile, and his 17-year-old nephew, Peter, was proclaimed King. The new government of General Simović[2] was soon faced with the inevitable German invasion, which it was ill equipped to meet. In the words of Winston Churchill, the Yugoslavs had 'saved the soul and the future of their country, but it was already too late to save their territory.'[3]

THE BAPTISM OF FIRE

The High Command of the Royal Yugoslav Army formally capitulated to the Germans on 17th April, 1941. The Nazi onslaught had come with such terrible swiftness that the Yugoslavs had been unable to complete their mobilisation before their country was overwhelmed by the enemy. Many of the first resistance fighters in Serbia were men who had been called to the colours too late to play their part in

[1] The orthodox clergy were led by the indomitable Patriarch Gavrilo. who was later to suffer imprisonment in a German concentration camp,

[2] Dr. Maček and Professor Slobodan Jovanović were vice-Premiers in the new government.

[3] Hansard, May 3rd 1941.

the desperate ten days of fighting before the final capitulation. Already, by April 17th, the King and his Government had fled abroad, first to the Middle East, then later to London. Yugoslavia was left to the tender mercies of the German tiger and his Italian, Hungarian and Bulgarian jackals, all eager for their share of the spoils. Worse still, there were enemies within the gates – the native Fascists – who saw in the ruin of their country an opportunity of realising their own selfish ambitions. Germany was not primarily concerned with annexations of territory. Her main concern was to ensure that her Balkan flank could not be turned as the Wehrmacht struck eastward into the Ukraine. Only the northern parts of Slovenia were formally annexed to the Reich, the Yugoslav areas of the former Austrian Provinces of Styria and Carinthia being reabsorbed into the Reichsgau of Kärnten and Steiermark. The Banat came under German military and civil administration. The rest of the country was partitioned amongst the various camp-followers, both Yugoslav and foreign. Italy took Slovenia south of Ljubljana, and most of Dalmatia, eventually incorporating these areas into the governmental system of the Kingdom of Italy. She also maintained a military occupation of Montenegro, and through her control of Albania she administered the Kosovo-Metohia region. Hungary was awarded the plains lying between her former state frontier and the rivers Tisa, Danube and Drava, as well as the two small northern areas of Prekomurje and Medjumurje. All of these areas except the Medjumurje were fully integrated into the Hungarian system of government. The Serbs of the Bačka were given the dubious privilege of electing representatives to the parliament in Budapest, and the Orthodox bishop of Novi Sad was made a member of the Hungarian Upper House. Bulgaria, from whose territory the main Panzer thrust had been made in 1941, was rewarded by the grant of most of Macedonia and part of southern Serbia, areas which she had long coveted.

When all the foreign satellites had been paid for their contributions to the defeat of Yugoslavia, Serbia south of the Danube, Croatia and Bosnia-Hercegovina still remained to be shared between the native Fascists. The egregious Pavelić returned from his exile in Italy even before the last rites had been performed over the corpse of the Kingdom of Yugoslavia.

On April 16th, 1941, he proclaimed the Independent State of Croatia, with Pavelić as its leader (Poglavnik), and King Tomislav II (Duke of Spoleto) as its king. Tomislav chose to reign from afar, and during the three years of his reign he never once tested the loyalty of his Croatian subjects by appearing amongst them. Had he inspected his domain he would have found that the hall-mark of the Poglavnik's stewardship was administrative inefficiency, combined with savage cruelty against his political opponents in general and against Serbs and Jews in particular. The frontiers of his state were gradually settled by negotiation with the Nazis and their allies. Bosnia-Hercegovina, most of the old province of Croatia-Slavonia and a part of Dalmatia all eventually came under the rule of Pavelić. As long as the Poglavnik and his Ustaši thugs concentrated on the murder of Serbs and Jews, his German masters were content to give them a free hand. The Gestapo maintained a careful watch over the affairs of the Independent State of Croatia, and saw to it that German troops were given every facility to conduct their operations against the Partisans.

Pavelić in Croatia enjoyed a degree of independence which was denied to his Serbian counterpart, General Nedić. Occupied Serbia did not have even the shadow of an independent Government. Nedić, a former Minister of War and commander of the southern group of the army during the fateful days of April 1941 was now content to perform a number of menial tasks as the puppet of the German military administration. The terms of reference under which he worked were to enable 'the German troops to relinquish the tasks which are the concern of the Serbs themselves, if they are willing to co-operate in reconstruction'. The area in which Nedić was allowed to perform his humble services on behalf of the occupying forces was restricted to the Morava valley, part of the Drina valley, and the Danubian plain south of Belgrade. Serbia was now smaller than she had been before the Balkan wars.

The unhappy story of conflict which had marked the relations between the South Slav peoples during the interwar period appears as an idyll of harmony and goodwill when compared with the terrible plague of hatred, mistrust and internecine strife which was unleashed in 1941. The seeds of disruption which were sown before the war, fertilised by the deliberate policy of the occupying powers and watered by the bitter tears of a betrayed, dishonoured and defeated people, now produced a hideous crop of dragons' teeth. The scars left by the humiliation of Kosovo Polje and the long night of Turkish occupation are as minor flesh wounds compared with the horrible lacerations which the Yugoslav nation received between 1941 and 1944. The ultimate bitterness was that many of these wounds were self-inflicted. Of the one and three-quarter million who died in battle or at the hands of the Fascist thugs, over six hundred thousand were murdered by their brother Slavs. The miracle is that the nation could emerge, united as never before, from this welter of treachery, violence and senseless fratricidal slaughter. The full story of the holocaust cannot be told here. We can only sketch the outlines of the tragedy. It contains elements of supreme heroism and despicable cowardice; of epic battles which fired the imagination of the world and of long, dreary months of despair under the daily humiliations of cruel occupation; of steadfastness and loyalty and of the blackest treachery and double – even triple – dealing. Men were seen at their best and at their worst. It was as if the God of War had sought out the unhappy people and called them to a day of judgement when their souls were laid bare to show to all the world the Olympian heights of virtue and the foulest cesspools of degradation of which mankind is capable. The printed word cannot convey to a people which has never known the combined horrors of civil war and Nazi occupation the full impact of the experience which Yugoslavs faced during World War II. One can only hope that something of its significance can be inferred from a bare recital of the chief events of the period.

In the spring of 1941, a battered remnant of the Royal Army took refuge in the hills of Ravna Gora in Serbia. They were led by a colonel called Draža Mihailović, who had been chief of staff to a division operating in Bosnia. Mihailović appropriated the name 'Četnik' for the forces under his command – a name which had been used by the nineteenth-century Serbian irregulars who fought against the Turkish invaders. There was already in existence an official 'Četnik' organisation, a combination of veterans' legion and Serbian Territorial Army, led by the 'Vojvoda' Kosta Pečanać. This organisation was seen by many non-Serbs to be an instrument of Serbian domination. Although nominally under the command of regular officers, who were supposed to supervise training, the Četnik bands were ill-disciplined, ill-trained and had a reputation for plundering and for paying off old scores against their personal enemies. Mihailović attempted to reach an accommodation with Pećanac, but the old Vojvoda soon threw in his lot with the quisling Premier of Serbia, General Nedić, and fused his official Četniks with the *Srpska Državna Straža* (Serbian State Guard) which was formed under German patronage in December 1941. Any appeal which the name 'četnik' still had in Serbia was thus lost, and outside Serbia the dislike of the organisation was merely strengthened. Mihailović could never aspire to be a national leader for the whole of Yugoslavia, despite the glowing recommendations of the exiles who formed King Peter's entourage in London. Nevertheless, Mihailović was in the field against the Germans some weeks before the first Partisan units organised their raid on Bela Crkva, near Valjevo, on July 7th.

The Communist-led Partisans made their appearance in the same wooded plateaux of the Šumadija which contained the Četnik stronghold of Ravna Gora. At first there was hope that the two groups could work together against the common enemy, but the co-operation broke down because the long-term aims of the leaders could not be reconciled, and neither was prepared to subordinate these aims to the temporary exigencies of war. The Communist party had hesitated for a short time after March 27th, when the people had demonstrated against the pro-Axis tendencies of Prince Paul's Government. As Communists, they had no interest in the patriotic slogans of the 'bourgeois' politicians. Their first loyalty was to the 'Fatherland of Socialism', the Soviet Union. Support for Yugoslav nationalism was simply a tactical position which could be taken up or dropped according to the over-riding strategy of the defence of the first workers' state. After the attack on the Soviet Union in June 1941, Communists throughout the world became fanatical supporters of the Allied war effort. They fought with great courage and self-sacrifice, because they believed that, on June 22nd, 1941, the Imperialist blood-bath had become overnight a war for the liberation of the workers.

Fortunately for the Yugoslav Party the period of indecision was short. Only a few weeks elapsed between the German attack on Belgrade and the invasion of Russia, and this period could always be represented as a time of preparation for the first attacks in the Šumadija in early July. Once they threw themselves into the struggle, the Communists showed that they had great advantages over their Četnik rivals. The Party had been illegal since 1921, and therefore had a generation of experience in the tortuous paths of underground organisation. The leaders had at their disposal trained cadres of disciplined revolutionaries. In 1939 and 1940 a number of Yugoslav veterans had returned from Spain after service with the International Brigade, and these men proved invaluable in training the first formations of Partisans in the art of guerrilla warfare. The fact that the Communists had played an insignificant part in Yugoslav affairs since 1921 proved to be of great psychological value, as they were not identified with any one of the embittered nationalist elements whose quarrels had driven wedges of iron between the various groups of South Slavs. The unspeakable atrocities of the Croats against the Serbs, which started from the moment when Pavelić and his Ustaši took control of Croatia, proclaimed to all the world in letters of blood and fire the utter bankruptcy of the pre-war political parties. The Communists had already benefited from the failure of the old régime in that a number of young intellectuals and army officers had turned to them as being the representatives of the only force that was not contaminated by the poison of national chauvinism. Typical of these new recruits were the Ribar brothers, sons of the former President of the Constituent Assembly, Olga Ninčič, daughter of a minister in King Peter's government in exile, Koča Popovič son of a millionaire, and Captain (later Partisan General) Arso Jovanović of the Yugoslav army. From the very first, the Partisans could claim a leadership which represented all nationalities and all walks of life in pre-war Yugoslavia. Mihailović and his Četniks could never make much of an appeal outside Serbia, and even amongst Serbs the appeal was limited to a small section of the community. Finally, and perhaps most important of all, the Partisans were led by a man of extraordinary ability, who was capable of inspiring his followers with his own example of courage and selfless devotion to the cause. Until the hour of national disaster provided Tito with his opportunity, the Communist leader was almost unknown in Yugoslavia. As an underground agitator and organiser he had shown himself to be an efficient servant of the Comintern, devoted to the Soviet Union and ruthless in suppressing deviationist factions within the party. During the three years from 1941 to 1944 he also showed himself to possess qualities of leadership which placed him among the giants on the world stage. Throughout the war, Tito never forgot that he was a Communist. In all the areas that he occupied People's Committees were set up, social reforms were instituted and political propaganda was carried out amongst the civilian population. The Partisan army became a great school, providing its rank-and-file members with instruction in the A.B.C. of Communism. When, in September 1941, the Partisans captured Užice, a small industrial town in the western Morava valley, they immediately set up a People's Court to try those accused of treason. Amongst those sentenced to death was a former secretary of the Communist Party, who was accused of deviationist tendencies.

Despite his uncompromising political views, Tito saw the necessity for collaboration with non-Communists. He would even accept deserters from the Ustaši and other Fascist organisations. In the autumn of 1941 he made efforts to bring about a common front with the Četniks against the Germans, but his terms included the setting up of People's Revolutionary Committees in the areas liberated by their joint action and this condition was unacceptable to Mihailović. The Četniks were not prepared to fight for a Communist Yugoslavia, but they soon showed that they were prepared to fight against the Communist Partisans, even if this meant 'arrangements' being made with the quisling forces of General Nedić. History has tended to paint the characters in the drama of Yugoslav resistance in uncompromising black and white. In practice, men's motives are very complex, and the line between misguided tactics and conscious treachery is hard to draw. Nedić claimed that his action in assuming the leadership of the puppet Government of Serbia was motivated by a desire to save lives and to prevent the senseless slaughter of innocent hostages. Mihailović also claimed that his overtures to Nedić were made in the same spirit. He believed that an attempt to attack the Germans in force would fail, and that the enemy would use the guerrilla attacks as an excuse to exact vengeance upon innocent Serbs. In the short run Mihailović was right, as the massacre at Kragujevać in October 1941 so tragically demonstrated. In the long run, Tito's policy of attack succeeded. Now, a generation later, Mihailović has long since left the stage and *les absents ont toujours tort.*

In the autumn of 1941 the disagreements between Tito and Mihailović on the conduct of the campaigns in the Šumadija were brought to an abrupt end by the intervention of the German army. In the first flush of battle the resistance forces had captured a number of important towns. Užice was in the hands of the Partisans, Čačak was held by the Četniks. Požega, between the two, was disputed territory. All attempts at agreement between the two groups broke down, and civil war between them encompassed their common ruin. By the end of November the Germans had re-established themselves in the Šumadija. Mihailović had dispersed his forces, and the remnant of the Partisans sought refuge in the mountains along the Serbian-Bosnian border. At Kragujevac in October the Germans had already shown their willingness to exact reprisals against the civilian population for the acts of the resistance movement. The Partisans had ambushed a column of German troops and had killed twenty-six of them. The population of Kragujevac was required to provide 100 victims for every dead German, and as 2,600 adult males could not be found, the number was made up by the inclusion of 200 boys from the upper forms of the local school. After the hostages had been riddled with machine-gun fire, tanks passed backwards and forwards over them, to ensure that all were dead. For days afterwards the bereaved relatives kept a silent vigil on the hillside by the light of thousands of flickering candles. The pinpoints of light on a hillside in Serbia symbolise the millions of mourners who followed in the wake of Germany's New Order in Europe. To the Yugoslavs the atrocity of Kragujevac was but the first of a thousand similar incidents which followed any activity against the Germans by any of the resistance forces. For those of us whose wartime experiences included nothing remotely resembling the horrors of a Nazi occupation it is perhaps unbecoming to attempt to judge those who felt that the price of armed resistance was too high.

M

The Partisans chose to risk all, and were rewarded by ultimate victory. The Četniks hesitated and lost.

The temporary successes of the first six months of the struggle were soon a distant memory. The story of the Serbian resistance had been repeated in Montenegro and in parts of Bosnia. In Croatia the Ustaši were in control, and had set themselves the grim task of exterminating the Serbs who lived within their 'Independent State'. The first stirrings of resistance were apparent in Slovenia, but they amounted to little more than isolated attacks against prominent collaborationists. In the winter of 1941–2, the enemy seemed to be invincible. Mihailović had withdrawn to his stronghold in Ravna Gora, and refused to contemplate any major operations for the time being. Tito and his Partisans were struggling across the mountains towards Bosnia, still licking their wounds after the defeat in the Šumadija, and in Montenegro a combined Četnik-Italian offensive had crushed Moše Pijade's attempt to make a Soviet state in the heart of the mountains. By the summer of 1942, however, Tito was in command of most of Bosnia outside the main towns, and had established his headquarters in the market town of Bihać in the upper Una valley. In six months the defeat of Užice had been avenged, and the Partisans were once again in command of a sizeable town in which they could introduce the elements of a Communist system of government. In November 1942 a body known as the Anti-Fascist Council for the National Liberation of Yugoslavia (A.V.N.O.J.) was set up. This embryo Government was headed by Dr. Ivan Ribar, a respected politician of pre-war days, and it included many non-Communists, but real power rested with Tito and the Partisan High Command. The Bihać Manifesto appealed to Yugoslavs of all political opinions and social classes to join in the struggle against the Germans, the Četniks and Ustaše, and promised that there would be no major changes in the social and economic system of the country. It seemed to envisage a federal system governed by the general principles of liberal parliamentary democracy. The Bihać Manifesto induced many non-Communists in Croatia, Bosnia and Slovenia to rally to the Partisans. In Serbia the response was less enthusiastic, partly because the Četniks still retained a following there.

The Partisans knew that they could not hold towns like

Bihać indefinitely, in the face of the aircraft, tanks and motorised columns which were at the disposal of their enemies. In order to prevent a catastrophe like that which overtook them at Užice they decided to evacuate Bihać and the surrounding area as soon as they learned of the enemy's plans to mount a major offensive against them. This offensive, known as 'Operation White', was the fourth which had been made during the course of the war with the object of obliterating the Partisans. It had been organised as a joint effort of the German, Italian and Ustaši forces, with the additional assistance of those Četnik units which were already working with the Italians in Dalmatia and Montenegro. Mihailović did not openly collaborate, although one of his chief lieutenants was present at the Rome meeting in January 1943, when the operation was planned. The fine distinction which the Četnik leader made between 'joint action' and 'parallel action' was too subtle to be appreciated by the Partisans. It was also too much for many of Mihailović's own men, and hundreds of them deserted to the Partisans when they realised that they were expected to fight on the side of the Germans and Italians. The armies which were ranged against the Partisans in 'Operation White' were a strange mixture. The Dalmatian Četniks, who had collaborated openly with the Italians were disowned by Mihailović, but they still clung to the prestige which they believed his name, and that of his Royal master, could give them. The Ustaše would have nothing to do with Četniks of any kind, because of the mutual exchange of bestialities which these two forces indulged in whenever the opportunity arose. Ustaši in Croatia had murdered Serbian Četniks, and Četniks in Dalmatia had been given a free hand by the Italians to murder Croats. The Germans mistrusted the Četniks, and warned the Italians of the unreliability of Mihailović. Mihailović in his turn, claimed that, although his first enemy was Communism, the Germans and Italians were not far behind in second place. His action, therefore, was against the Partisans and not for the foreign occupiers of his country. If the latter chose the same time to make their offensive this was a pure coincidence. The ramifications of treachery, collaborationism, opportunism and sheer incoherence, the tangled web of motives, the tortuous labyrinths of plot and counter-plot have an air of Gilbertian absurdity

– until one realises that the future of a heroic people was at stake.

Operation White failed in its major objective – to annihilate the Partisans. Tito led his men, women and children across the snow-covered mountains of Bosnia to the banks of the Neretva near Jablanica, and there forced the crossing of the river, placing over 25,000 Partisans on the other side. Within a few weeks the Četniks had been driven out of Hercegovina and most of Montenegro. Their 'quasi collaboration' with the Germans and Italians had ended in failure. For a few months the Partisans enjoyed a respite from attack, and the time was used to reorganise the shattered units which had survived the crossing of the Neretva. During this period, contact was made with the Albanian Partisans, under Enver Hoxha, and an emissary was sent to meet representatives of the Greek and Macedonian resistance movements. Tito's contacts with his Balkan colleagues were more fruitful than those which Mihailović had sought to establish at about the same time in 1943. Mihailović had sent representatives to Hungary, Rumania, Albania, Greece and Bulgaria to discuss the possibilities of a Balkan alliance against Communism, but any hopes of success were swept away in the flood which engulfed the old order in Central Europe during 1944 and 1945. Another international contact which was strengthened at this time was that of the Partisans with Britain. On the eve of the German Fifth Offensive, Captains Stuart and Deakin arrived by parachute to take up their mission at Tito's headquarters. Soon supplies of war materials from the West were to reach the Partisans, and all support to Mihailović was withdrawn. By the end of 1943 considerable assistance was being given to the Partisans, but when they faced the Fifth Offensive they could count on little more than moral support from our side.

Tito's answer to this new German attack was the same as that which he gave to the grotesque alliance of Germans, Italians, Ustaši and Četniks which opposed him during the Fourth Offensive (Operation White). He knew of the plan to encircle his Partisans in their Montenegrin hideout, and he decided to break out from behind his mountain ramparts before the steel trap closed around him. Hungry, ill-equipped, worn out through lack of sleep, harassed by aerial bombing and machine-gunning, the heroic army forced its way across the Sotjeska torrent and trekked wearily into the mountains of eastern Bosnia. They did not rest there for long. The crossing of the Sotjeska took place in June 1943. By November the Partisans were in control of a large part of Bosnia and Dalmatia, and the Anti-Fascist Council (A.V.N.O.J.) had met at Jajce to proclaim the Provisional Government of Yugoslavia. Tito had become a Marshal of Yugoslavia, as well as the acting Prime Minister and Minister of Defence. A challenge had been thrown out to King Peter and the exiled politicians not to return without permission to the homeland from which they had fled in 1941. A programme had been drawn up which sketched the main outlines of a federal republic, and wherever the Partisans were in control the change to a new way of life was being introduced. The remarkable improvement in the position of the Partisans during the second half of 1943 was partly attributable to the collapse of Italy and the opportunities which this afforded for direct contacts between Tito and the Allied troops across the Adriatic. Many Italians in Dalmatia had given up their arms to the Partisans rather than to the Germans. Some of them formed a Garibaldi Brigade to fight with the Partisans. More important than arms and men, the Italian surrender gave the Yugoslavs the control of a number of Dalmatian islands and ports, to which supplies could be sent from the Adriatic coast of Italy.

The British military mission led by Brigadier Maclean,[1] which joined the Partisans during the autumn of 1943, sent reports which confirmed the impression given earlier by Captain Deakin and Captain Stuart. The forces under Tito's command were indisputably the only serious military opposition to the Germans in Yugoslavia. Mihailović and his Četniks had been unable to maintain their precarious balance between anti-Communism and anti-Nazism, and had slithered farther and farther down the Gadarene slope of collaboration with the enemy. Mr. Churchill summed up the position in a statement to the House of Commons on May 24th, 1944:

'The reason why we have ceased to supply Mihailović with arms and support is a simple one. He has not been fighting the enemy, and, moreover, some of his subordinates have

---

[1] Fitzroy Maclean, *Eastern Approaches*, Part III. Cape. 1949.

made accommodations with the enemy, from which have arisen armed conflicts with the forces of Marshal Tito, accompanied by many charges and counter-charges and the loss of patriot lives to the German advantage. We have proclaimed ourselves the strong supporters of Marshal Tito because of his heroic and massive struggle against the German armies. We are sending, and planning to send, the largest possible supplies of weapons and to make the closest contact with him.'[1]

Three months earlier, the Commons had been told that the Partisans were holding down fourteen out of the twenty German divisions in the Balkans. Speaking of the Partisans, Mr. Churchill had said:

'Around and within these heroic forces, a national and unifying movement has developed. The Communist element had the honour of being the beginners, but, as the movement increased in strength and numbers, a modifying and unifying process has taken place, and national conceptions have supervened. In Marshal Tito, the Partisans have found an outstanding leader, glorious in the fight for freedom.'[2]

British support was reaffirmed during the summer of 1944, when Tito met Churchill at Caserta. During these discussions Tito assured Churchill that he would not force the Serbian peasantry to abandon their private farms, and that he would be prepared to work with Dr. Šubašić and some of the ministers in King Peter's government. The question of an Allied landing in Istria was also discussed.[3] Tito laid claim to Trieste, but the Allies were unwilling to see the port change hands. The issue was left undecided until the Commonwealth forces met the Yugoslavs face to face in the spring of 1945, and Tito's men were forced to withdraw.

By 1944 it was obviously only a matter of time before all Yugoslavia was in the hands of the Liberation Army. When the Russians entered Serbia along the Danube in October 1944, part of Belgrade was already in Partisan hands. Slovenia was cleared by the O.F. (Freedom Front) forces under Tito's friend,

[1] Parliamentary Debates, *Hansard*, vol. 400. pp. 776–7.

[2] Parliamentary Debates, *Hansard*, vol. 397. pp. 692–4.

[3] Churchill, Sir Winston, *The Second World War*, Vol. VI, 'Triumph and Tragedy', pp. 78–84.

Kardelj. The Bulgarians left most of Macedonia when their Government sued for peace with Russia in September 1944. In the last hours of defeat the Germans and Ustaši wreaked a terrible vengeance on the civilian population in the areas which they still held. A few days before the Bosnian capital fell to the Partisans in April 1945, Ustaši gangs were rounding up Serbian men and women and hanging them from the trees along the main street. Also, at the eleventh hour, Nedić made frantic efforts to prove that he really was the Serb patriot he always claimed to be. He attempted to form a common front with Mihailović against the Germans and the Partisans, but before they could begin to work out their desperate plans the tide of war had passed over them. Tito was installed in Belgrade as the head of a government controlled by the Communists, and supported by the mass of the Yugoslav people. Dr. Šubašić of the London Government became Foreign Minister, and the Government was officially recognised by King Peter.

Chapter 4

The Establishment of the People's Republic

WHEN THE war ended Tito and his Communists found themselves the undisputed masters of Yugoslavia. For twenty years before the war they had been a despised and hunted minority, rent by bitter doctrinal disputes and manipulated from abroad by the agents of the Comintern. When the party was declared illegal in 1921 it had fifty-eight seats in the Constituent Assembly, and was the third largest party in the country. Its greatest strength was in Macedonia and Montenegro, two areas where the people felt themselves to be second-class citizens in the Kingdom of the Serbs, Croats and Slovenes. Following the dissolution of the party in 1921, a legal front organisation was formed, which obtained only 10 per cent of the votes which had been cast for the Communist Party in the elections for the Constituent Assembly. In 1924, the front organisation, the Independent Workers' Party (*Nezavisna Radnička Partija Jugoslavije*) was banned and police action against the Communists was intensified. By 1928, the party membership was down to 3,000. The decline of the party between 1921 and 1928 was not due, however, to the oppression of its members by the police. In his report to the 1948 Party Congress Tito reviewed the history of this period, and summed up in the following words :[1]

> 'The blame for all this (i.e. the decline of the party) of course cannot be put solely on the exceptionally difficult conditions under which the party worked as an illegal organisation, under the white terror . . . but the fault is mainly that of the fractional struggle within the party. Fractionalism – that is the evil that obstructed the development of bolshevisation of the C.P.Y.'

[1] Political Report of the Central Committee of the C.P.Y. Josip Broz Tito. Belgrade 1948. p. 29.

The 'bolshevisation' of the party meant the subordination of the Yugoslav Communists to the discipline of the Comintern, and the removal of 'the ballast of opportunism and reformism which was a left-over from the pre-war Socialist movement and the ballast of petty bourgeois irresoluteness and faint-heartedness, in a word – lack of faith in the forces of revolution'.[1]

In the process of jettisoning this ballast the party was weakened by internal dissensions, and alienated from the Yugoslav working class in whose interests it claimed to act. The spontaneity of the early days was eventually replaced by a blind obedience to the Comintern. During the period of royal dictatorship between 1929 and 1934 most of the leaders who stayed in Yugoslavia were imprisoned or executed, and the direction of the party fell into the hands of a group of *émigrés.* From 1932, when the Comintern appointed Milan Gorkić to the leadership, until 1937, when Tito assumed the position of Secretary-General, the history of the Yugoslav Communist Party was really the history of the intrigues and squabbles of a group of Comintern agents operating from Vienna and Moscow. It has no relevance to the history of Yugoslavia. In 1937 there was a complete purge. The only prominent survivor was Josip Broz, alias 'Comrade Walter', the leader of the Zagreb Section of the party, the most able and loyal of Stalin's adherents in Yugoslavia. 'Comrade Walter' returned to Yugoslavia to reorganise the party and to win acceptance for the new line of co-operation with all anti-Fascist groups against the rising tide of Nazism. In the three and a half years which remained before the old Yugoslavia disappeared, the new leader built the nucleus of the underground movement which provided the experienced cadres for the Partisans. 'Comrade Walter' soon became known throughout the world by his new alias, 'Comrade Tito'. It is significant that, during the ten years after Tito's ascendency over the Yugoslav Communists had been established, death in battle was the only cause of vacancies in the Central Committee of the Party. The period of factions and purges was over. The new leadership was united behind Tito, and together they saw an insignificant conspiracy under foreign patronage grow into a national movement capable of seizing the

[1] *Ibid.*, p. 33.

levers of power and of manipulating them in order to change the face of Yugoslavia.

The Communists had no illusions about their ultimate aims. They may have assured Winston Churchill that they did not intend to change the property relations within the country; they may have accepted a government which included Dr. Šubašić and other members of King Peter's exiled Ministry in London; they may even have agreed to leave the question of the future of the Monarchy open until the end of the war. These were merely necessary tactical moves in the face of pressure from the Western Allies, but once the war was over such agreements could be swept aside at the first opportunity. By the end of 1945, Subašić and his colleagues had been isolated and forced out of the Government, the Karageorgević dynasty had been abolished, and Yugoslavia had been proclaimed a Federal People's Republic. In January 1946, the newly elected Constituent Assembly voted for a new Constitution, and a year later the first five-year plan was inaugurated.

The new constitution contained certain provisions which are part of the common currency of most such documents which have appeared since 1777. All citizens are equal before the law; there is no discrimination on the grounds of race, property status, degree of education or religious creed; freedom of conscience and freedom of religion are guaranteed; the inviolability of the home is respected; freedom of the Press, freedom of speech, freedom of association, freedom of assembly and freedom to hold public meetings are all guaranteed. Articles in the Yugoslav constitution relating to these matters might well have been written by Thomas Jefferson or by the revolutionaries of 1789. There are two aspects in which the Yugoslav Constitution of 1946 is of special interest, however. Firstly, it makes a serious attempt to deal with the nationality problem, the reef on which old Yugoslavia had foundered. Secondly, it has a section on social and economic organisation which writes into the fundamental law of the state the principles of a socialist economy.

On the nationality problem, recognition is given to the autonomy and right of secession of each of the six federal units. Each of the six units has some historical significance, and in most cases an ethnic and cultural personality. The *banovina* of old

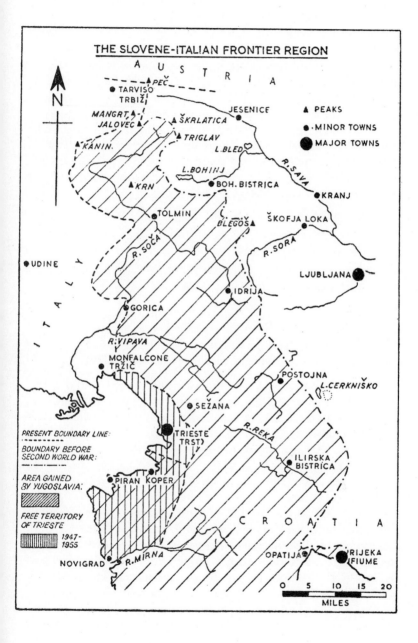

THE SLOVENE-ITALIAN FRONTIER REGION

A U S T R I A

▲ PEAKS
● MINOR TOWNS
⬤ MAJOR TOWNS

PEČ
TARVISO
TRBIŽ
JESENICE
MANGRT ▲
JALOVEC ▲
▲ ŠKRLATICA
KANIN ▲
▲ TRIGLAV
L.BLED
R.SAVA
L.BOHINJ
▲ KRN
● BOH. BISTRICA
KRANJ
TOLMIN
BLEGOS ▲
ŠKOFJA LOKA
R.SOČA
R.SORA
UDINE
LJUBLJANA
● IDRIJA
GORICA
R.VIPAVA
MONFALCONE
TRŽIČ
POSTOJNA
L.CERKNIŠKO
● SEŽANA
TRIESTE
(TRST)
R.REKA
ILIRSKA
BISTRICA
PIRAN KOPER
C R O A T I A
NOVIGRAD   R.MIRNA
OPATIJA
RIJEKA
FIUME

I T A L Y

PRESENT BOUNDARY LINE:
BOUNDARY BEFORE
SECOND WORLD WAR:
AREA GAINED
BY YUGOSLAVIA:
FREE TERRITORY
OF TRIESTE
1947-
1955

0   5   10   15   20
MILES

Yugoslavia were units devised to suit the administrative convenience of the Central Government, and often divided people from their compatriots. The six republics are Serbia, Macedonia, Montenegro, Slovenia, Croatia and Bosnia. In addition, there are two autonomous regions within the Republic of Serbia – Kosovo-Metohia, which is peopled mainly by Shqiptars, and Vojvodina, where there is a large Magyar population. Each republic has its own government and legislature, and has some initiative in local affairs, but in all major policy decisions the Federal Government in Belgrade, with its bi-cameral legislature, is the supreme authority.

The 1946 constitution declared that all authority is derived from the people and belongs to the people.

'It is the duty of every citizen to work according to his abilities; he who does not contribute to the community cannot receive from it.'

By Article 14 all mineral wealth, power resources, means of communication and all foreign trade are under state control:

'The state directs the economic life and development of the country in accordance with a general economic plan, relying on the state and co-operative sectors while achieving a general economic control over the private economic sector.'

Although private property rights are guaranteed, and the continuation of a private sector in industry is envisaged, the emphasis throughout Chapter 4 of the constitution, which deals with economic matters, is on the importance of the nationalised sector as 'the mainstay of the state in the development of the national economy'.

The first task which faced the new Government was that of physical reconstruction. The country had emerged from four years of bloody war. Apart from the irreplaceable loss of human life, the mutilated bodies and sick minds of hundreds of thousands of the survivors, there were the wrecked houses in hundreds of devastated villages and towns, and the factories and transport facilities blown up by the saboteurs. The Yugoslav railway system was inadequate before the war. In 1945 it was almost non-existent. Even where the lines and bridges had not been blown up there were hardly any engines capable of hauling the trucks which remained. Away from the big towns most roads were little more than rough tracks, fit only for the carts of the peasants. Without transport there would be no possibility of restoring agricultural and industrial production even to the low levels of the 1930's. Immediate first aid was given by U.N.R.R.A. to reconstruct the most important railway lines and to provide motor transport for the carriage of essential supplies. The Yugoslavs set themselves the task of laying new tracks to supplement the inadequate railway network. Many of these new lines, including the famous Šamać-Sarajevo Youth Railway, were built by unskilled volunteers, helped by groups of young people from abroad.[1] From the first, these schemes were seen as something more than construction projects. They were used as a means of educating the youth in the principles of the new state. There is no doubt that the enthusiasm of the young people for the project on which they were engaged was genuine. Having worked alongside them, the author cannot believe that fear of physical compulsion could have evoked the spirit and self-sacrifice that the young Yugoslavs displayed. They believed that they were contributing to a new society. They could see with their own eyes the needs of their country, and they flocked in their thousands to make their contribution, regardless of political opinions or social origin. In the years immediately after the war it seemed that all Yugoslavia was engaged on the task of reconstruction. The volunteers sang as they built:

'We build the railway
The railway builds us.'

They returned from their task with a new outlook on life. The intensive propaganda campaign which had been part of their everyday life on the construction scheme, the slogan shouting, the lectures, the whole atmosphere of camp life, moulded the habits and thoughts of thousands of young Yugoslavs. They came home convinced that nothing was impossible for them, no task too formidable to those who combined the ardour of youth with an understanding of Marxist philosophy. It would be too much to expect that this spirit could have

[1] An account of the work of a group of British volunteers is given in *The Railway: An Adventure in Construction.* Edited by Edward Thompson. British-Yugoslav Association. London. 1948.

remained undimmed through the years that lay ahead. The pace was too strenuous to be maintained at the same feverish pitch. The years since 1948 have brought disillusion to many, but it is doubtful if the new régime could have weathered the storms of the late 1940's without the enthusiastic backing of the heroic youth of Yugoslavia.

At the same time as this great effort at reconstruction was being made, many of the surviving features of old Yugoslavia were being eliminated. The monarchy was abolished, the remnants of the old administrative machine were dismantled, and the leaders of the old political parties were either won over to co-operate with the new régime or were made politically ineffective. A number of pre-war leaders who had either collaborated with the enemy or who had adopted a hostile attitude to the Partisans were put on trial. Draža Mihailović was executed, Ante Pavelić fled to Argentina, and Bishop Rožman of Ljubljana to the U.S.A. Archbishop Stepinac of Zagreb was imprisoned but he was later released and lived in restricted residence in a Croatian village until his death in March 1960. A strict watch was kept on the few leading members of the Social Democratic and Croat Peasant parties who remained behind in the new Yugoslavia. Any sign that these former leaders were attempting to revive their political organisations was instantly suppressed. The Communist Party grew from 12,000 in 1941 to half a million in 1948. In addition, over six million members were enrolled in the People's Front, an organisation led by the Communist Party, but composed of members whose political development was not considered adequate for full party membership. The People's Front was not a coalition of political groups, although it included members of the pre-war parties. In fact it was seen as an instrument for breaking up the old political loyalties, especially amongst the peasants. In Edvard Kardelj's words, 'There is no doubt that the form of such a political organisation as the People's Front greatly eases the breaking up of the remnants of the old reactionary parties with our masses, who are accustomed to political organisation and who are politically active.'[1]

---

[1] Edvard Kardelj. *The Communist Party of Yugoslavia in the struggle for New Yugoslavia*. Report to the Fifth Congress of the C.P.Y. Belgrade. 1948. p. 81.

By 1947, the most urgent reconstruction work had been put into effect, and the next step forward to a new order of society could be taken. The announcement of the first five-year plan was seen as a milestone on the road towards the socialist state. All remaining major enterprises, both industrial and commercial, were nationalised, and a start was made towards a planned agriculture. Marxists have always mistrusted the peasantry. In his report on the fifth Communist Party Congress in 1948, Tito quoted Lenin on this question: 'The peasant holding continues to remain small-scale production. It is here that we have a boundlessly broad and very deep-rooted basis of capialism. It is on this basis that capitalism preserves itself and regenerates in the fierce struggle against Communism. The forms of this struggle are fraud and speculation against the state buy-up of grains (and other products) and against the state distribution of supplies in general.'[1] Tito accepted this description as a true picture of the state of affairs in Yugoslavia. But old Yugoslavia was a peasant state, with more than 70 per cent of the population living off the land. The habits of centuries could not be changed by the passing of laws and resolutions in Belgrade. The peasant, bound by an almost mystical attachment to his tiny plot, had always suspected the activities of the town-bred politicians, who seemed to him to come from another world. Old Yugoslavia never solved the problem of the peasantry: inefficient farming methods, rural over-population, and all that this meant in low standards of housing, health and education. In pre-war days Yugoslavia had a density of population five times that of Denmark; its yield of wheat was less than a third of that in Denmark. These figures give some indication of the poverty of the Yugoslav countryside.[2]

The new Government wrote into the constitution the classic slogan of agrarian radicalism: 'The land belongs to those who cultivate it.' Land was taken from the *kulaks*; i.e. those who owned more than seventy-five acres (thirty hectares); and the Church was forbidden to own more than ten hectares in any parish. Every encouragement was given to the peasants to join co-operative or collective farms, but outright compulsion was

---

[1] Political Report. p. 124.

[2] For an account of the pre-war farming system see D. Warriner *Economics of Peasant Farming*. O.U.P. 1939.

not used. At a time when many goods were still rationed, peasants who joined a co-operative were given an opportunity to buy extra rationed goods at specially low prices. Any farm machinery which was available was put at the disposal of the members of the co-operative. In spite of the inevitable resistance of the peasantry, by 1951 almost a quarter of the farms had been brought under some form of communal management. In this respect the Yugoslavs went further and faster than any of the other Eastern European People's Democracies, and there was no foundation to the accusations made by the Cominform in 1948 that the Yugoslavs had been unduly tender to the kulaks. After 1951, there was a gradual change in policy, and much of the land under communal management has now returned to private ownership. The latest official figures[1] show that co-operatives and state farms occupy only 2.5 million acres of the total cultivated area of almost 30 million acres. More than half of the 2.5 million holdings are under twelve acres in area. Crop yields have risen but little from the low levels of the 1930's. The average wheat yield in the period 1930–39 was eleven quintals per hectare. The average during the last ten years was only twelve quintals per hectare. Yields of maize, cotton, hemp, sunflower, tobacco, sugar beet and beans were all below pre-war levels, and only potatoes and cabbages showed substantially better yields in the 1950's than in the 1930's. In numbers of livestock, Yugoslavia has made good the terrible losses of the war years, but the numbers of cattle, pigs and sheep kept on the farms are still hardly greater than in 1931. The general picture in the countryside is therefore still the same as before the war. There are still the same small, inefficient peasant holdings, many of them hardly more than allotments, and many peasants are still unable to earn a decent living from the produce of their land. A new feature of the rural scene, however, is that there are now more opportunities for the sons and daughters of peasants to find work in the growing towns and so earn money wages to supplement the meagre income of the family plot. In many villages which the author has visited, the older folk still follow a way of life which belongs to another century, but their children are away in the towns, studying to be engineers, doctors, architects and even agronomists.

---

[1] *Statistical Pocket Book*, 1955

The biggest changes in the economic life of the country have been in industry; before the war, manufacturing industry hardly existed outside Slovenia and a few urban centres in Serbia and Croatia. Mining was the chief industrial occupation and most of the mines were worked by foreign companies. For example, the great copper mines at Bor were controlled by French capital; Shell and Standard Oil had a monopoly over oil extraction, and even the Slovene textile industry was in foreign hands. Often technical backwardness and lack of transport facilities inhibited the exploitation of Yugoslavia's rich mineral resources. At Jezerina in the Kosovo-Metohia region, 8,000 tons of chromium ore were extracted every year by hand. The ore was carried by pack-horse for the first five miles and then transferred to bullock-carts for the next fifteen miles of the journey to the nearest railhead. One of the first acts of the new Government was to nationalise all large industries, including those in foreign hands. The Five Year Plan announced in 1947 envisaged the expansion of the basic heavy industries under public ownership and the introduction of a large number of industries which were entirely new to Yugoslavia. As in Russia, and the other eastern European countries, the emphasis was on capital goods. Iron and Steel production was to be increased by 300 per cent on the 1939 figures, coal by 250 per cent, and chemicals by 900 per cent. The labour force to man these new industries was to be drawn mainly from the peasantry. That vast reservoir of under-employed, untrained, backward-looking people was to be given a new purpose in life, learning new skills and earning for themselves and the whole nation a higher standard of life than they had ever before enjoyed. At the same time, food production was to be expanded. This was to be achieved by a general increase of over 20 per cent in the productivity of the land during the five-year period of the plan. In fact, the agricultural and industrial targets were not reached. Nevertheless, over half a million peasants left the land to find work in the growing industries. The output of the mines increased according to plan but manufacturing industries and agriculture lagged behind. The textile industries have still not reached the targets set for them in the Five Year Plan of 1947.[1]

---

[1] *The Law on the Five Year Plan 1947–1951.* Passed by the National Assembly. April 28th, 1947.

N

The failure of the Plan was partly due to the over-enthusiasm and lack of experience of the planners. Their paper schemes were often remote from the needs of the people and set unreal targets which could never have been attained with the inadequate resources, human and material, which Yugoslavia possessed at that time. The Minister in charge of the Plan, Andrija Hebrang, was dismissed for this reason in 1948. Far more serious, however, was the blow delivered by the Cominform in June 1948. The plan had been based on the assumption that the countries of Eastern Europe would supply Yugoslavia with certain materials and trained personnel which she lacked. This assumption was shattered by the resolution passed at a meeting of the Cominform in Bucharest in June 1948. In the non-Communist world, the news of this resolution was received with incredulity. At the time, Yugoslavia's relations with the Western world were particularly bad. The Trieste dispute, the shooting down of American planes over Yugoslav territory, Yugoslav support for the Greek Communists, Anglo-American influence in Italy during the 1948 election campaign – all these factors contributed to the state of tension and hostility which existed between Yugoslavia and her former allies in the west. Western journalists spoke of Tito as the principal lieutenant of Stalin outside the U.S.S.R. To many Communists, Yugoslavia appeared to be the model 'People's Democracy', and few of them, outside a small circle in Eastern Europe had any inkling of the gravity of the dispute between the Communist Parties of Yugoslavia and the U.S.S.R. Tito himself is said to have reacted 'as if a thunderbolt had struck me'[1] when he received the letter from Stalin and Molotov on 27th March, 1948, which rejected his answers to previous criticisms by the Soviet leaders. The letter began, 'We consider your answer untruthful, and therefore wholly unsatisfactory', and went on to berate the Yugoslav leaders as 'dubious Marxists', Trotskyists and slanderers of the Soviet Union. It soon became apparent that relations between the Yugoslav and Soviet leaders had been deteriorating throughout 1947. The core of the problem lay in the refusal of the Yugoslavs to grant special privileges to the U.S.S.R. which would have led eventually to the complete political and economic subordination of their country. For example, there

[1] Vladimir Dedijer, *Tito Speaks*, p. 341.

had been a proposal to set up joint trading companies on the pattern of the *Sovrom* companies in Rumania. Two such companies were in fact established – the *Justa* Air Transport Company and the *Juspad* River Shipping Company. The experience which the Yugoslavs had in these two cases did not encourage them to proceed further with arrangements which would have given the Soviet Union a stranglehold over their whole economy. Faced with the tenacious opposition of the Yugoslavs, Stalin temporarily abandoned any further projects for joint companies. He only ceased his activities in this sphere, however, in order to concentrate his pressure in other directions. He thought that he could isolate Yugoslavia from her Balkan neighbours, Albania and Bulgaria, and then proceed to isolate the leadership of the Yugoslav Communist Party from the rank and file members. The latter aim was to be accomplished by the infiltration of Soviet experts and agents into every aspect of Yugoslav life, from the Army to the world of learning and the arts. The Yugoslavs were prepared to go to great lengths to placate the Russians. Kardelj, the Yugoslav representative at talks in Moscow in February, 1948, signed an agreement that his government would consult with the Soviet leaders on all issues of foreign policy. The tone of the discussions can be judged from the following extract given by Dedijer in 'Tito Speaks'.[1] At one of the meetings Kardelj had mentioned Benelux. Stalin retorted sarcastically, 'Benelux, that's nothing'. 'There is Belgium, there is Luxemburg', Kardelj continued.

Stalin 'And nobody else.'

Kardelj, 'There is the Netherlands.'

Stalin, 'No.'

Kardelj, 'Yes, the Netherlands are in. Look at the name of Benelux. It means Belgium, Netherlands and Luxemburg.'

Stalin, very angry. 'When I say no, it means NO.'

Despite the rudeness and stupidity of the Soviet leader, Kardelj, 'boiling with rage', agreed to sign the document promising consultation on matters of foreign policy. He did so in order not to complicate a situation which was already tense. He felt, as did Tito and the other Yugoslav leaders, that an open break with Russia was unthinkable. They continued to

[1] Vladimir Dedijer, *Tito Speaks*, p. 330.

hope for a reconciliation for some months after the dispute had become public knowledge. Gradually, as the propaganda campaign of the Cominform became more and more hysterical, they began to hit back, and their tone changed from one of sorrow and bewilderment to one of bitterness and anger. Stalin hoped that new leaders, more amenable to the wishes of the Cominform would replace those who had dared to challenge the Soviet Union's right to interfere in the internal affairs of Yugoslavia. No greater psychological blunder could have been made. To the dismay of the Stalinists, few Yugoslavs showed any disposition to take the Cominform's side in the dispute. General Arso Jovanović, Sretan Žujović and Andrija Hebrang were the only important figures who were alleged to have acted as agents of the Cominform.[1] Many Yugoslavs who may have been lukewarm in their support for the new régime had no doubt that they preferred the native Communists to the representatives of Stalinism. Unlike many of the Communist leaders who took power in Eastern Europe in the wake of the Red Army, Tito and his colleagues had remained with their people throughout the occupation. Their reputation did not rest upon the protection of the tanks and bayonets of the Red Army. Thus the Yugoslav party leaders had little to fear politically from the Cominform campaign. Economically, there was, perhaps, more to fear. The Soviet bloc countries sealed off their frontiers with Yugoslavia and refused to trade with the Titoist traitors. They refused to make deliveries under the trade agreements which had been concluded during the previous two or three years. Often Yugoslavia had sent grain and

---

[1] On April 13th, 1948 – before the publication of the Cominform attacks – a Party commission was set up to investigate the activities of Hebrang and Žujović. Amongst the charges made against Hebrang were that 'he hindered the Five Year plan from being brought out on time'; 'he left chaos behind him in the Economic Council and the Planning Commission; and attempted to carry out a policy of state capitalism'. He was also accused of attacking the leadership of the Yugoslav Communist Party 'in front of our friends from the Soviet Union'. A year later Tito attacked Hebrang as a former agent of the Ustasa. In November 1950 Žujović published a confession, in which he described himself and Hebrang as agents of the Cominform. Žujović was released from prison, but Hebrang refused to recant and remained a prisoner until his death. After 1950 the main charge made against the two former leaders was that they were agents of the Cominform. Their alleged sabotage of the Five Year Plan is no longer mentioned.

agricultural produce and was awaiting payment in machinery and raw materials. Oil from Rumania, fertilisers from Russia, heavy machinery from Czechoslovakia and other goods, equally important to the Yugoslav economy, were now no longer available. By the end of 1948 it was apparent that the Five Year Plan would have to be abandoned, but there was a more serious problem than that of a failure of the economy. What was at stake in 1949 and 1950 was the very existence of Yugoslavia as an independent state. This fact was gradually recognised by the Governments of the Western powers. In 1948 Yugoslavia's relations with Britain and America were at a very low ebb, particularly because of the Trieste affair. By 1950, both Britain and America were sending economic and military aid in order to help Yugoslavia to survive. When they recovered from the first shock of the Cominform campaign, the Yugoslav Communists began to adjust their policies to meet the needs of the new situation. Tito has summarised the position as follows:

'The campaign against our country and methods of socialist reconstruction, which for the last decade, has been waged by leaders of the countries of the Eastern bloc and some Communist leaders of the West, has so far inflicted great damage on us, particularly in the material respect. But it has also brought some benefits, particularly in the field of Marxist ideology; in the more rapid liberation from dogmatism and in the better recognition of negative features in the development of Socialism, thus enabling us to avoid such shortcomings ourselves.'[1]

The new approach to Marxism, more flexible than the old Stalinist line of pre-1948 days, and more concerned with immediate practical problems, was first expounded fully at the Ljubljana Congress of the League of Communists in 1958. One of the chief authors of the new line is the former schoolmaster from Slovenia, Edvard Kardelj. Kardelj further developed his ideas at the 1960 Congress of the Socialist Alliance. He argued that the bureaucratic state capitalism, highly centralised economic planning and rigid political

---

[1] *Forty Years of the Communist Party of Yugoslavia.* Text of a speech by Tito to the Central Committee of the League of Communists. Belgrade. 1959. p. 40.

dictatorship which were features of the early days of the Yugoslav Revolution, are no longer necessary. Once the revolution is firmly established, the state, and even the party, can begin to 'wither away', and power can be diffused throughout the community by means of self governing workers' organisations. Local government, based on the commune (*opština*), can be given a more important role at the expense of the central agencies. It is no longer thought that the Communist Party should arrogate to itself a position of privilege and power, but at the same time any talk of a second party is considered to be unreal and reactionary.[1] It is characteristic of Yugoslavia today that these ideas should have been expounded after many of the changes to which they refer had already been put into effect. Some of the changes were embodied in the new Constitution of 1953, but Kardelj now says that this Constitution is unsatisfactory. 'Our present Constitution is wholly obsolete, and its spirit has, one may say, nothing in common with the present situation in the country . . . an ever stronger need is felt to give a comprehensive formulation of the changes that have taken place in our society.'[2]

In contrast to the 1946 Constitution, that of 1953 allowed individuals who were not members of the Party or the People's Front (now Socialist Alliance) to stand for election to the Federal Parliament.[3] In fact four such individuals were returned for Macedonia, one of them defeating a well-known

---

[1] See the account of the Djilas affair, pages 207–9.

[2] Kardelj's speech to the 1960 Congress is printed in *Four Factors in the Development of Socialist Social Relations*. Edition Jugoslavija, Belgrade 1960.

[3] Since 1953 the Communist Party has been known as the 'League of Communists' and the People's Front has become the 'Socialist Alliance'. The Communists no longer claim a monopoly in laying down 'the political line of struggle for the construction of socialist relationships in our country'. This work is now the joint responsibility of the League of Communists and the Socialist Alliance. To the outsider it would appear that there is little difference between the two organisations. Tito and his leading Communist Party colleagues hold official positions in the Socialist Alliance. The Socialist Alliance has a membership several times larger than that of the League of Communists and it demands less from its members. It would seem that the Communists see themselves as a 'ginger group' within the broader organisation. There is no possibility that the two might develop independent policies. It was the suggestion that this might be desirable which led to the downfall of Djilas. In January 1954 he wrote : 'No class or political movement can claim the exclusive right to represent society as a whole or to proclaim their ideas as objective truth.

Communist. This system of election is comparable to that introduced by Gomulka in Poland for the elections of 1957. There are no opposition parties, but occasionally strong local dissatisfaction with the individual Communist leaders can result in a successful protest vote being recorded. In the elections for the Presidency which took place after the election of the parliament, one M.P. actually voted against Tito!

The system of recall of candidates by their constituents is incorporated into the new constitution. This can occasionally result in some strange reversals of fortune. In 1954 Djilas was recalled by his constituency in Montenegro two months after he had been elected by a majority of 99.8%. Such fickleness of public opinion would be hard to match even in the West!

The 1953 Constitution provided for a new legislative body to replace the old Council of Nationalities. This was a Council of Producers, chosen by the representatives of organisations of industrial workers, professional bodies and agricultural co-operatives. The other house, called the Federal Council, is chosen by universal adult suffrage. The recognition of the right of the representatives of industrial and professional bodies to elect candidates reflected the growth during the years between 1950 and 1953 of a number of self governing workers' organisations. The most important of these were the Workers' Councils in the factories. Since 1953 there has been a great increase in the number and variety of such organisations. It is perhaps too early to pass judgement on the success of this experiment. There is no doubt that Yugoslav ideas on worker' self-government have a strong appeal in other countries of Eastern Europe. In Hungary and Poland during the exciting days of 1956 the demand for the introduction of workers' councils was raised by the leaders of the 'revisionist' movement against the old Stalinist bureaucracy. Time alone can tell whether Yugoslavia has developed a new and higher form of democracy. All that can be attempted here is a brief review of the main features of the new system.

Chapter 5

The New Yugoslavia

FOR SEVERAL years now tourists, scholars and technicians from the non-Communist world have been able to visit Yugoslavia and to move about the country without restriction. Many Yugoslavs have been given visas to study or work abroad. Technologists have gone to Germany, agricultural students to Britain and Scandinavia, social scientists and economists to the U.S.A. There have also been exchanges with students of the 'uncommitted' countries of the Middle East and South East Asia. No other country in Eastern Europe has been so willing to learn from the experience of the industrially more advanced nations of the West; no other Communist Government has been so prepared to permit its citizens the opportunity of exchanging ideas with people living in the liberal parliamentary democracies. The latter may think that they can teach the Yugoslavs something about political freedom, but the Yugoslavs are convinced that the rest of the world can learn from them an important lesson in economic democracy. Their ideas have already made some headway in Eastern Europe. In the ferment of October 1956 in Poland and Hungary the demand for Workers' Councils on the Yugoslav pattern was made by some of the Communist rebels. The old heresy of 'Titoism' has been renamed 'Revisionism' by the high priests of Communist orthodoxy, and both Khrushchev and Mao Tse-Tung have warned the faithful of its baleful yet seductive appeal.

The experiment in economic democracy originates in the period immediately following the Cominform's attack on the Yugoslav Party. By bitter experience the Yugoslavs learned at this time that Stalin, 'the great genius of mankind' could be wrong on an issue of fundamental importance. They realised that Soviet insistence that there was only one road to Socialism was merely a cloak for Soviet imperialism. Up to 1948 the Yugoslav Communist Party had appeared as one of the most faithful bands of Stalinists in Eastern Europe. The events of

1948 forced them to think again about the fundamentals of their policy. By 1950 they had abandoned all thought of copying Soviet methods of economic planning. In place of the rigid centralisation and unreal targets of their first Five Year Plan, they sought to introduce a more flexible system based on decentralisation and workers' management. A law passed in 1950 defines the basic concept of workers' self-government.

'Factories, mines, carriers, transport, trade, agricultural, forest, public utility and other state economic enterprises, as the general people's property, shall be managed by the working collectives on behalf of the social community within the framework of the state economic plan, and on the basis of the rights and duties established by the laws and other legal prescriptions.

The working collectives shall exercise this right of management through Workers' Councils and managing boards of the higher economic associations with which are affiliated a number of economic enterprises.'[1]

This basic law has been subject to many amendments since 1950, in the light of the experience gained by the operation of the new system. At first over-enthusiasm led to many mistakes. It was too much to expect that workers newly recruited from the ranks of the peasantry, could adjust themselves overnight to the responsibilities of self government.[2] It was too much, also, to expect administrators and Communist Party dignitaries to take easily to a system which denied them the privileges and the power which they had enjoyed during the period of rigid state control. Many of the paper schemes which were drawn up in the first flush of enthusiasm for the new idea were found to be unworkable. At times wasteful competition between enterprises working in the same field resulted in the closing of factories.

[1] Basic Law on the Management of State Economic Enterprises. Article 1. English text from *Social Government in Yugoslavia*. Yugoslavia Information Service, Belgrade 1957.

[2] In order to develop trained cadres of working people who are capable of playing an effective part in the running of industries there has been a great development of adult education schemes under the auspices of the 'Workers' Universities'. At the 1960 Congress of the Socialist Alliance a number of speakers referred to the importance of adult education not only as a means of improving technical efficiency, but also as an instrument of social change.

The shortage of competent managers, and the problem of discipline within the factories created many problems. These were referred to in a speech by Dr. Pavle Kovać at the Congress of Workers' Councils in 1957.

'It is a familiar fact that management of enterprises in the conditions of the contemporary economy constitutes a highly complex task, requiring extensive professional knowledge and ability. Consequently, one of the basic problems that had surrounded the introduction of workers' self government bore on the creation of an organisation such as would enable the workers, who in the majority of cases lack special professional, technical, economic and other knowledge, to manage enterprises successfully. In effect, the case has been one of resolving the social-economic antagonism between the direct producers and the professional managers which neither capitalism nor the system of administrative management of the economy could solve, notwithstanding the fact that in the latter the means of production had passed to state ownership.'[1]

The new system attempts to solve one of the problems which has affected all countries where private industry has been replaced by some form of state monopoly. The worker in the industry feels no more responsible to his new masters than he did to his former private employer. Often, in fact, he feels less important and less responsible than he did under the old system. The theory that by virtue of his voting rights as a citizen he has a voice in the running of his industry, has little meaning to him. The idea of some more direct form of workers' participation in the management and control of industries is not new, but Yugoslavia is the first country to have embarked on an experiment of this kind on a national scale. There is a superficial similarity between the methods used in Yugoslavia and those advocated by Mrs. Besant in *Fabian Essays* published in 1889. She advocated a system whereby industrial enterprises would be placed under the control of communal councils elected by all the workers living in a particular area. In Yugoslavia the *opština*, or communal council, is responsible for the economic

---

[1] *The New Yugoslav Law.* April-December, 1957, p. 119. Bulletin of the Union of Jurists Associations, Belgrade.

policy within its area. It draws up the targets after consultation with the factory representatives and the Republican Government. The *opština* also appoints the managers to the factories within its area, and can remove them if asked to do so by the Workers' Council of the factory concerned. Each enterprise has its Workers' Council which is elected annually by the employees. This council can decide on the spending of the surplus which has accrued to the enterprise during the preceeding year. This surplus can be distributed partly in the form of a bonus payment to all workers, and partly in the form of social expenditure on housing, cultural facilties or improved amenities. In the day-to-day running of the factory the manager has complete control. The basic law defines his duties as follows.

'A director shall organise the process of production in an enterprise and directly conduct the realisation of the plan and the operation of the enterprise, enforcing the laws and other prescriptions, the conclusions of the managing board of the enterprise and the orders and instructions of the appropriate state organs, as well as of the managing board and the director of the higher economic association.

A director shall be directly responsible for the enforcement of the laws, or other legal prescriptions and the orders of the appropriate state organs, and he shall ensure their application in an enterprise.

Within the economic plan and conformably to the conclusions of the managing board of an enterprise, the director . . . shall make contracts and allocate the working assets. A contract shall be valid as soon as made by the director.

A director shall represent an enterprise before the state organs and in the legal relations with different physical and legal persons. He may authorise another person to represent the enterprise in determinate legal matters.

The director of an enterprise shall hire workers and appoint other employees in the enterprise, except those concerning whom it was otherwise decreed by the special prescriptions, and he shall issue the decisions relating to their labour relations with the enterprise.

The director . . . shall make decisions relating to the termination of employment of the workers and office employees, unless this power was delegated to other persons in the enterprise on the basis of general prescriptions.

The workers and office employees have the right to file objections and appeals with the managing board of an enterprise against every decision relating to termination of employment or assignment to another job, and final decision shall rest with the managing board.

The director . . . shall assign the workers and office employees to the individual jobs and determine their duties.

The workers and office employees . . . shall be accountable to the director for their work in the enterprise.

The director . . . shall ensure discipline in the work and operation of the enterprise.

The director need not consult the workers' council in routine matters but he does consult them when major changes in policy are envisaged.'

The introduction of Workers' Councils has not had an adverse effect on efficiency, although there was some disorganisation and loss of production in the early days. Textile production, for example, had passed the 1939 figures by 1947, but it fell to two-thirds the pre-war output in 1952. By 1953 it had recovered, and has steadily increased ever since.[1] Throughout industry as a whole there has been a continuous growth since 1955. To the outside observer there are unmistakable signs that the economic well-being of the Yugoslav worker has materially improved during the last few years. There are more consumer goods in the shops, and their quality and variety is a welcome change from the drab uniformity which was so much in evidence during the first post-war decade. It is perhaps inappropriate for an outsider to attempt to assess the effect which Workers' Councils have had in helping to bring about these changes, or how far the ordinary worker feels that his lot has been improved materially and spiritually by the attempt to give greater flexibility and variety to the forms of economic organisation.

Despite the post-war changes Yugoslavia is still primarily an agricultural country, and Workers' Councils do not yet affect the majority of the peasantry. The chronic evils of pre-war

[1] See Appendix – Economy of Yugoslavia 1959.

Balkan agriculture – over-population and under-production – have been alleviated to some extent by the expansion of industry in the towns, but the peasantry still constitute almost a half of the population. It is therefore only the workers in industry and commerce who are directly affected by the new economic experiments.

The peasants resisted the formation of peasant work co-operatives and similar organisations which smacked to them of the dreaded Russian 'Kolkhoz'. Since 1951 there has been a relaxation in the pressure and most peasants who had been influenced to join co-operatives during the previous five years exercised their right to become completely independent farmers again. In recent years general co-operatives which are merely concerned with the buying of equipment and seed, and the sale of produce have had more success. These general co-operatives are also concerned with rural education, and in co-operation with Workers' Universities, Peoples' Universities and Women's organisations they are helping to bring the peasants into the twentieth century. Nevertheless Yugoslav agriculture is still technically backward and it seems unlikely to make any great advance until the peasantry are willing to accept some form of co-operative exploitation of the land.

We have seen how the shock of excommunication from the Cominform led to re-examination of the social and economic policies of the Yugoslav Communists. The same shock led eventually to a change in foreign policy. The exigencies of the economic situation were sufficient explanation of the need for better relations with the West, but there were also compelling political and military reasons. The first important departure from the old Stalinist line came in 1949 when the Yugoslavs closed their frontier with Greece, and so prevented the Communist guerilla forces from regrouping on Yugoslav soil when they were being hard pressed by the Royalist army. Another important step was the decision to give qualified support to the United Nations' action in Korea in 1950. These moves preceded the negotiations for economic, and later military, aid from the U.S.A., Britain and France. In the difficult years after 1950 dollar aid from the West made a great contribution to the economic recovery of Yugoslavia, and enabled her to survive in face of the ferocious hostility of the Soviet Union and its satellites. After the death of Stalin, there was a change in Soviet policy, and relations with the countries of Eastern Europe now have a semblance of normality. Khrushchev and Bulganin came to Yugoslavia in 1955 on a good-will mission, and astounded the Yugoslavs by confessing that their previous enmity had been misconceived. The Yugoslavs were naturally wary, and their suspicions seemed confirmed when the Soviet leaders showed their bad faith over the treatment of Imre Nagy at the time of the Hungarian revolt. Although they reacted against the first Soviet intervention in Hungary, and although they admitted a number of Hungarian refugees, the Yugoslavs leaders have since recognised the government of Janos Kadar, and have attempted to improve relations between Hungary and Yugoslavia. If relations between Yugoslavia and her former friends in Eastern Europe[1] are now on a more reasonable basis than they were between 1948 and 1955, they are still far from cordial. Only with Poland has there been any real warmth and understanding. Gomulka has been called the 'Polish Tito', and there are undoubtedly similarities between the careers of the two men. But Poland is not Yugoslavia. Poland has a greater need to remain on good terms with the Soviet Union. Geographical realities prevent her from following the same course as Yugoslavia, although Gomulka may occasionally make demonstrations of support for the Yugoslav line.[2]

Events caused the Yugoslavs to change their foreign policy. After the changes, has come the rationalisation about them, and the gradual evolution of a policy of 'active co-existence' with all countries, regardless of their social systems. Yugoslavia's closest friends in this policy are the uncommitted countries of Asia and Africa. She supported the Bandung declaration of the Afro-Asian countries, and has recently developed close cultural and economic links with Egypt, India, Burma and the mergent nations of Africa. As Tito showed in his

---

[1] Except for Albania, under Enver Hoxha, which still follows the pre-Khrushchev line.

[2] The last important occasion when such demonstration was made was in 1958 at the Ljubljana Congress of the League of Communists of Yugoslavia, when the Polish Ambassador refused to join his East European colleagues in a concerted withdrawal from the meeting in protest against Yugoslav criticisms of the Soviet Union.

speech in September 1960, in the U.N. debate on the Congo, the policy of 'active co-existence' rejects the idea of military power blocks and looks to the machinery of the United Nations as a means of settling international disputes.[1] Yugoslavia did, however, initiate talks which led to a Military Treaty with Greece and Turkey in 1953. At the time she was anxious to strengthen her position by an alliance with her two Balkan neighbours, both of whom were members of the NATO. This pact is now of no importance. Yugoslavia's need for it diminished after the death of Stalin, when a more friendly attitude towards her was taken up by the Soviet Union and the East European satellites. At the same time Turkey and Greece found it impossible to co-operate during the period of the Cyprus emergency. These two events ensured the early death of the Balkan Pact as a military alliance, but for a time it still had some validity in the sphere of cultural and economic co-operation.

In the more relaxed climate of international relations during the last few years political freedom in Yugoslavia has made a slow advance. Conformity in all aspects of art, literature and philosophy is no longer demanded. Criticism is permitted within limits, but the limits are drawn tightly enough to prevent fundamental criticism of the economic and social basis of the new régime. The attitude to criticism varies from time to time according to the international situation, and particularly to the state of relations with the Soviet Union. During the Hungarian rising there was a tightening of censorship and control, but this has now relaxed. Nothing like the outburst of criticism against the Communist way of life which was permitted in Poland during the first months of Gomulka's return to power has ever been seen in Yugoslavia. Nevertheless a steady relaxation is discernible since the days of 1945–8 It has been said with some truth that in Poland one can say anything one likes about Gomulka, but nothing against the Soviet Union, whereas in Yugoslavia one can say what one likes about the Soviet Union, but nothing against Tito.

---

[1] Yugoslavia seemed ready to depart from these principles when she mobilised along the Italian frontier in 1953, after the Anglo-American decision to leave Trieste. Fortunately, the dispute was settled by negotiation, and since the Udine (Videm) agreement of 1955 Italo-Yugoslav relations have steadily improved.

Those schooled in the liberal political traditions of the West may feel that experiments in economic democracy are unreal and fraudulent when they are conducted within the framework of a one party state. It should not be assumed that Yugoslav Communists are insincere because they use the words 'freedom' and 'democracy' about a society which, to the Western reader, lacks those political institutions which appear to us to be prerequisites of a free social order. Words mean different things at different times and places. In Britain in the last two hundred years 'political democracy' has ceased to be a term of abuse, signifying mob rule and anarchy, and has come to denote a form of government based on two main political groups, both of which accept the basic premises of our unwritten constitution, and contend peacefully for the control of Parliament. In pre-1914 Yugoslavia the word 'freedom' meant primarily the absence of foreign, political and military domination, as it does today to many Africans and Asians. But the removal of the foreign rulers did not satisfy the aspirations of the Yugoslavs for 'freedom'. They found as much to complain of in their new national state as they had previously done under Habsburg or Turkish rule. Once alien control had gone, they began to struggle amongst themselves for the achievement of what they considered to be new freedoms. The rulers of old Yugoslavia were faced with demands for economic emancipation by their people, and with pressure from Croat and Slovene nationalists against their subjection by Serbia. Since the collapse of the old régime, however, the national question is no longer of major importance. It is true that one often hears Slovenes complain that their Republic is paying more than its fair share in taxation in order to provide capital for new industries in the backward areas of Macedonia, Bosnia and Montenegro. Such complaints do not come only from those who hanker after the 'good old days'. The author recently listened to a diatribe by a local Communist leader in Slovenia against the savagery of the Montenegrins. But there is little or no support for the kind of separatist movement which tore old Yugoslavia asunder. Especially amongst the younger people (and well over half the population is under twenty-five years old) the chauvinism of the past means nothing. They consider themselves to be Yugoslavs first, and Croats, Serbs or Slovenes second.

If the Yugoslavs are more united nationally than they have ever been in the past, are they also more united politically, in view of the fact that there is no official opposition? To the western reader the absence of parliamentary opposition parties is in itself proof of the denial of freedom. In this connection the affair of Milovan Djilas is instructive.[1] He was a Communist of long standing, and a close friend of Tito both during the war and in the struggles against the Cominform in the years after 1948. In November 1953 Djilas was elected to the new Federal Council by a vote of 99.8% of his Montenegrin constituents. In the period immediately before these elections – the first under the new Constitution – there had been an attempt by the leadership of the party (now called the League of Communists) to reimpose party discipline. During the period of doubt and confusion following the break with the Cominform, Communists had lent support to a bewildering variety of heterodox views. The central committee had met at Brioni in June 1953 to attempt to put a stop to some of the wilder excesses, and to reimpose a strict party discipline, Djilas revolted against this tightening of control, and from his powerful position within the party leadership he began a campaign to win support for his views. At first he was encouraged to express his opinions, even by Tito. In December 1953 he wrote in *Borba*, the official organ of the Party, 'The new enemy, bureaucracy, is even more dangerous than the previous one, capitalism'. In January 1954 he went further and stated that . . . 'the Leninist type of party and state are outdated, as must always happen when conditions for revolution no longer exist, and democracy begins to live.' In the same article he attacked the 'caste system' which had grown up amongst leading Communists, and he urged that the courts and the police should be freed from interference by the Party. Letters were published from Communists in various parts of the country supporting the general line taken in the articles. It does not seem that Djilas's doctrinal heresies enraged his colleagues in the party leadership, as much as his personal satires directed against certain unnamed, but identifiable, figures, and their wives. In fact, up to the publication

[1] See Fitzroy Maclean, *Disputed Barricade*, pages 413–344 for an account of the Djilas affair up to the first trial in 1955. For later developments see F. W. Neal *Titoism in Action* and Ernst Halperin, *The Triumphant Heretic*.

o

of these satires he continued to maintain his position in the party and the government. On December 25th, 1953, he was elected President of the National Assembly. A month later he had been given his 'final party warning' and sacked from all his public offices. In the public debate which ended in his disgrace, one member of the Central Committee spoke in his defence – Vladimir Dedijer. Tito's reply to 'Comrade Djilas' was more in sorrow than anger. Tito felt that if Djilas continued to propagate his ideas, there would be 'a bloody struggle' in the country within a year. He agreed that the party must eventually 'wither away', and he admitted that the idea was originally his own. But Djilas seemed to think that this could happen within a few months, whereas Tito believed that it would be a lengthy process, only capable of realisation when 'the broadest masses of our people had come to accept a Socialist outlook.' Djilas remained unconvinced. In April 1954 he resigned from the party, although still retaining his membership of the Socialist Alliance. For a time no more was heard of him. Then in December 1954 he deliberately trailed his coat again, by making a statement to the *New York Times* advocating the formation of a new party. 'I thought that the Communist Party must permit freedom of discussion. Now I see that this is impossible. Another political formation should be constructed.' At the same time Vladimir Dedijer continued to express his agreement with the Djilas line. The two former leaders were brought to trial, charged with spreading hostile propaganda against the State. Djilas was given a suspended sentence of eighteen months' imprisonment, his colleague one of six months. The sentences were not to be carried out unless the offences were repeated during the next three years. The mildness of the punishment led some Western correspondents to suggest that the verdict was tantamount to an acquittal. But Djilas was not disposed to accept the implied olive branch. He seemed determined to force the authorities to make an example of him. He chose every opportunity to embarrass the government by publishing articles in the foreign Press which attacked the foreign policy of his former associates. Thus, when Tito was in Moscow, trying to make some accommodation with the new Soviet leaders, Djilas published articles in the *San Francisco Examiner* attacking Khrushchev and his friends, and implying that Tito's mission was a waste of time. In November 1956, Djilas again published articles in the Western Press, this time expressing disapproval of the Yugoslav policy towards Hungary. He was now tried for 'conducting hostile propaganda and mispresenting Yugoslav foreign and domestic policies in articles contributed to the foreign Press,' and he was sentenced to three years imprisonment. Dedijer published an open letter to Tito protesting against the arrest of his friend, but no proceedings were taken on account of this. In fact, shortly afterwards, Dedijer was allowed to visit Scandinavia, where he lectured on foreign affairs. Although his lectures were criticised by Tito, and although he was refused a passport later in the year to visit Manchester, Dedijer remained at liberty, and was allowed to complete his doctoral thesis at Belgrade University. Two years later Dedijer was given a passport in order to take up a fellowship at Manchester University. Djilas, however, continued to defy the authorities, and to suffer the full rigours of the law for his temerity. Even imprisonment did not silence him. In 1957 a book called 'The New Class' appeared in America, the manuscript of which had been smuggled out of Yugoslavia shortly before its author's arrest. In it he bitterly attacks the Communist leaders, accusing them of irresponsible and arbitrary use of power. The book was banned in Yugoslavia, and Djilas was sentenced to a further seven years in prison, but he was released in January 1961. He still maintains that his views have not changed 'in essence', and that he has given 'no dishonest undertaking or guarantee', in order to obtain his freedom. The Djilas case illustrates to the Western reader the extent of political freedom in Yugoslavia.

In Western eyes Djilas does not appear to be a criminal. In Britain and America the publication of attacks on the government in foreign newspapers is not, at least in peace-time, a criminal offence. A different view, of course, is taken in war-time. A different view, also, may be taken in some other countries in the West. But the Communists see themselves as fighters in a class war, and Djilas is regarded by them in the same light as the traitor William Joyce was regarded in Britain in 1945. Many non-Communist Yugoslavs, who do not accept the Marxist view of life, shed few tears over the imprisonment of Djilas. To them the formation of opposition parties does not suggest a development towards a system in which the choice before the electorate is one between a Kennedy and a Nixon, or a Macmillan and a Gaitskell. Their experience of parliamentary forms of government is of the chauvinism and sham democracy of Old Yugoslavia. They do not think of opposition in terms of Her Majesty's Opposition which accepts the fundamental assumptions of the unwritten constitution, and provides an alternative government should the one in power be defeated at the polls. They think rather of their own experiences – of Radić, shot in parliament by a government supporter, of the rigged elections of the 1930's, of the intrigues of the Čarsija clique and the imprisonment of Croat and Slovene opposition leaders. They think also of the misery brought about by the factionalism and terrible fratricidal strife which the old régime engendered, and which reached its apotheosis in the nightmare of World War II. There is a great yearning for security, and a fear that the creation of opposition groups might re-open some of the old wounds. One cannot expect them to forget their own history.

Occasionally, representatives of the old parties engage in quasi-political activities, and such manifestations are quickly and severely dealt with. In 1957, for example, a group of elderly socialists received prison sentences for political offences. They were accused of maintaining contact with emigré groups in Paris, and in particular with Dr. Mladen Žujović, brother of one of the accused.

Mladen Žujović was sentenced to death, *in absentia*, in 1946, at the same trial as Draža Mihailović, for alleged treachery during the occupation. The accused represented themselves as a group of old men who met to reminisce about their past activities, but one of them admitted writing a book advocating opposition to the present régime, which was to be smuggled to Paris for publication. There was an outcry against this trial in Western political circles, and an international Socialist deputation was formed, headed by the late Aneurin Bevan, with the intention of interceding on behalf of the prisoners. The deputation was refused admission to Yugoslavia, but the prisoners have since been released. In January, 1960, a Franciscan monk was sentenced to fifteen years imprisonment for forming a group which intended to propagate Croat nationalist ideas.

Several young men connected with the group were also imprisoned at the same trial.

It can be seen from the above that no political opposition to the present form of government has any opportunity to develop in Yugoslavia. The Government would say that organised political opposition has no chance because political parties are based on economic interest groups, and when large scale private enterprise has been abolished there is no basis for opposition parties. It is significant that in all the political trials of recent years the accused have been convicted after allegations that they had maintained contact with anti-Communist groups outside Yugoslavia. Fear of foreign intervention seems to lie behind the government's suspicion of the Roman Catholic Church. This Church represents to them an international movement against Communism, inspired by the Vatican with the object of undermining the authority of the State. It is thought that before the war something like a third of the people of Yugoslavia, most of them in Slovenia and Croatia, belonged to the Roman Catholic Church. The Church now maintains over 6,000 churches, served by 3,500 priests, and there are 135 Catholic monasteries. In 1952 over 2,000 students were training for the priesthood. Any visitor to Yugoslavia can see that the the Churches are well attended. The author visited a number of villages in Slovenia on Easter Sunday, 1960, and in every case it seemed that the majority of the population were attending the local parish church. But the Roman Catholic Church still argues that there is no freedom of religion in Yugoslavia. Its position is that the freedom of worship is not the same as freedom of religion. Because the churches are open, and because most of the clergy are able to perform their ecclesiatical duties, because children can be accepted for confirmation and religious instruction in the church, and those who wish can marry in church after first performing a civil ceremony, one should not assume that the church is free. In new Yugoslavia 'Marriage and family are under the special protection of the State . . . only marriages concluded before competent state authorities are valid. After the conclusion of marriage citizens are authorised to undergo a marriage ceremony in accordance with religious rites.'[1] To the Roman Catholic such a situation is a denial of religious rights. The removal of Roman Catholic schools from the authority of the Church, the alienation of Church properties, the suppression of Catholic newspapers and propaganda organisations are described by Catholic authorities as examples of religious persecution.

It would seem that the Church did not feel that its liberties were so limited and circumscribed during the brief period of rule by the Croat State of Pavelić, nor during the Italian occupation of Slovenia and Dalmatia. It was obvious at the end of the war that many of the Catholic leaders who had been identified with these régimes would probably receive rough justice at the hands of the Partisans. Many of them fled abroad in the last months of the fighting. Archbishop Sarić, of Sarajevo, for example, whose 'Poglavniku Oda' (an ode of doubtful literary merit, which sang the praises of Ante Pavelić) appeared in the weekly *Katolicki Tjednik* on Christmas Day, 1941, was one of those who did not wait for the arrival of his enemies. Archbishop Stepinać, however, stayed at his post as Archbishop of Zagreb. In May, 1945, he was arrested after expressing his disapproval of the way in which trials of alleged war criminals were being conducted. He was released after a brief detention, only to be re-arrested in the following year, after he had issued a pastoral letter denouncing the policy of the new government towards Catholic property and schools. At his trial in 1946 he was accused of collaboration with the Fascist régime of Ante Pavelić. He pleaded not guilty, but refused to answer any questions put to him by the prosecution. These questions concerned the behaviour of his subordinate clergy towards the Fascist régime, the attitude of the Church to forcible conversions to Catholicism of Orthodox Serbs, and the relations of Stepinać himself to Pavelić and the Ustaši. The Croat puppet state undoubtedly had good relations with the Church. Inspired by a Catholic fanaticism Pavelić expelled all non-Catholics from government offices, and there is no doubt that this action received great support from members of the clergy. None who collaborated with the régime were ever disciplined by their ecclesiastical superiors. The Vatican was one of the first powers to accord full diplomatic representation to the Croat

[1] From *Church and State*, a pamphlet published by the Yugoslav Government.

state. Did Stepinać approve of all that was done by Pavelić, often in the name of the Church? Stepinać and his supporters claimed that whilst he maintained formally correct relations with the authorities, he secretly aided Jews and Serbs who were the victims of oppression by the Ustaši, and that he only accepted forced converts into the Church in order to save them from further persecution. They also made counter charges of terrorism and religious persecution against the Partisans. Stepinać was sentenced to sixteen years imprisonment, but in December, 1951, he was released from prison and allowed to live in restricted residence in his native village of Krasić, where he performed the functions of parish priest. His diocese was left in the hands of an apostolic administrator, Mgr. Franjo Seper.[1] In 1952 there was an attempt to reach an understanding between the government and Stepinać, but the Archbishop remained adamant that no compromise was possible unless the State recognized the Roman Catholic marriage service, reopened the Church schools, and gave complete freedom to the Catholic press. These conditions were unacceptable to the authorities, and the negotiations broke down.

In the same year Stepinać was made a Cardinal, and the Government announced that they would allow him to travel to Rome for his installation, on condition that he did not return to Yugoslavia. This offer was contemptuously rejected, and the Yugoslav Government then broke off diplomatic relations with the Holy See. It seemed that nothing further could be done as long as Stepinać lived. The Cardinal continued to perform his duties as a parish priest at Krasić and was occasionally allowed to receive visitors from abroad. He died on February 10th, 1960, and was buried in the Cathedral of St. Stephen on Zagreb in the presence of a large congregation. Since his death there has been a slight improvement in the relations between the State and the Roman Catholic Church. One sign of this was the honour done to Mgr. Ujčić, Archbishop of Belgrade in the conferment on him of a high state decoration on the occasion of his eightieth birthday. Another was the surprisingly light sentence passed on the Bishop of Skopje, Mgr. Čekada, in a trial in March, 1960. The Bishop was accused of receiving money from the Vatican in contravention of the currency regulations.

[1] Appointed Archbishop on the death of Stepinać.

The Bishop admitted to receiving fourteen million dinars from the *Congregation de Propaganda Fide* which was used for religious purposes in the Dioceses of Skopje and Sarajevo. He claimed that smuggling of the money would have been unnecessary if relations between Church and State had been on a proper basis, and that the money had been for church purposes only, and was not for his own use. After a two day trial, he received a suspended sentence of eighteen months.

So far, we have considered mainly the position of the Church and its clergy. What is the position of the Roman Catholic laity? The thousands who flock to the Churches on important religious occasions include many peasants who, although not politically active, have shown in the past that they will resist passively government policies of which they disapprove. There are also Catholic intellectuals, especially amongst the older academics, trained in the Universities of Austria and Germany before the First World War. They are viewed with suspicion, but they are not considered to be a potent force of opposition. The author knows many practising Catholics who pursue their professions without interference or persecution. It is quite certain, however, that their chances of promotion are small compared with those of their Communist colleagues. A Yugoslav University, for example, would be as unlikely to promote a devout Catholic to a senior teaching post, as an American state Univeristy would be to offer a chair to a prominent Communist.

In such matters as the granting of passports and travel permits, scholarships, priorities in securing accommodation in new housing areas and in countless other ways, the State favours those who support it and work for it rather than those who are thought to be hostile to it. The active member of the Catholic Church may find life more difficult for him than it is for the non-Churchgoer, but it is not made impossible.

The Serbian Orthodox Church is in a somewhat different position from that of the Roman Catholic. It was the national church of Old Yugoslavia, and was always in the forefront of the Slav nationalist movement. Almost half the population of Yugoslavia have been brought up in the Orthodox tradition. As a national church it does not fall under the same suspicion as does the Roman Catholic Church because of its international contacts. Its leaders were identified with the struggles of the emergent Serbian nation in the nineteenth century. In the last war many of its priests fought and died with the resistance forces; its Patriarch was imprisoned in Dachau; its leaders refused to compromise with the Quisling régime of Nedić in occupied Serbia. Although it has not always agreed with the new régime, it has not, like the Roman Catholic Church, openly clashed with it. Its influence, however, has suffered a decline since the war. Before the war the Patriarch could force governments to modify policies which were thought to be against the interests of the Church – as for example in the dispute with the Stojadinović Government over the proposed Concordat with the Vatican. In 1935 the Concordat between the government and the Vatican had been signed, but it required the ratification of the Skupština.

After a lengthy battle against ratification led by Patriarch Varnava and backed by the Holy Synod of the Orthodox Church, the Government was forced to give way. The ratification had been passed by the lower house, but was never submitted to the Senate. Today no Church in Yugoslavia could hope to influence the government in this way. The Orthodox Church has lost its influence in education, much of its property and all of its political power.[1] It is materially somewhat better off than the Catholic Church because the greater number of its clergy have joined the government sponsored associations of priests and through them receive certain material benefits.

The other important religious community is that of Islam, whose members number about 12% of the population – mainly in Bosnia, Kosmet, Macedonia and South Serbia. Their existence bears witness to the long period of Turkish rule in these areas. Although they have nominal links outside the country, as a militant international body opposed to Communism the Moslem Community cannot be compared with the Roman Catholic Church. Although some Moslems did support the Pavelić régime in the early days of its rule in Bosnia, especially after the visit of the pro-Nazi Mufti of Jerusalem, they later turned more and more to the Partisans. Their relations with the new régime have been comparable with those of the

[1] Two theological faculties are maintained – one of the University of Belgrade, the other of Prizren.

Serbian Church, although a number of government measures have undermined traditional Moslem ideas concerning the role of women in society.

It is perhaps naïve to assume that a country which has suffered so much from internal faction and dissension, and which has known the horrors of foreign occupation and the pettiness of native autocrats, should adopt overnight both the outward forms and the inner spirit of a political democracy which has developed through the centuries in the entirely different social climate of Western Europe. We have seen in the preceding pages how the outer garments of parliamentary machinery often cloaked the reality of a society at war with itself; a society where extremes of poverty and wealth, and the legacy of centuries of alien rule and internecine strife made a mockery of the rule of law. There is no doubt that the new Yugoslavia is offering the opportunity for a higher material standard to many of its citizens. There is no doubt also that the worst excesses of the struggle between the nationalists which warped the development of Yugoslavia between the wars are now only a bitter memory of the past. These two achievements stand to the credit of the new régime. They provide a starting-point from which to build a society which is capable of offering a fuller life to all its members. It remains to be seen whether the new way of life which is being fashioned under the leadership of the Communist Party will satisfy the deeper, non-material needs of the people.

We hope that the outline which we have given of the history of the Yugoslav people will help the English-speaking reader to understand some of the differences between our way of life and theirs. Their experience has been totally different from our own; because of it the pattern of their lives, their institutions and their ways of thought have been cast in a different mould. Underlying these differences, however, is our common humanity. Every year more and more visitors from Western Europe are discovering the fascination of the beautiful land of Yugoslavia, and are finding that they are received with warm hospitality and friendship. We would like to think that the foregoing pages will make some contribution to the furtherance of this friendship.

Bibliography

(Place of publication London unless otherwise stated.)

THIS SHORT bibliography includes a number of books in English and French which are likely to be available to the reader who wishes to follow further some aspects of the story of the Yugoslav people. In the second section there are a number of the more important works in Serbo-Croat and Slovene which have been consulted by the authors.

I BOOKS IN ENGLISH
1. *General Background of Balkan History*
a. Pre-Nineteenth Century

Dvornik, F. *The Slavs: their Early History and Civilisation.* (Boston: American Academy of Arts and Science, 1956)
Based on a series of lectures given at Harvard in 1951. A standard work on the origin, migration and settlement of the Slavs, and their history to the twelfth century.

Obolensky, D. *The Bogomils* (Cambridge University Press, 1948)

Ostrogorsky, G. *History of Byzantine State. Translated by* J. M. HUSSEY (Oxford: Basil Blackwell, 1956, Princeton, N.J.: Rutgers University Press, 1957)
A classic work by a distinguished Yugoslav scholar.

Porphyrogenitus, Constantine. *De Administrando Imperio. Edited by* GY MORAVCSIK, *English translation* R. J. H. JENKINS (Budapest: 1949)

Vaughan, D. M. *Europe and the Turk: The Pattern of Alliances 1360–1700* (Liverpool: University Press, 1954, New York: Gregory Lounz, 2nd Revised Edition, 1960)

b. The Balkans in the Nineteenth Century

Hertslet, Sir E. *The Map of Europe by Treaty*, 4 vols (London: H.M.S.O., 1875–91)
Standard work of reference shows changes in Europe after 1814.

Marriott, Sir J. A. R. *The Eastern Question* (Oxford: Clarendon Press, 3rd edition, 1925, New York: Oxford University Press, 1940)

Oakes, Sir A. and Mowat, R. B. *The Great European Treaties of the 19th Century* (Oxford University Press, 1918)
Texts of treaties and notes on the background of diplomatic history. Chapter XI refers to Turkey, Russia and the Balkan States between 1871 and 1914.

Pribram, A. F. *The Secret Treaties of Austria–Hungary, 1879–1914*, 2 Vols. (Harvard University Press, Cambridge, Mass., 1920–21)

Seton-Watson, R. W. *The Southern Slav Question and the Hapsburg Monarchy* (1911)

Sumner, B. H. *Russia and the Balkans, 1870–80* (Oxford University Press, 1937)
A scholarly study of Russian policies in the Balkans during the period of the Russo–Turkish war.

Taylor, A. J. P. *The Habsburg Monarchy, 1809–1918*. (London: Hamish Hamilton, 1948, New York: The Macmillan Co., 1948)
Valuable for its treatment of the relations between the Monarchy and its Slav subjects.

Taylor, A. J. P. *The Struggle for Mastery in Europe, 1848–1918* Oxford History of Modern Europe, Vol. 1 (Oxford U. Press, 1954)
A study of European diplomacy during the period 1870–1914. Scholarly and readable.

c. The First World War

Edmonds, Sir J. E. *A Short History of the First World War* (Cambridge University Press, 1951)

d. The Balkans Between the Wars

Pribićević, Stoyan *Living Space* (Heinemann: London, 1940)
A study of the problems of Slav Nationalism in S.E. Europe and a plea for federation of the Slav countries, by the son of a former Serbian Minister.

Seton-Watson, H. *Eastern Europe Between the Wars, 1918–41* (Cambridge University Press, 1945)

e. The Second World War

Churchill, Sir Winston S. *The Second World War*, 6 Vols. (London: Cassell, 1948–54, Boston: Houghton Mifflin Company, 1948–54)

f. Background to East Europe since 1945

Betts, R. R. (Editor) *Central and S.E. Europe, 1945–58* (Oxford University Press for Royal Institute of International Affairs, 1950)
Chapter 3 on Yugoslavia by Phyllis Auty gives a concise account of developments between the outbreak of the war and the Cominform resolution.

Seton-Watson, Hugh *East European Revolution*, 3rd edition (London: Methuen, 1956)
A general survey of political and social developments in East Europe. 3rd edition brought up to date March 1955.

Warriner, Doreen *Revolution in Eastern Europe* (Turnstile Press, 1950)

Wolff, R. L. *The Balkans in Our Times* (Oxford University Press, 1956, Cambridge, Mass.: Harvard University Press, 1956)

2. *Yugoslavia – General Works*

Buchan, John (Editor) *Yugoslavia* (Hodder & Stoughton, 1923)
Useful chapters on the formation of Yugoslavia after the First World War.

Kerner, Robert J. (Editor) *Yugoslavia* In United Nations Series (University of California, 1949)
A useful introduction to the geography and pre-war history of Yugoslavia. Most valuable for its chapters on Yugoslavia between the wars. A brief account of the First World War and the immediate post-war period also included.

3. *Yugoslavia – Geography, Travel and Description*

Ancel, J. *Peuples et nations des Balkans*, 2nd edition (Paris: 1930)
Cvijić, J. *Les Pays Balkaniques* (Paris: 1917)
Cvijić was the father of Jugoslav geography.

Hodgkinson, H. *The Adriatic Sea* (Cape, 1955, New York: The Macmillan Co., 1955)
A description of both shores of the Adriatic. A pleasant, readable and well illustrated introduction to Dalmatia.

Le Play Society *Slovene studies. Edited by* L. DUDLEY STAMP (The Le Play Soc., 1933)
Study of the human geography of an Alpine valley in Slovenia.

Mackenzie, G. Mary Muir and Irby, Adelina P. *Travels in the Slavonic Provinces of Turkey in Europe*, 1st edition (Bell and Dalby, 1867) 2nd edition, 1877.
An account of the journeys of two English ladies in Bosnia during the last decades of Turkish rule. Miss Irby settled in Bosnia and died there.

Moodie, A. E. *The Italo–Yugoslav Boundary* (George Philip, 1945)
A study in political geography which deals with the problems of demarcation after the First World War. Good maps.

Milojevic, B. *Yugoslavia: Geographical Survey. Organisation of the Yugoslav State.* (Belgrade: Committee for Cultural Relations with Foreign Countries, 1958)

Whelpton, E. *Dalmatia* (Hale, 1954, New York: W. S. Heinman, 1954)

West, Rebecca *Black Lamb and Grey Falcon*, 2 Vols. (Macmillan 1942, New York: The Viking Press, 1941)
An account of a journey through Yugoslavia in 1937, but much more than a travel book.

4. *Yugoslav History*

a. Serbia before 1914

Temperley, Sir Harold *History of Serbia* (Bell, 1919)
Vuchinich, Wayne S. *Serbia between East and West: The Events of 1903–8* (Stanford University Press, 1954)

Remak, Joachim *Sarajevo* (Weidenfeld & Nicholson, 1959, New York: Criterion Books, 1959)
A vivid account of the events leading up to the murder at Sarajevo in 1914. Leans towards the pan-German point of view.

b. Yugoslavia in the Second World War

Clissold, Stephen *Whirlwind: An Account of Marshall Tito's Rise to Power* (Cresset Press, 1949)
The story of the Partisans.
Maclean, Sir Fitzroy *Eastern Approaches* (Cape, 1949)
Includes a section of the author's personal experiences as head of the British Mission to the Partisans.

c. Yugoslavia – Modern Politics

Byrnes, R. F. (Editor) *Yugoslavia* (London: Atlantic Books, Stevens, 1958 for Mid-European Studies Centre of the Free Europe Committee, Inc., New York: Frederick A. Praeger, 1957)
One of a series of books on East–Central Europe, largely written by refugee scholars. Openly anti-Communist, but contains much useful information on economic geography. Deliberate omission of chapters on religion, literature and labour.
Djilas, Milovan *The New Class* (Thames & Hudson, 1957, New York: Frederick A. Praeger, 1957)
A bitter attack on the leadership of the Communist Party of Yugoslavia by one who was a leading member of it until 1953.
Halperin, Ernst *The Triumphant Heretic: Tito's Struggle Against Stalin* (Heinemann, 1958)
Of particular interest for its treatment of Soviet–Yugoslav relations from 1948 to the Hungarian revolt of 1956.
Neal, F. W. *Titoism in Action* (Cambridge University Press, 1958, Berkeley: University of California Press, 1957)
An excellent account of developments since the Cominform Resolution of 1948.
McVicker, Charles P. *Titoism: Pattern for International Communism* (Macmillan, 1957, New York: St. Martin's Press, 1957)
A thorough analysis of the theoretical and practical aspects of developments after 1948, by an American who worked as a diplomat in Yugoslavia.
The Trial of Dragoljub-Draža Mihailović (Union of Journalists Associations of the F.P.R. Yugoslavia, Belgrade, 1946)
Record of the Stenographic minutes of the trial of Mihailović.
Ulam, Alan *Titoism and the Cominform* (Oxford University Press, 1952 for Harvard University Press, Cambridge, Mass: Harvard University Press, 1952)

A study of both the theoretical and practical issues involved in the dispute.

d. Biographies of Tito

Dedijer, Vladimir *Tito speaks: His Self Portrait and Struggle with Stalin* (Weidenfeld & Nicholson, 1953)

Dedijer was a close associate of Tito during and immediately after the war. Contains a very full account of relations with the Soviet Union immediately prior to the break in 1948.

Maclean, Sir Fitzroy *Disputed Barricade: the Life and Times of Josip Broz-Tito, Marshal of Jugoslavia* (Cape, 1957), *Heretic: The Life and Times of Josip Broz-Tito* (Harper & Brothers, 1957)

A most readable biography of Tito by a British Conservative M.P. Sympathetic, scholarly and fair-minded in its treatment of controversial events.

Zilliacus, Konni *Tito of Yugoslavia* (M. Joseph, 1952)

A biography of Tito by a British left-wing Labour M.P. who is a friend and admirer of the Yugoslav leader.

5. *Miscellaneous*

Barker, Elizabeth *Macedonia, Its Place in Balkan Power Politics* (Royal Institute of International Affairs, 1950)

Djilas, Milovan *Land Without Justice: An Autobiography of His Youth* (Methuen, 1958, New York: Harcourt, Brace & Company, 1958)

A brilliant study of life in Montenegro seen through the eyes of a sensitive youth.

Federal Statistical Office *Statistical Pocket-book of Yugoslavia.* Published annually since 1954 (Belgrade)

A useful pocket-book of statistical information.

6. *The Peasantry*

Trouton, Ruth *Peasant Renaissance in Yugoslavia (1900–1950)* (Routledge, 1952, New York: Humanitas Press, 1952)

Emphasises the role of education in the social life of the peasantry during the first half of the twentieth century. Historical background of less value than material on modern trends.

Lodge, Olive *Peasant Life in Yugoslavia* (Seeley, Service & Co., 1941)

A very full account of peasant life before the war, based on personal impressions.

Warriner, Doreen *The Economics of Peasant Farming* (Oxford University Press, 1939)

Halpern, J. M. *A Serbian Village* (Oxford University Press, 1958, New York: Columbia University Press, 1958)

An absorbing account of a year spent by an American social scientist in the Serbian village of Orašac, the birthplace of Karageorge.

Tomasevitch, J. *Peasants, Politics and Economic Change in Yugoslavia* (Cambridge University Press, 1955, Stanford, Calif.: Stanford University Press, 1954)
Written by a scholar who is of Dalmatian peasant origin. Very full treatment of many social and economic problems of the peasantry.

7. *Folk Lore, Poetry, Music, the Arts*

Subotić, Dragutin *Yugoslav Popular Ballads: Their Origin and Development* (Cambridge University Press, 1932)
Rootham, H. Trans. *Kosovo Polje* (Blackwell, 1920)
Translation of the great Serbian epic of the struggle against the Turks in the fourteenth century.
Njegoš, P. *The Mountain Wreath* (Translated by J. W. Willis) (Allen and Unwin, 1930)
An epic by the great Montenegrin poet, Bishop Njegoš (1813–51)
Norman, L. R. *The Sculpture of Ivan Meštrović* (Syracuse University Press, New York, 1948)
Churchin, M. (Editor) *Ivan Meštrović* (Williams & Norgate, 1919)
Morison, W. A. *The revolt of the Serbs against the Turks (1804–1813)* (Cambridge University Press, 1942)
Heroic ballads of the Serbian Revolt.
Janković, J. *Dances of Jugoslavia* (Max Parrish, 1952, Chester Springs: Pa.: Dufour Editions, 1952)
Ballads of Marko Kraljević (Cambridge University Press, 1922)
Parry, M. and Lord, A. *Serbo-Croatian Heroic Songs*, Vols. I–II. (Geoffrey Cumberlege, 1953–54, Czmbridge, Mass: Harvard University Press, 1954)
Matthews, W. K. and Slodnjak, A. *Selection of Poems by Francè Prešeren*. Translated from the Slovene (Oxford: Basil Blackwell, 1954)
Translation of some poems by the great Slovene romatic poet (1800–49). Introductory essay on Slovene history.
Bartók, Bela and Lord, A. D. *Serbo-Croation Folk Songs* (Oxford University Press, 1951, New York: Columbia University Press, 1951)
Texts and transcriptions of 75 folk songs.
Rice, D. Talbot, *Byzantine Art* (Pelican Books, 1958)
The Beginnings of Christian Art (Oxford; Basil Blackwell, 1958)

8   *Modern Literature*

Andrić, Ivo *The Bridge on the Drina* (Allen & Unwin, 1959, New York: The Macmillan Co., 1960)

Translation of *Na Drini Ćuprija*, one of the novels in his Bosnian trilogy. A vivid account of life in the Bosnian town of Višegrad under Turkish and Hapsburg occupation.

Andrić, Ivo *Bosnian Story*. Translated by Kenneth Johnstone. (Lincolns-Prager, 1958)[1]
A novel of Bosnian life in the early nineteenth century.

Levstik, Fran, Translated by F. S. Copeland *Martin Krpan* (Ljubljana: Mladinska Knjiga, 1960)
A folk tale written by the nineteenth-century Slovene nationalist, Fran Levstik, (1831–87).

Articles in English Journals

Articles on Yugoslavia have appeared from time to time in the following journals. One or two examples are given, but the reader is advised to consult the index to the appropriate journal for further references.

The Slavonic and East European Review

Athlone Press, for School of Slavonic and East European Studies. There is usually an article on Yugoslavia in every issue. Subjects covered include history, language, literature, and politics.

Warriner, D. 'Urban Thinkers and Peasant Policy in Yugoslavia, 1918–59' (Vol. XXXVIII, No. 90, December 1959)
Excellent concise account of the 'peasant problem' in modern Yugoslavia.

Jelavchich, Barbara 'The British Traveller in the Balkans: the Abuses of the Ottoman Administration in the Slavonic Provinces' (Vol. XXXIII, No. 81, June 1959)
A survey of the writings of English travellers in the Balkans during the nineteenth century.

Geographical Journal

Royal Geographical Society, Kensington Gore

Roglić, J. 'Geography in Yugoslavia' (No. 118, June 1952)
A short survey of the work of Yugoslav Geographers.

Bičanič, R. 'Effects of War on rural Yugoslavia' (No. 103, Jan.–Feb. 1944)
Contains useful maps and diagrams showing agricultural geography of Yugoslavia between the wars, and a discussion of the problems facing the country at the end of the Second World War.

---

[1] One of a series of 12 Yugoslav novels to be published by Lincolns-Prager.

Geography

Journal of the Geographical Association, Park Branch Library, Sheffield 2.

Cornish, Vaughan 'Bosnia: The Borderland of Serb and Croat' (No. 110, Vol. XX, part 4, December 1935)

Lebon, J. H. G. 'The Jezera: A Mountain Country in S.W. Yugoslavia' (No. 110, Vol. XX, part 4, December 1935)

The Royal Institute of International Affairs publishes a quarterly, *International Affairs* and a monthly review *The World Today*, both of which have published articles on Yugoslav affairs. *Keesing's Contemporary Archives* should be consulted for summaries of current events. It is available in most reference libraries.

II SHORT LIST OF SOURCES IN SERBO-CROAT

Melik, A. *Yugoslavija–Zemljopisni Pregled* (Zagreb: 1952)
General geographical survey of Yugoslavia.

Lah, A. *Gospodarstvo Jugoslavije – prisperek k ekonomiski geografije F.N.R.J.* (Ljubljana: 1959)
The economy of Yugoslavia – a contribution to the economic geography of the F.P.R. Yugoslavia.

Istorija Naroda Jugoslavije (Zagreb: Vol. I 1953)

Skrivanić, Gavro A. *Kosovska Bitka* (Historical Instutute of Montenegro, Cetinje, 1956)

Pavlovic, Dragoljub *Iz Naše Knizevnosti feudalnog doba* (Sarajevo: 1954)

Jovanović, Slobodan *Vlada Milana Obrenovića 1868–1899* (Belgrade: 1925–7)
One of the most important histories of nineteenth-century Serbia, by the leading historian of Old Yugoslavia.

Jiraček, Konstantin, *Istorjia Srba* (2nd revised edition, Beograd, 1952)

Kardelj, Edvard *Sperans* (Belgrade: Kultura, 1958)
History of the Slovene National Movement.

Novak, V. and Zwitter, F. Editors *Oko Trsta*
Geography, ethnographic structure and history of the Julian Region.

Mihovilovic, Ive *Trst Problem Dana* (Zagreb: 1951)
For further information on recent Yugoslav sources see Vuchinich, Wayne S., 'Post-War Yugoslav Historiography,' *Journal of Modern History*, Vol. XXII, Chicago, U.S.A.

III PAMPHLETS AND JOURNALS

a. World War I

Between 1915 and 1919, Yugoslav emigrés in London who believed in the formation of a South Slav State published journals and pamphlets in support of their views. The following are of particular interest.

South Slav Committee
South Slav Library
Vol. I, 'The South Slav Programme'
Vol. V, 'The Idea of South Slav Unity' (Nisbet, 1915)

Jugoslav Committee
Southern Slav Bulletin (No. 38, Jan. 15th 1919)
This number contains the Declaration of aims of December 1918, made by the newly formed first Jugoslav Government.
Smodlaka, J. *Yugoslav Territorial Claims* (Paris: Lang, Blanchong, 1919)
Reprint of a speech by a Dalmatian member of the Yugoslav delegation to the Peace Conference.

b. Yugoslav Embassy Pamphlets
The Yugoslav Information Service of the Embassy in London publish pamphlets on current problems from time to time. The following brief selection indicates the nature of the topics which are dealt with.
'Yugoslavia: The Church and the State' (Information Office, Embassy of F.P.R. Yugoslavia, 1953)
The official account of relations between the post-war régime and the various religious groups. Particularly detailed on position of Roman Catholics, trial of Stepinać etc.
Kardelj, E. 'Trieste and Yugoslav-Italian Relations' (Information Office, F.R.P. Yugoslavia, 1953)
Reprint of articles in *Borba*, October 25th and 26th, 1953.
Pijade, Moša 'About the Legend that the Yugoslav Uprising owed its Existence to Soviet Assistance' (Yugoslav Embassy, 1950)
Taylor, A. J. P. 'Trieste' (Yugoslav Information Office, 1945)
A pamphlet putting the case for Yugoslav possession of Trieste.

c. Miscellaneous Pamphlets
Ernjaković, G. 'The Yugoslav Educational System' (Edition Jugoslavija, Belgrade, 1959)
Kardelj, Edvard. 'Four Factors in the Development of Socialist Social Relations' (Edition Jugoslavija Belgrade, 1960)
Speech by Kardelj at the 5th Congress of the Socialist Alliance, April 1960.
Thompson, E. P. Editor 'The Railway' (British-Yugoslav Association, 1948)

The story of the British Brigade on the Šamac to Sarajevo Railway in the summer of 1947.

Tito, Hebrang and Kidrić 'The Five Year Plan' (Belgrade: 1947) Speeches in the National Assembly, April 26, 1947.

Tito, Josip Broz 'Political Report of the Central Committee to 5th Congress of CPY' (Belgrade: 1948) Includes Tito's account of the history of the party.

'Programme of Yugoslav League of Communists'

        Worcester Park, Press Books Ltd., 1959
The programme adopted at the Ljubljana Congress of the League of Communists in 1958.

'The Soviet–Yugoslav Dispute: Text of the Published Correspondence' (Royal Institute of International Affairs, 1948)

Trieste and the Italo–Yugoslav Frontier

A spate of books and pamphlets on various aspects of the boundary dispute with Italy has appeared since 1945. Below are some of the more important of them.

Memorandum of the Government of F.R.R. Yugoslavia on the Economic Problem of Trieste, and Annex to Memorandum (No date)
Argues that Trieste belongs to Yugoslavia economically. Annex contains excellent maps and diagrams.

Melik, A. *The Development of the Yugoslav Railways and Their Gravitation Towards Trieste* (Belgrade: 1945)

Čermelj, Lavo *Recensement de 1910 d' Trieste ; d'apres les proces-verbaux de la Diète Provinciale de Trieste et du Parlement Autrichien* (Institut Yugoslave d'Etudes Internationales, Belgrade, 1946)
The criteria used for ethnic statistics in the census examined.

Kos, Milko *Developement historique de la frontier Slovene occidentale.* (L'Institut Scientifique, Ljubljana, 1946)

University of Ljubljana, Institute for Questions of Nationality. *Who Should Have Trieste?* (Ljubljana, 1953)

Ilešić, S. *The Population Development of Trieste and Its Near Environs.* (Ljubljana: Research Institute, 1946)

Čermelj, Lavo *The Life and Death Struggle of a National Minority.* Translation by F. S. Copeland.
The story of the ill-treatment of Slovenes in the Trieste area and Istria during the Fascist period.

Institute for International Politics and Economics *Italian genocide policy against the Slovenes and the Croats: a selection of documents* (Belgrade: 1954)

Index

Printed in Great Britain by
Lowe & Brydone (Printers) Ltd., London